Get Your Short Film Funded, Made and Seen

THE SHOOTING PEOPLE SHORTS DIRECTORY

Edited by Trica Tuttle

Contributors and writers
Chris and Ben Blaine, Katie Bradford,
Méabh O'Donovan, Andy Gordon and
Christos Michaels, Lisa Gunning, Ingrid Kopp,
Cath Le Couteur, Marilyn Milgrom,
Jess Search and Tricia Tuttle

Interviews and case studies
Matthieu de Braconier, Mark Craig, Ben Crowe,
Matt Dentler, Evan Fleischer, Catherine Des Forges,
Andrew Goode, Trevor Groth, Brent Hoff, Neil Hunter,
Philip Ilson, Lee Kern, Joe Lawlor, Peter Mann,
Rebecca Mark-Lawson, Jason Meil, Luke Morris,
Daniel Mulloy, Penny Nagle, Sydney Neter,
Dan Nuxoll, Anne-Claire Pilley, Nik Powell,
James Fabricant, Fabien Riggall, Steven Starr,
Laura Thielen, Simon Young

First edition 2007

Shooting People Ltd
P.O. Box 51350
London N1 6XS
www.shootingpeople.org

Copyright 2007 Shooting People Ltd

ISBN 0-9544874-2-7
Printed April 2007

A CIP catalogue record for this book is available from the British Library.

Design by Giles at Pixeco, www.pixeco.com

Our warm acknowledgments and thanks go out to the following people who helped to make this book possible:

Matthew Andrews, Aspen Shortsfest, The Bureau, Channel Four British Documentary Film Foundation, Current TV, Mike Figgis, James Franklin, Future Shorts, Paul Hewlett, Briony Hanson, Independent Cinema Office, Independent Film Channel (IFC), Don Knee at the Cruet Company, Lifesize Pictures, London Short Film Festival (Halloween), Giles Marsh, James Mullighan, MySpace, Jo Phipps, Pixeco, Revver, Rooftop Films, Marsha Rosengarten, Quinny Sacks, The Script Factory, Shooting People Films, Short Circuit Films, Short Film Central, Shorts International, Sound Films, South by Southwest, SND Films, Sundance Film Festival, Jessica Thomas, Stu Tily, Wholphin

"Short films are as important as feature films... not only in developing talent but also in providing filmmakers with alternatives to express their visions".
Trevor Groth
Sundance Film Festival

"Short films allow a filmmaker to express their vision in its purest form".
Rebecca Mark-Lawson
Managing Executive,
UK Film Council's short film schemes

Tricia Tuttle,
Editor, *Get Your Short Film Funded, Made and Seen*

Tricia Tuttle works as a freelance film researcher, writer and producer. She is the Editor of *Filmmakers' Yearbook* from A&C Black. She is also the producer of Shooting People Films' *Best v Best*, a DVD series of major award-winning short films. *Best v Best Volume One* was released in December 2005, and *Vol Two* in March 2007. Tricia is also the Film Editor for DIVA magazine.

Previously, she worked as an events producer for The Script Factory, and for the London Film Festival for 3 years co-producing talks and special events. She also co-programmed the British Film Institute's London Lesbian and Gay Film Festival at the National Film Theatre. She has an MA from the British Film Institute and Birkbeck College in Film Studies and she has also lectured in Media Studies for Birkbeck College, University of London, and Middlesex University.

For additional information, and to download extra materials and clearance forms which are in this book, go to www.shootingpeople.org/shortsbook

Contents

Let's Start

A foreword from Shooting People

Hello there.

All of us at Team Shooters are very proud to be publishing this book on short filmmaking. We feel a short film resource like this is long overdue; it's a book which provides, not just a wealth of must-have information and contacts for anyone thinking about making a short film, but one which also reflects a multitude of direct film experiences from so many of our friends, peers and colleagues right across the independent film sector.

You may already be a 'Shooter' reading this book. If you are not, then come and join us! Shooting People is a massive online community of filmmakers in the widest sense: directors, writers, producers, actors, cinematographers, editors, make-up artists, animators, composers, festival organisers, funders, exhibitors and more. We share resources, skills and experience, which help films get made and seen. Members (over 31,000 last count!) receive daily email bulletins covering all aspects of filmmaking. Through these bulletins and our site, members of Shooting People can post messages and queries to each other for advice; find and advertise work; add events and screenings to our indie film calendar; upload their films for others to watch; and comment on and debate all aspects of the craft. We also network with each other online, and at parties, salons and screenings in the UK, NYC and beyond.

Everyone who works at Shooters HQ is involved in filmmaking in its various guises. We are passionate believers that Shooting People will continue to make a major contribution to building a strong independent film scene - one that can offer alternatives to mainstream cinema, not only in how films are made, but also in how they are distributed.

Our grateful thanks goes to the wonderful Tricia Tuttle for her exhaustive work in editing such a great resource.

And to everyone who is venturing into the sometimes tough, but always thrilling world of short film: HAPPY SHOOTIN'!

Cath Le Couteur
Shooting People Co-Founder
www.shootingpeople.org

Introduction

Trica Tuttle

Shorts chic? Short films are sexy. From Robbie Williams and the Arctic Monkeys to major brands like Audi and Cobra, everyone wants to get in on the act. There has never been a more fertile and exciting time for short films and short filmmakers. OK, so there isn't necessarily more money to be made in selling them, but it is cheaper to make them, and a new festival or screening initiative seems to pop up somewhere around the world every week dedicated to screening them. Audience interest in shorts is at an all-time high, and with the explosion of VOD [video on demand] markets, there are more places to get your film seen than ever before.

If you are thinking about making a short film, then this is your time, and you've found the right book to get you started.

A very potted history of shorts

Short films have been around longer than their feature-length cousins; the roots of cinema are in the short film. The earliest films by Edison and the Lumiere brothers were short reels showing everyday events like workers leaving a factory or women drinking tea on a summer lawn (and these are still worth watching, by the way, and can easily be found on the internet). These 'short films' were born out of a necessity to test the new technology, but the short form has never subsequently disappeared, even as the ability to create longer narratives and multi-reel films developed throughout the first part of the century. Until the 60s, cinema audiences could expect shorts – animation, comedies and documentary newsreels – to screen before feature films as part of a longer programme.

Since then, the form has taken on new life creatively but it has rarely been a commercial prospect. Very few short films make their money back, much less a profit of any sort. Rather, until recently, they have often been seen as the territory of experimental and artist filmmakers, or student filmmakers looking to gain invaluable experience and a 'calling card' for future work. All that is changing.

Over that last 5 years the perception of short films has been undergoing a seismic shift. There's been a renewed interest in short forms from the public and industry alike, and it's one that has coincided with a crossover in the fields of art, design, music, film and commercials. Short filmmakers are being recruited to make adverts and music videos (such as Ken Wardrop, whose award-winning short *Undressing My Mother* got him a gig to make a Robbie Williams video in 2006).

User upload sites like MySpace and YouTube have also seen an explosion of DIY short films with an eager audience. Admittedly, these aren't normally very good – unless you're in the mood for a hilarious Jackass-style 'cat on a skateboard' film – but the format has taught online distributors a few tricks about viral distribution and spawned other great, more selective sites like revver, pawky (which are both mentioned in Meabh O'Donovan's article covering distribution), and Shooting People's new online film channel.

Why should you make a short film?

Some filmmakers claim that a short film is as much work as a feature. It's true that, unless you are one of the very lucky few who are commissioned to develop and produce a short, and who get a good sales agent to do all the leg work selling your film and placing it at festivals around the world, you will need to do everything yourself or find a small team of collaborators. You will write a short script; secure funding (or pay for it yourself); book and hire equipment and crew; manage the shoot; supervise or handle post production; and then get your film into festivals and hopefully sell it to distributors and broadcasters. It's hard to see how this could take much less that a year of your life. So why should you make one?

While it may be surprising how long it takes to make something so 'small', it's an intensely gratifying process if you end up with a film you are very proud of, and even better, if it launches you as a filmmaker 'to watch'. There are so many benefits to making a short film:

> it's an invaluable way to learn about the production-distribution cycle and see the industry in microcosm;

> for aspiring career filmmakers, the craft experience you get is the best teaching you could wish for;

> the low-risk environment allows you bend rules, experiment, and make mistakes (without damaging your career);

> they allow you to find your voice as a filmmaker and define and refine your visual style;

> the limited length will help you to learn the most economical ways to tell story;

> you will build up a portfolio of work which will help with funding-raising for future films; and

> you can establish and test some creative relationships and partnerships for future collaborations

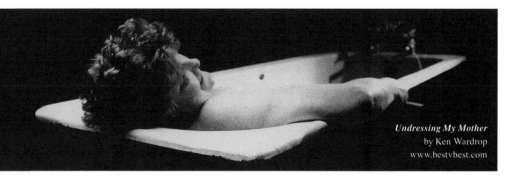

Undressing My Mother
by Ken Wardrop
www.bestvbest.com

It's important then that you not only know what you want to get out of the process, but that you are really passionate about your idea – you're going to be spending a lot of time with it.

Funding for short films is out there but, like any funding, it's a very competitive market and you will need to think about how you can make yourself an attractive prospect and one which seems worth the investment. Unless you are hitting up rich Uncle Albert for £5000, you will rarely receive investment – either public or private, for a short or a feature – unless the investor can see evidence of your talent, and of the fact that you have the discipline and desire necessary to finish and deliver a project. Your first short film will be the start of that portfolio, and as it's such a huge investment of time (and possibly, though not necessarily, money), you'll want to make sure that it is the best it can possibly be. Every step of the process needs to maximise your potential and make sure that you create the film that you want to represent you as a filmmaker.

How to use this book

Get Your Short Film Made, Funded And Seen is designed to be used as on ongoing resource throughout the production and distribution process. You don't need to read it in the order we've set out, though if you are brand new to filmmaking, you might want to at least scan everything before you even put pen to paper. While the sections are broken down into the stages of making a short film - from idea development to getting in front of an audience - that's not to say you won't find useful information on all stages of the process throughout the book. It's all connected. For example, you might find some of the best tips on content and ideas in the GET IT SEEN section where we have interviewed many of the major players from the short film exhibition world, especially those from the big US and UK markets. These people have *seen* more short films than most of the other people in the book – funders and filmmakers alike – and they generally have good instincts for what makes a short film work.

If that sounds like we are saying that there are hard and fast 'right' and 'wrong' ways to making a short, then let's clarify that that isn't the intention; We don't want this book to be prescriptive. One of the reasons we've included so many articles and interviews from different filmmakers and film professionals is that we want to give you a number of perspectives to digest as you define your own style and approach. As Philip Ilson says in his interview, sometimes it just comes down to subjective personal tastes. There are a million different ways to approach a film. You will have your own.

However you approach this book, it should be a companion text to *watching* other short films to see how other filmmakers have done it. Nothing can replace this stage of your short film education. To this end we have included a list of 25 of the best short films you can watch for free on the internet - and in a shameless plug (for what we think is a good cause), you might note that Shooting People Films also produces a series of the year's best award-winning short films, *Best v Best* (bestvbest.com), available in two volumes, which will give you an excellent sense of what kinds of films are getting into festivals and winning the major awards.

Indisputably, for those of you planning a career in film, making a short film is a valuable step on that ladder. While there are many other ways to learn – working as a runner on feature shoots, taking film courses or even undertaking a film degree – working on a short film should be seen as a essential part of that education.

Short films are also a viable art form in their own right and with so many new platforms emerging, good shorts are reaching wider audiences than they have since the days when they screened before features.

Presumably you are reading this because you are about to make a short film of your own. If you are a newcomer, welcome to our mad, passionate family of filmmakers. We hope this book will help you to make the film you have playing in your head.

Section One:
Define Your Idea

The writing and idea development part of any film, whether short or feature, is likely to be one of the more challenging areas for any filmmaker. Short films are more forgiving than features to the writer in many ways: your plot can be the simplest single idea, character development is less rigorous for the writer, and quite simply, short screenplays take less time to produce. Yet paradoxically, there is even less room for manoeuvring: any indecision or tendency to over-elaborate will be more obvious, and narrative fat will seem even more flabby.

Whether you are making a drama or a doc, you'll need to approach the idea generation and writing stage of your short film with much consideration – get this right and you are well on your way to making a good short. Most programmers we interviewed for this book say that a good idea is far more important to them than uber-technical proficiency and slick production values on a short film. Many also add that the most frequent problem they see in otherwise decent doc and drama shorts is that filmmakers almost always want to include too much information for the short form. Think carefully about this and try to avoid the urge to put every idea you have into this single film. Be brutal with yourself in the writing/developing stage and you will save much time, energy and money – the latter is almost always a scarce resource for filmmakers.

Marilyn Milgrom's article on The Script will help you drama short writers think about developing and honing your own script ideas. If you are working on a doc short, check out Jess Search's The Short Doc for a checklist of things you'll want to consider before you start. To complement these, we've included sample documents and several interviews and case studies with filmmakers who have successfully navigated this stage of the short film production process. This section also includes the first part in a running interview with Chris and Ben Blaine, the UK-based fraternal filmmaking duo responsible for more than ten shorts and half a dozen music videos in less than ten years. They've generously allowed us to use their short *Death of the Revolution* as a case study in the book as well, so you will find related script, storyboards, budgets, etc. in the relevant sections as you read through.

Drama

The Script
Marilyn Milgrom, script consultant

This is a short article in which to deal with a big subject: how to write a good script for a short film. There is a huge range of short films and there will always be those that break all the rules and somehow manage to succeed. So, rule number one: there are no hard and fast rules. But, if your aim is to get your film funded, there are definitely some guiding principles that will help to ensure that your project is taken seriously.

In most cases the first and most important consideration for potential funders will be your script, and so this chapter aims to give you an overview of those guiding principles and to raise questions along the way that will help you clarify your idea and suggest practical ways to develop it.

Why Am I Making this Film?
No-one makes a living out of writing or directing short films. Most people see short films as a tool for learning and testing ideas, or a way of demonstrating that they have the talent to do something else. Generally that 'something else' is to make features.

> **"It's worth saying that there are films that please audiences and win awards that are neither 10 minutes long nor inherently dramatic."**

A lot of directors are also writers but just as many are not and are simply driven to writing their own short film script out of frustration and the desire to get on with making something. Whether you are working alone or as part of a writer/director team make sure that the project you are developing plays to your strengths and is achievable within your budget. Don't make an intense character study if you're scared of actors or develop an action story that will require stunts, car chases and special effects if you know you will only have £5K to make it.

What is a short film?
The most important thing to say is that a short isn't a feature film and that it is generally a bad idea to try to squeeze a story you are developing (or have written) as a feature into a short. It's like having an idea for a novella and then deciding to tell it as a haiku: the two are different forms and just as a haiku can only explore one idea, the

same is true of the short film. This depends to some extent of course on how short it is: most festivals will accept as a short anything that is under 30 minutes, but many programmers and curators also say that they find it difficult to place longer short films (ones over 20 minutes). If your film *is* over 20 minutes long it may well need and be able to cope with more characters and a secondary story strand. But the majority of funding in the UK is aimed at films that are around the 10 minute mark so dramatic narratives of that length will be the primary focus of this chapter.

It's worth saying at the outset that there are a lot of films that please audiences and win awards that are neither 10 minutes long nor inherently dramatic. *Who Killed Brown Owl* (w/d: Christine Molloy and Joe Lawlor) for example is a film that consists of a single 9 minute crane shot that features a hundred people in Enfield who the directors choreographed to create a snapshot of an apparently typical summer afternoon in the park. As the film's title suggests, there is a darker element that makes it memorable for more than its sheer technical brilliance but this is not explored in any dramatic sense and the overall effect of the film is more like a tone poem.

There are other successful shorts that contain no drama, they simply want to make us laugh, and that's fine too. But if your film is basically going to function like a joke then keep it short (2-3 minutes max) and make sure the audience won't see the punch-line coming a mile off. Films like this will make far more of an impression if they not only make us laugh but also manage to allude to something that gives us pause for thought. Christopher Nolan's 3 minute film *Doodlebug*, made when he was a student at London University, features a man in a room desperately trying to kill something we assume to be a huge bug scuttling across the floor, concealed by a rag. But when the man pulls off the rag he reveals a tiny version of himself trying to kill a bug… and as we cut to the face of the first man we see, looming behind him a huge face: it is a huge version of himself, trying to kill a bug… The film always gets a laugh but it also suggests a filmmaker with a serious interest in deeper philosophical questions.

> "A lot of the best short films play out more or less in 'real' time"

Finding the Story

Any kind of dramatic story requires 3 basic elements:

> A world

> A character

> A problem

Short films are no different; you just have less time to establish and develop each element. Most successful short films focus on ONE moment or event in the life of ONE main character. Because of that it is unusual for a short film to take place over a long period of time – it's usually just looking at the immediate build up to and/or consequences of that one event. A lot of the best short films play out more or less in 'real' time, and a story that spreads over more than a few days is unlikely to work well as a short film. There are exceptions to this at the longer end of the short film duration but, in general, stick to a story that follows one character and focuses on one event.

The World

Because of the need to establish an instantly recognisable world in order to get on with exploring a character's problem, it can be useful to set your film around a familiar event or ritual: a wedding, a birthday party, the first day at school, tea with stuffy relatives, Christmas Day etc. With a setting of this sort you can take for granted the audience's familiarity with the situation and you have immediately placed your characters

Daniel Mulloy, notes on developing short ideas

When writing *Antonio's Breakfast*, I knew I would have almost no money to shoot it, so I set the film in a single location. It was written with Antonio (lead) in every scene so that the film, although short, would convey a strong sense of Antonio's character and dilemma.

Dad was written as the antidote to *Antonio's Breakfast*. Set in the same building, the characters were almost the reverse of those in *Antonio's Breakfast*. In the latter, a young man looks after his father. In *Dad* a middle-aged man doesn't have the mental strength to leave his elderly parents small flat. The strong sexual scenes in *Dad* counter a suppressed sexual tension in *Antonio's Breakfast*.

I write my films aware that I will need to finance them with very minimal funds. This means that I am able to translate the scripts to film from my own company and do not depend on a producer to pick the project up.

When writing, I have a strong sense of what needs to be communicated. I then work with the artists in rehearsals until they have made the performances their own. In *Antonio's Breakfast* this meant that the young guys spent time working out what they thought would feel natural for them to say and I trusted them implicitly and went with it.

I find that because a script is so ephemeral, i.e. based on the writer's instinct of what will work, it is easier to show it to readers once the script has a developed shape. This is because it is easy to be waylaid by criticism if the work is incomplete. I try to remember that people tend to read or watch what is there in front of them and no more, be that extra scenes in a script or the missing sound on a rough off-line edit.

Daniel Mulloy studied fine art at University College, London, and Hunter College, New York. His first film, *Dance Floor*, won many accolades, including a BAFTA Cymru Award for best newcomer. Mulloy's second short, *Sister*, was released in 2005 and screened at more than 30 festivals winning the ARTE Grand Prix in Hamburg and another BAFTA. *Antonio's Breakfast* premiered at Sundance Film Festival and screened all over the world, winning the Short Film BAFTA in 2006. Daniel's most recent short film, *Dad* premiered in the Edinburgh Film Festival in 2006.

Antonio's Breakfast is on Best v Best Vol. Two (bestvbest.com)

into a story world full of barely suppressed emotions, which is always useful for generating dramatic tension and story events. The other advantage to choosing a setting of this sort is that it gives the story a finite time frame.

Another popular setting for the short film is the journey. Most short films focus on a pivotal, significant event in the life of the main character so that the story inevitably takes the character on a metaphorical emotional journey and it can work well to use a literal journey as its setting.

The Character & the Problem

The most important questions to ask yourself when you begin to develop your story are:

> Who is the main character?
> What is their problem?
> How will the audience recognise the problem?
> Are the stakes high enough?
> Am I telling the story from the best point of view?

The audience must be clear from the outset who the film is about and they won't be if you aren't. Your main character is the one who has the problem and if there isn't a character in the story with a problem then you don't have a film, or at least not one that will work as a dramatic narrative.

What is driving your main character through the story must be one of the following:

> a want
> a need
> an obligation

And in all cases it must be clear to the audience, even if it isn't to the character, what this is. But what must also be present in the story - and apparent to the audience - is something that is making it hard for the character to pursue their want, need or obligation. The fact that something is making it hard is what turns it into a problem and, like we said before, no problem, no film.

The most straightforward kind of problem is where there is an external obstacle confronting the character: the car breaks down, they get locked in the bathroom or out of the house. Such an apparently simple event can be the basis of a great short film. But in lots of films there is no obvious external force of opposition, the problem comes from inside the character: they are shy, insecure, too young to understand, etc. In fact, lots of short films are about children or teenagers precisely because their age and lack of experience of the adult world provide a rich source of universally recognisable problems.

Making Problems Manifest to the Audience

The way in which you turn a character's inner problem into the heart of your film and make sure that the audience can SEE it is one of the most important ways that you can demonstrate your skill as a filmmaker and not just as a story-teller. When we're reading books we can be inside a character's head but when we're watching films we need to see characters DOING things that show us what they are thinking and feeling.

Lynne Ramsay's *Gasman* has a brilliant example of this (you can watch this film on Cinema 16: British - www.cinema16.co.uk). The main character is a young girl (Lynne) who discovers at a Christmas party that her father has another family and that the wee girl she has been happily dancing with is actually her half-sister and competition for her Daddy's affections. At the end of the film the father and his four children walk back along a disused railway line, retracing the journey they had earlier taken to the party but now in a very different mood. Lynne watches sullenly as the other girl and her brother are collected by their mother and walk off. Unseen by her father, she picks up a rock that we fear she will throw at their departing backs. In fact she doesn't throw it, she lets it drop to the ground but because we have watched her almost do it and then decide not to, we understand all the confusing and contradictory feelings that she is dealing with: anger at

Neil Hunter, notes on writing a short film

I wrote a short film that was so autobiographical I had to get my friends' permission before I went ahead and made it. Three lives crammed into 28 minutes - it was both too short and too long. You can do a short that covers a lot of ground, but that has to be part of the point of the piece, part of its style. This I didn't know at the time. However, it probably remains one of the few Bresson-inflected coming out stories of the early 1990s.

For *The Sickie*, Rupert Jones had a simple idea - that a character overhears the voice-over of the film he's in. It seemed an ideal short subject, and after chasing a few false scents, we came up with a script that tried to keep things simple, direct, funny, short, and with a point. Peculiarly, Hollywood has taken the same simple idea, and expanded it into a vehicle for Will Ferrell (*Stranger Than Fiction*).

My advice to a writer working on a short film is: 'end it before they're expecting you to'.

Neil Hunter is the co-writer and co-director of *Boyfriends*, *Lawless Heart* and a new feature, *Sparkle* which will be released in 2007. Neil also co-wrote the short film *The Sickie* which premiered in the London Film Festival in October 2006.

the other wee girl and her mother; understanding that it's not really their fault; yearning to have a sister; fear of having competition for her father's love and attention; and anger that her whole world has changed.

Are the Stakes High Enough?

Ensuring that there is something at stake in the story means that the audience can understand what the character stands to lose if they do not solve their problem. If the story hinges around a life or death situation then it is clear what is at stake but if it is simply that the car breaks down think about how you set the film up so that the audience knows why it really matters that the character completes this particular journey.

Am I Telling the Story from the Best Point of View?

Think about the story of *Cinderella* and imagine if you told it with one of the ugly sisters as the main character. You could still make a good story but it would not have a happy ending (in one of the earliest versions of the story the sisters have their eyes pecked out by blackbirds at the end!) and therefore would have a very different meaning – it would function more as a cautionary tale than as a feel-good fairy story.

In other words the meaning of any story is attached to the character through whom it is told and what happens to them at the end. In fairy stories we are totally clear who is being tested or changed by the events of the story and we are in no doubt about what their story 'means', but many short film scripts fall down because they have chosen a main character whose journey does not chime with what the writer is trying to say.

Another common point of view problem is that the script starts out being very clearly about one character but then switches to another, leaving the audience unable to identify strongly with either and so inevitably weakening the overall impact of the story.

What Does My Story Mean?

You probably don't set out to write a film with a moral or even with a conscious awareness of what your story means but every story communicates some meaning to the audience. You may start out with just the vaguest idea of your main character and their problem and no idea where they are going to end up, or you may know how you want the story to end but be less sure where to start from and how to get there. But once you are sure how the story begins and ends then you have a clear indication of its meaning and this will help you make important choices as you refine and develop your script particularly in relation to...

The Tone of the Film

Tone is intimately connected to genre and though genre is less of an issue in shorts than in features it is still important to think about what kind of film you are writing in broad terms. If you discover that the story you want to tell is one that takes a bleak view of life then don't set the film up in a way that is broadly comic. In a short film you simply don't have time to make shifts in tone: the audience is looking for clues about the kind of story this is from the outset and they will be confused or even downright angry if you change the contract half way through.

> **"If you can't sum up the basic story of your film in ONE sentence then either you don't really know what your story is yet or it is simply too complicated for a short film."**

The tone of the film emerges from the way in which each element supports the underlying 'meaning' of the story: hence the fact that a dog flattened by a car in a broad comedy may be a 'tragedy' for the owner but is a joke for the audience, whereas a dog hit by a car in a drama (in which the tone is very 'real world') is a shocking moment for both the characters and the audience. Much of the work of establishing this tone will be achieved through choices made by the director, production designer, composer etc but the first indication of the tone comes from the script.

To summarise so far:

A good short film needs a story in which something happens that has a discernible effect on the main character. All successful short films focus on **one** moment/event. That moment is likely to be:

> one of universal significance

> a moment that is of significance to the protagonist (whether s/he knows it at the time)

> one that produces a situation in which the stakes are high for the protagonist

Developing Your Story

It's extremely rare for the first draft of any short film script to be the one that is finally shot, and anything up to 20 drafts is not that uncommon. The fact that the form is short does not mean that it is easy to execute.

23

Most scripts that are submitted to funding bodies have had far too little development work done on them, so put yourself ahead of the pack by ironing out the bumps in your script before you send it out.

One thing that everyone can do is to give the script to friends to read and then interrogate them. Don't tell them anything about the story or the film in your head, just ask them open, searching questions to see if they have 'got it'. If they are confused about anything it is far more likely that there is a problem in your script than that they are stupid. They may not be able to tell you how to fix things but they will certainly help you to see where the problems are.

Another way to test the spine of your story is to see if you can pitch it in under a minute using this 10-point plan:

> Title;

> Genre/Tone;

> Setting (Time & Place);

> Main character;

> Want/Need/Obligation;

> Opposition;

> Catalyst for change;

> Climax;

> Resolution; and

> And the audience feels…. (Theme)

(In some films the catalyst for change will precede the main character's want/need/obligation)

> "If you are finding it hard to follow the 10 point plan then the chances are that you have too much plot"

Here's an example using *The Girl in the Lay-by* (D: Sarah Gavron W: Denise Whittaker – watch it on: http://www.atomfilms.com):

The Girl in the Lay-by is a drama about an 18 year-old girl called Coll who works in a hotdog van by a Scottish loch. (**Title, genre, setting, main character**)

She hates her job and dreams about travelling to New York. (**Want**)

She lacks the confidence to defend herself when her boss ridicules her dream but then she meets a strange old man who takes her seriously. (**Opposition and catalyst for change**)

When the old man dies Coll realises that she must seize her moment or sacrifice her dream. (**Climax**)

She walks out of her job and the audience knows that she is setting off for a brighter future now that she believes in herself (**Resolution and theme**)

Doing this exercise helps you clarify the BEATS of your story: it makes it really clear what are the significant facts that you have to ESTABLISH and therefore what you have to SHOW the audience in order for them to understand your story. It also helps you be clear about the TONE of your film.

In *The Girl in the Lay-by* the film opens with a wide shot of a hot-dog van by a loch. It's grey and raining and we cut to a close-up of Coll in the van staring into space and twiddling her hair. Then we cut to her sticking a picture of the New York skyline onto the wall of the van. The audience now knows what kind of world we are in (real, bleak), who the film is about and what she wants. The remaining beats in the 10 point plan don't tell you exactly what happens but they do indicate the significant shifts in the story and who is involved in each one. We know that we need to see the boss being contemptuous, Coll meeting the Old Man, some exchange between them that indicates that he has faith in her, evidence that he has died, the moment of realisation for Coll that she must move on and Coll leaving the van for good.

If you are finding it hard to follow the 10 point plan then the chances are that you have too much plot and/or too many characters in your film. Remember that a 10 minute film can only focus on one idea, does not need any sub-plots and can only cope with a small number of characters. There should not be a single character in your script that does not have a function, i.e. all your characters should be making a contribution to driving the story forward or increasing the main character's problem. Are there characters you could remove entirely without fatally compromising the story? Can you combine two characters into one to make the action feel more focussed?

So now you're clear about the spine of the story, but are you sure that every moment of the script is contributing something useful? In such a short form there is no room for a scene that is not pulling its weight. Remember the two principles that govern all good cinematic storytelling: UNITY and CAUSALITY

Unity
Every scene must be revealing something that increases our understanding of the character and their problem.

Causality
Each scene must MOVE THE STORY ON so that what happens at the end could not have happened any earlier – it is only possible now BECAUSE of each scene that came before.

The Girl in the Lay-By

The Step Outline
A good way to check that you have no slack in your film is to do a step outline on large filing cards. Use one card per scene and on each card write:

> One sentence that summarises what happens.

> What is revealed that is significant to the plot?

> What is revealed that is significant to the audience's understanding of the characters?

> Is there an indication of significant theme?

There may be a couple of very short scenes that simply establish time or place and nothing more, but every scene of significant action should ideally be working to deliver something on at least two out of the three possible fronts (plot, character or theme). Play around with your cards to see if you can combine scenes to make each one do more work, lose some altogether, etc.

Once you know that you have a watertight story then you can make decisions about the most effective order in which to tell it, e.g. forwards, backwards, with flashbacks etc. When you are making shorts at the beginning of your career you have an opportunity to take risks that may not come your way again, so you should certainly make the most of it and be bold and innovative. But if your story will work best as a straightforward linear narrative (as do most of the films quoted in this chapter and many others that have won countless awards), then you don't have to play with non-linear structure simply for the sake of it. Audiences instinctively know when something is pretentious or dishonest but no-one ever tires of a good story well told. If you are a writer/director, you can demonstrate your talent through the way in which you visualise the story, and in the quality of performances that you elicit from your cast. As a writer, what you are looking for is a way of telling the story that adds to its meaning and keeps the audience engaged... not one that will leave them totally confused!

Remember it's a Film

Now you are clear that you have a good story how do you make it CINEMATIC?

> ESTABLISH the world and the character with maximum speed and minimal dialogue

> Remember to use visuals AND sound; sound is a brilliant way to suggest a whole world outside the frame that you can't actually afford to shoot. You can also use sound in creative ways to enhance the impact of your story

> Establish a tone and keep it consistent

> Make sure that your main character is ACTIVE i.e. that they are making choices and/or doing things that allow us to understand them

> Remember that it's better to SHOW a change in a character (via props – significant objects, relationship to others etc) rather than indicate it through dialogue

> Use cinematic devices such as parallel action and montage to build tension and move the story forward with maximum economy

> Go back to your step outline and check that everything that is significant is made manifest to your audience in the most visual way possible

The Final Words

The dialogue should always be the last thing you write and generally the less of it you need to tell the story the more cinematic and the less like television your film will feel. Of course there are some great shorts which are dialogue-heavy but they succeed in establishing themselves as films through other means, e.g. *Je T'aime John Wayne* (D: Toby MacDonald, W: Luke Ponte), a romantic comedy that is a clever and affectionate homage to the Nouvelle Vague.

The Audience for the Script

Finally, remember that the first 'audience' for your film is a reader of the script and one of these may have the power to begin the process of getting it funded. There are loads of you out there with great visual imagination and directorial flair, and a lot of funding schemes will ask for supporting material, but there's no getting away from the fact that you will be at a disadvantage if you can't put the film in your head down on the page. Do everything you can to help the reader 'see' your film as they read and not get irritated:

> Follow the screenwriting conventions (you can check these out on www.scriptfactory.co.uk)

> Read scripts (features and/or shorts) – there are lots of websites where you can find them (e.g. www.scriptpimp.com, www.script-o-rama.com) to familiarise yourself with ways of conveying action and tone on the page

> Avoid writing camera directions and stuff that is going on inside a character's head that the audience for the film can't see

Many of the people who watch short films are hoping to spot the feature filmmaking talent of the future; they are looking for writers and directors with something to say and a unique way of saying it. So be bold and inventive and don't let anyone talk you out of taking creative risks if they are ones that are essential to telling your story. But don't ever make the mistake of thinking that SIMPLE means superficial or facile. A small story can make a big impression if it is told with cinematic flair that captures all the depth and thematic resonance of the idea.

Looking for a script or a writer to work with? Join Shooting People's Screenwriters' Network, a collection of short and feature film writers from the UK and US, edited by Andy Conway (www.shootingpeople.org/cards/andyconway)

Chris and Ben Blaine, interview

Part 1 – Writing Short Film Scripts

What are the major differences between writing for shorts and features?

CHRIS BLAINE: Time. There's a huge difference. We've managed to write shorts in an evening and features have taken at least a weekend...to five years. Some shorts have taken longer of course. Plus the form is very different.

The most effective shorts seem to be those which have a simple idea and a simple plot, all well told. If you've got a really simple basic premise then you can spend time creating the world the film exists in, stuff which makes it feel special and unique and real without necessarily being another idea that the audience have to take in.

Chris and Ben Blaine have written and directed more than ten short films with budgets ranging from £50-50,000, and including *Free Speech*, *Death of the Revolution* (which is a case study in this book), and their latest Cinema Extreme short, *Hallo Panda*. In the first excerpt from an in depth interview which runs throughout this book, Chris and Ben Blaine talk about the writing process for short films.

That said if we ever make another short film I think it'll be one so stuffed full of ideas it does the complete reverse of what I've just been saying.

BEN BLAINE: Yeah, actually the difference for me is not so much between short and feature length, as between stories and ideas. A lot of our best short films are driven not so much by the narrative as by the central idea behind them. This can work quite well at 5 to 10 minutes because it means you can share a thought with the audience without getting bogged down in the mechanics of the story. *Death of the Revolution* is a good example of this, the story is so simple as to be almost non-existent and what really gives the film its momentum is the unravelling of the idea. Same with our film *Free Speech*, where the story of the couple's relationship is told by implication rather than explicitly through the narrative.

Films like this can only really be written quickly because, like a sketch, they either work or they don't. We once 'developed' an idea like this with a Screen Agency and they made us spend the best part of a year on a simple five-page thought about love and maths. By the end of that year I'd have gladly killed myself. We never made that film...

Films with an actual story, something driven by the gravity of getting from A to B, they can take longer and the length of the story doesn't really relate to the length of time they take to write. I mean of course it's physically quicker to write 15 pages than 150 but to perfect the mechanics of a narrative in miniature is probably harder than getting them right on the grand scale. Our latest film, *Hallo Panda* is 30 minutes long and whilst all the characters and ideas fell into place in the first draft it took us about 8 or 9 rewrites to really make the story work, and we ended up having to do some quite big structural re-shaping in the edit too.

Based on your experience of making more than 10 short films – what general advice would you give other filmmakers about writing short film scripts?

CHRIS: Keep it simple! Very simple! Pace yourself! Most of the time you can't wring out all the meaning you want in a single line of dialogue or a single shot - it all comes from everything that has gone before in setting up that payoff...

I suffer from this greatly: I think way too hard about each line of dialogue and action and try to pack so much meaning into each one and it simply washes over anyone who reads or sees the film. You have to set up the idea, so when you have your line with all its meaning, it can mean something because you've put the thought in the audience's head before you get there. Ben can write and it flows, but I usually talk about the idea a lot before putting anything to page - in fact, I'll avoid sitting down and writing as much as is humanly possible.

I do the same with editing. I love it when I'm in there...but you just try getting me there. I think this is because I want to have figured it out before I sit down. I think the best shorts I've written have been after I've dreamt the whole film on an extremely long night bus / walk / 2nd night bus / 2nd walk home or I've written it as a joke to amuse Ben without thinking and haven't realised all the subconscious meaning that was in there. "

BEN: All the usual stuff for screenwriting holds true for shorts. Think about writing visually, use dialogue sparingly and to purpose, think about structure and the overall shape of the piece... but most of all put your work in the bin and burn it.

That may sound harsh, well, OK, it is harsh, but for me the most

Death of the Revolution

important thing is to accept that as a writer you have lots of ideas. If this one doesn't work out, fine, bin it and do something else. This holds true for features but as I said before, the good thing about shorts is, if nothing else, they take less time to type out. Also with shorts, there are fewer hiding places than with a feature script, so it's usually easier to see if it not really working.

There's no shame in writing a bad script. No shame in admitting that a brilliant idea is just a brilliant idea and not, actually, a brilliant film. I've got an idea I love about a man who goes to a tailor to get a suit made and the tailor takes loads of measurements and the man goes away and the tailor, who is obviously down on his luck, works night and day drawing patterns and cutting them, and pining them and sewing this suit together. A week later the customer returns and the tailor has made him a pinstripe coffin.

> **"there are fewer hiding places than with a feature script, so it's usually easier to see if it not really working"**

I love this. I especially love the moment where the tailor proudly unveils it and the customer has to try and express his thoughts without wanting to offend the tailor. It's comic, it's tragic, it says something I quite can't put my finger on but I like. It also has no real ending. Or at least not one I've ever thought of and liked. It's a great idea, but it's a bloody awful film, which is why we never made it.

Don't get too proud and possessive of your work. If you find that your idea won't fall into the shape you want it to be then find another idea."

How do you know when a script or idea is ready to shoot? Do you ask friends to read work and give feedback?

BEN: Well it helps there being the two of us. It's a really good sounding board for whether something is working or not. I think we're both pretty harsh, which is how it should be. If it gets past us then on the whole we can usually justify it to other people, especially in a short film.

I think the best thing is that both of us understand scripts and filmmaking... that's the toughest thing about giving a script to friends. Both with scripts and finished films everyone knows when something isn't working, but very few people actually ever know *what* isn't working, which is the most important thing. If you give a script to your mates then their feedback is always going to be brilliant, but you need to be able to decipher what they mean from what they say... For instance, often people will say the end of something doesn't work when really this is because you're doing something wrong in the middle, which is undercutting what could be a brilliant ending.

It's what Chris was saying earlier, writing - and editing - is a process of giving meaning by association. You see a man crying and you think 'how sad', you see exactly the same shot of a man crying, but after having first watched him kill his children - well it's a different scene. The accumulation of events and significance in a narrative is probably the single most powerful tool you've got. Consequently it can be very hard to detach a scene or image from the meaning that it has been given, even if that meaning is not intrinsic but implied. It's often very hard for non-filmmakers really to be able to unpick this process and see which part of your story is giving them the bum steer.

I suppose an important thing to underline though is that filmmaking is always a collaboration whether you work with your brother or not. As long as you're working with a creative team you trust and respect then that should be all the sounding board you need.

> **"often people will say the end of something doesn't work when really this is because you're doing something wrong in the middle"**

CHRIS: We also worked with a script editor called Carolyn Young on the Featurelab scheme run by Screen East and wrote *Helicopter Land*, which is probably our most accomplished feature script to date. She improved our writing ten-fold and we're really, really keen to keep working with her because she's great.

I'm sure many other script editors are great too, if you can find one, then do (try asking The Script Factory for people who've done their script editing courses; that's a starting place). As we said earlier, it's really easy to try and pack your ideas up tight and something a script editor will be great at, is getting you to pace yourself, making sure you're putting the information over at a decent pace.

Can you talk a little bit about the writing process on *Death Of The Revolution*?

CHRIS: Ben and I collaborate fiercely when it comes to feature scripts and wouldn't do it any other way, but shorts can be written so quickly that we've most often written them alone. That said we wrote *Hallo Panda* together so it might just be a case of our collaborative relationship changing over time. Anyway, I had nothing to do with it, Ben just dumped a bunch of short scripts in front of me one day and I said I liked this one best.

BEN: The idea largely comes from life. Adam, the naughty boy who smashes the calculator is my friend Adam Waine who now runs the Warner Village in Leicester Square in London. Leyla Fuyad is also a real girl who was in my class at primary school, and she did indeed fail her cycling proficiency test because the pedals of her bike drove her forward whichever way she pushed. Charlotte, who gets her pencil stolen, is based on Charlotte Nolan. I had a crush on her, though I don't think I ever stole her pencil. I was actually a very well behaved boy at school, though I did once get into trouble for graffiti-ing desks with quotes from Shakespeare. I've always been a ponce.

Anyway, about six or seven years ago I met up with Susie Jacobsen [UK-based filmmaker] who was looking for someone to write a short film for her to direct. I set myself the challenge of writing a new script every night for a week and *Death Of The Revolution* was Tuesday night's. Susie optioned it but never made it. When Chris and I were finally in a position to make it ourselves we redrafted it a bit, but just to tighten the argument up in places. Including everything - except thought - it must have taken about twelve hours work over six years. It's one of those ideas, it either works or doesn't.

CHRIS: I was a little annoyed that someone else might get to make the film, so when Susie's option expired it pretty much became the next film we were going to make - although as we felt we had to make it on film, we couldn't do it through the UK Film Council's Digital Shorts programme, and as we'd found a producer who wanted to make *Free Speech* we did that instead... but always with this script in the back pocket...

Hallo Panda
Photo by Jessica Thomas

Sample Script

Death Of The Revolution.
By Chris and Ben Blaine.

FADE IN.

EXT. PRIMARY SCHOOL - MORNING.

Through the windows of a ground floor classroom a maths lesson
is underway.

INT. PRIMARY SCHOOL, CLASS ROOM - MORNING.

CHARLOTTE HANSON is searching for her pencil.

PETER UPSON, a jolly boy with floppy hair, makes a noise like a
FART and everyone GIGGLES.

ADAM TRAVIS, a naturally malevolent child, notices Charlotte and
nudges his friend TONY PALMER, who grins.

With the reactions of an assassain Charlotte looks up and sees
the two boys starting to laugh.

Morally appalled her hand shoots indignantly into the air.

                    CHARLOTTE
          Miss!!

The TEACHER looks up from her marking.

Tony's eyes are wide with panic.

BLACK.

SUPER IMP. - TITLE.

BACK TO SCENE.

Tony stands by the Teacher's desk. He is small with messy hair
and a look of shame. The Teacher is quite young, although in
this setting she is older than the hills.

                    TEACHER
          Why did you hide Charlotte's
          pencil Tony? Don't you know it's
          wrong?

                    TONY
               (quietly)
          Adam told me.

Disappointed she shakes her head.

Adam squrims in the corner of the room.

> TEACHER
> And if Adam Travis told you to
> jump off a cliff - would you do
> that too?

> TONY
> No miss.

The Teacher nods at him, the logic of her argument plain to see.

> TEACHER
> Well then! Go on, give Charlotte
> her pencil back and get on with
> your long division.

Sullenly Tony takes the pencil and starts the long walk back.

The other children watch darkly from their moral high ground.

> TONY (v.o.)
> It's not fair. I wish *she'd* jump
> off a cliff.

His bottom lips juts out in depression.

Mechanically he sticks out the pencil for Charlotte, who takes
it from him in a prissy fasion.

> CHARLOTTE
> Thank you very much Tony.

She gets on with her work and he sits down again.

> TONY (v.o.)
> What if *Miss* told me to jump off a
> cliff?

Adam punches him on the arm.

> ADAM
> (hissing and furious)
> GRASS!

Tony turns away and ignores this, starting to do his Maths.

> TONY (v.o.)
> No, I wouldn't jump off a cliff if
> Miss told me to. Does that mean I
> shouldn't do what she says either?

Tony looks up from his sums, his forehead furrows in
concentration.

>   TONY (v.o.)
>   If you apply her logic to any
>   authoritarian relationship then -

Tony sticks his tongue out to make more space in his head for
thoughts.

>   TONY (v.o.)
>   Surely that means obeying the
>   commands of any ruler is *always*
>   the first step on the road to
>   totalitarianism!

The pencil slips from his hand and bounces on the floor.

>   TONY (v.o.)
>   Of course! The sublimation of
>   personal responsibility to the
>   will of either a single leader or,
>   in the broadest possible sense,
>   the society into which one is
>   born, what Rosseau describes as
>   the General Will"- is not onl y
>   the avoidance of our natural duty
>   - but - it lays us open to abuse.

His jaw drops open in astonishment.

>   TONY (v.o.)
>   If we simply accept what we are
>   told then what is to stop our
>   acceptance of future actions being
>   taken for granted and thus our
>   name being put to deeds we would
>   not wish it put to!

He folds his arms and sits back on the small wooden chair.

>   TONY (v.o.)
>   E.G. the German public and the
>   holocaust of the Jewish nation in
>   the 2nd World War!

Charlotte is staring at him like he is mad.

Another thought strikes him and he looks around the room at the
collection of seven and eight year olds.

> TONY (v.o.)
> My GOD! I must explain this to the
> others! I must, inject them with
> the revolutionary zeal necessary
> to bring about the overthrow of
> the oppressive establishment and
> thus bring about the birth of a
> utopian future!

The Teacher is still marking maths books.

Adam is fighting with Peter.

> TONY (v.o.)
> All children will be equal! Black,
> white, Asian and Leyla Fuyad, who
> isn't really any of those but does
> have a bike that can't go
> backwards.

LEYLA is chewing her pencil and staring vacantly out of the
window.

SUSIE is drawing horses on her maths book.

> TONY (v.o.)
> No one would work unless they felt
> inspired to!

The Teacher is subtly reading her horoscope below the table.

ANDY is picking his nose.

> TONY (v.o.)
> We would learn with the beauty of
> nature and everyone would have an
> EQUAL TURN IN THE SANDPIT!

INT. SANDPIT - DAY.

A child drives a toy car wildly through the sand.

INT. CLASROOM - DAY.

Tony's eyes are wide with inspiration.

Leyla is still staring out of the window.

> TONY (v.o.)
> I must leap to my feet and say:

DREAM SEQUENCE:

INT. CLASSROOM - DAY.

Tony is on his feet, his fist raised - he takes a deep breath.

The rest of the class look at him.

                    TONY (v.o.)
          Friends! Romans! Countrymen! And
          Leyla Fuyad! Do not submit to the
          mindless crush of authority!

END DREAM.

INT. CLASSROOM - DAY.

Adam is trying to break the solar cell on his calculator.

                    TONY (v.o.)
          Do not so passively bow your heads
          in the face of Mr.Green the
          Headmaster just because he can
          simultaneously point and click his
          fingers!

INT. SCHOOL HALL - DAY.

MR.GREEN simultaneously points and CLICKS his fingers.

DREAM SEQUENCE:

INT. CLASSROOM - DAY.

The rest of the class listen to Tony as he talks, arms
outstretched.

                    TONY (v.o.)
          Throw off your shackles and tear
          down these walls! You have nothing
          to lose but your break time
          biscuit and the year five's
          superior rights on the climbing
          frame! Who is with me?

Thirty eager hands rise into the air.

INT. LONG CORRIDOR - DAY.

The doors swing open at the far end and the children start to
charge SCREAMING down it.

> TONY (v.o.)
> Put down your Berol pens and pick
> up your swords and let us storm
> the Nature Gardens!

EXT. THE NATURE GARDEN - DAY.

Children charge across the grass - one boy has a large flag.

INT. SCHOOL HALL - DAY.

The children are singing hymns in Assembly.

> TONY (v.o.)
> Together as a single nation with
> one pure, out of key voice, let us
> sing rude words to the hymns in
> assembly!

> PETER
> (singing)
> "Someone's weeing Lord, cuym by
> ahhh!"

EXT. PLAYGROUND - DAY.

The children run around with their anoraks zipped up.

> TONY (v.o.)
> Let us unite in putting our coats
> on backwards and zipping our
> Parkas up until we can NO LONGER
> SEE OUT!

INT. LONG CORRIDOR - DAY.

The children charge SCREAMING.

> TONY (v.o.)
> And let us charge into battle,
> running down all the corridors
> wearing nothing but the INCORRECT
> FOOTWEAR!

END DREAM.

INT. CLASSROOM - DAY.

Tony smiles.

With a rush of adrenaline and a SCREETCH of chair legs, Tony stands up.

Charlotte and Adam stare at him, the room falls silent.

The Teacher looks up from her horoscope and fixes him with a hard stare.

                    TEACHER
          Tony?

Tony clears his throat.

Peter Upson makes a noise like a FART and everyone LAUGHS.

Tony pales, swallows hard and sits down.

He shoots Peter an evil glare, Peter is still LAUGHING.

                    TONY (v.o.)
          I bet no one never did that to
          Lenin.

                                        FADE OUT.

Docs

The Short Doc

Jess Search, Chief Executive,
Channel 4 British Documentary Film Foundation

Compared to short fiction films, fewer short documentaries get made in the UK - a shame because they can be completely wonderful and a passport to making longer films, both documentary and fiction. One of the reasons that not many short docs have been made in the UK recently is that our documentary filmmaking has revolved around television and there are very few slots for shorts there. It's quite rare these days to even see a half hour documentary (Channel 4's long running 3 Minute Wonders after the news are a notable exception). But documentary filmmakers should be looking beyond traditional terrestrial television because, as this book proves, there are now loads of new places for short documentaries to screen. They are a great counterpoint to the wealth of short fiction films, and they are great way to draw attention to your skills as a storyteller.

New broadcast possibilities

Firstly, it's worth mentioning that new broadcasters (or narrowcasters) are entering the market for short docs. Current TV, which launched on the SKY platform in the UK in 2007, will be looking for plenty of short documentary content. Current are an MTV-style documentary-only digital channel and website, often represented in the media by one of their backers Al Gore (you can read our interview with Jason Meil from Current TV on page 209). Al Jazeera English was launched in 2006 and is also looking for short documentaries – under 30 minutes (though they mainly want them told by local people, not by western filmmakers travelling the world). Channel 4's broadband docs channel 4Docs is also worth checking out – they don't pay for films but it is a place to put your short and get it seen by audiences as well as Channel 4 new talent commissioning editors (see www.channel4.com/4docs). Keep an eye on the market; other players will emerge in the next couple of years.

Fests and exposure

Remember, with shorts, it's not just about selling your film. Among other benefits, shorts are a passports to the very stimulating and fun festival circuit, which is a great way to expand your horizons and contacts. Fests are so important to a filmmaker's development, I'd go so far as to say that if you are working on a longer form doc, it's worth thinking about cutting a short out of it – not quite a trailer, but a self contained work that you can freely use to promote the longer film whilst it is being finished. You may find this expands your festival

The Channel 4 British Documentary Film Foundation
www.britdoc.org/foundation
Katie Bradford

The Channel 4 British Documentary Film Foundation is an independent, not-for-profit organisation, which was set up by former commissioners from Channel 4 with a grant from the Channel in October 2005 to support new British documentary work. The Foundation's Katie Bradford contributes this case study of several of the short films they supported in their first year:

Funding short docs is a core part of the Foundation's mission to ensure a creative and ambitious future for British documentary. The short films that we support allow us to discover new directors that we haven't worked with before and also to facilitate films which are more formally and stylistically experimental. Whilst not as common place as fiction shorts, short docs can be brilliant as a calling card to commissioning editors and as a way of securing first or longer commissions, as well as allowing you to work the festival circuit if your film does well (though bear in mind most festivals won't pay for you to attend for shorts).

Making a great short doc is really hard – what works for a short wouldn't usually work for a feature and vice versa. It's essential when you're pitching or making a short documentary really to consider the structure and form - you need to relay information quickly and in many cases stylistic and/or structured pieces work better than a purely observational approach. On a basic note, your camera work and sound need to be good – a lot of short docs are let down by the quality of the filming, which ruins the overall impact.

In our first year, we funded 6 shorts, all between 10 and 40 minutes long, with budgets ranging from £5,000 to £20,000. They're all total one-offs, but the one thing that they do have in common is that the people making them have a real vision for their subject. None of them would be sustainable as a longer piece but work brilliantly at their natural length – as we aren't tied to TV slots, we can work with directors to see what duration is going to be most powerful for their film.

Oddly, we don't get pitched enough brilliant short doc ideas – what we look for in a short doc proposal is a gem of an idea, a subject that is immediately engaging, that will take the audience on a short journey. Different rules apply – shorts don't necessarily need to be big impact like feature docs, there's a chance to try new things and cover quirkier subjects, as long as they have a wholeness to them that can be captured in short-form.

A common problem when working with filmmakers making a short is that they get so involved in their subject and their film that they want to include too much. The most common bit of editorial feedback that we give is 'it's great, but it could do with being 6 minutes shorter!' and our rule of thumb is that most shorts work best at under 20 minutes. The exception to this amongst the films that we've funded so far is *Sargy Mann* (see case study below) – here, both because the mood of the film is quite ambient and because Sargy Mann's re-discovery of his artistic process is quite a slow and involved experience, there's enough development to the story to keep you engaged over a longer duration.

Another way that we get involved with short documentaries is by programming them for BRIT-DOC, our annual documentary event in Keble College, Oxford, which takes place each July. Entry for the shorts programme is by open submission and we put out a call for entries in the spring.

For more information about the Channel 4 British Documentary Film Foundation (and to apply for funding) and the BRITDOC festival, visit www.britdoc.org

42

potential even more (Shooting People members can download the chart to the world's top 40 documentary festivals from the site shootingpeople.org – listed in order of the entry dates throughout the year).

Doc shorts are very popular screenings at festivals. In fact, too many feature docs at film festivals feel too long for their subject – like they have been stretched to turn it into a theatrical property. Tell your story well in as many minutes as it actually *needs* and you'll have a much better film. If you try to expand it solely to make it a theatrical 80 or 90 minutes, that will be obvious to commissioners, distributors and audiences alike. The strategy may not have the desired effect. The BBC used to have a great documentary strand called 40 minutes which was, you guessed it, 40 minutes long. While 40 minutes would be considered a short film by Cannes and many other film festivals, it is actually a very good length for many stories. Interestingly, Sundance Film Festival does not distinguish between fiction and documentary in its short film category and documentaries have beaten the fiction to win Best Short there twice in the last 5 years. For examples of good short doc filmmaking, these recent winners are both worth checking out. *Terminal Bar* by Stefan Nadelman tells the story of a down and out bar in New York owned by the filmmaker's grandfather through the photographs he took of patrons over the years (available on Cinema 16); and *Family Portrait* by Patricia Riggen catches up with a Harlem family famously photographed by Gordon Parks in 1968 for Life magazine to see what's happened to them in the intervening years. It's a damning pre-Hurricane Katrina look at how America treats its poor urban black population (available on Shooting People's Best v Best Vol One collection).

> **"if you are working on a longer form doc, it's worth thinking about cutting a short out of it – not quite a trailer, but a self contained work that you can freely use to promote the longer film whilst it is being finished"**

Family Portrait by Patricia Riggen

Notes on developing a short film idea

If you are working on a short documentary, here are a few tips to keep in mind:

1) *Think before you shoot.* Treat your idea like a squash ball and get it nicely warmed up by thrashing it off as many walls as possible before you start shooting. It's truly very rare that a great short doc is exactly what the director first imagined it would be. Your idea should change and develop at all stages. Before you go to

TALK TO ME directed by Mark Craig

Covering 22 years in 22 minutes, *Talk to Me* tells the story of director Mark Craig's life entirely through answer phone messages that he has meticulously kept, heard over a single tracking shot of photographs and general ephemera from his student years through to the present day.

Mark: In 1985 I bought an answer machine. I then kept every message that was left for 20 years! I always knew I'd end up doing something with them - originally it was going to be an art installation with flashing lights and dozens of retro phones and different ringing sounds etc. But I had no joy in obtaining any art grants or even corporate sponsorship, and some even thought I was a sad anorak for keeping thousands of old answer machine messages in the first place. Then the Foundation was born - I filled in the easy peasy application form on their website and in due course was called in to meet 'the panel'. One pitch later, I was amazed to be walking out the door with a cheque. Those gals certainly don't hang about.

But then the hard part began. What made things tough in my case was first having to do a sound-only edit with an exceptionally large amount of material, especially when it duly crashed the Avid and was lost. Argggh! With the final audio sequence assembled, my plan to shoot the visuals on a rostrum camera in one take. A little tricky as it was over 20 minutes long and had a couple of hundred separate stops, starts & moves... Hmmm... The Foundation were on hand to remind me that 'less was more' and not to let clever tricksiness obscure the inherent power of the raw material. Good advice.

Talk To Me is now doing the rounds of the festival circuit, which, despite having a reasonable amount of broadcast experience, is a first for me. The opportunities to learn more and meet key industry players have inspired and invigorated me at a time when many of my contemporaries have become jaded with the industry, and so big thanks to the Foundation for giving me a break when I needed it. Perhaps I'm a maverick and perhaps they are too, but in a world of forgettable telly it's great to have a bunch of people prepared to stick their necks out, take a chance, and maybe help something get made that makes a difference...

SARGY MANN directed by Peter Mann

Director Peter Mann follows his father Sargy Mann, a successful figurative painter, as he rediscovers his artistic process after going completely blind.

Peter: Initially I wanted to make a film about how my father worked when he still had a small amount of vision in one eye, which had been the case for the last few years before he went totally blind. I felt that through watching him try to see and paint you could learn a lot about visual perception in general as well as about him and his type of figurative painting. Also the relationship between visual art and how we actually experience the world is something that, almost certainly because of my father, has always fascinated me.

I was going through the submission process for Britdoc during the time I was filming. I found it extremely frustrating writing proposals trying to pretend I knew what I was doing and what the film would be about, and at the same time shooting it. My main problem was that all the time I was filming I was only thinking about what was happening at that moment and I hated having to think in terms of where it might lead to and what the story was. (continues...)

make it you need to have an excellent plan of action, but life has a funny habit of turning out differently than expected and you need to be able to move with it.

2) *Ask WOULD I WATCH THIS?* …seriously? Would you read the description and turn on your TV/ computer? Be honest with yourself. If your subject or concept feels familiar or uninspiring even to you – it needs radical shaking up, or maybe you should move on.

3) *Don't convince yourself there are no problems.* Every film has them and you better be aware what your biggest weaknesses are. If something is going to go wrong, what will it be? How are you going to ensure that it doesn't go wrong, and what are your B and C plans if it does? Wishful thinking will sink you. Admitting that there's a risk - your access to the key location could fall through or your main character hates being interviewed - will be essential to preparing creative solutions.

> **"Documentaries differ from fiction most dramatically in the edit. This is where documentaries are really made"**

4) *Be prepared to re-think it in the edit.* Documentaries differ from fiction most dramatically in the edit. This is where documentaries are really made (arguably, dramas are forged in the script stage). There are many ways to skin a cat in the edit room and you may want to try a few before settling on your final approach. The other wonderful thing about documentary is that it's very often possible to continue filming during the edit (as opposed to the huge costs of re-shooting fiction scenes) when it becomes clear what else you might need.

5) *Be creative.* One of the things I particularly love about the short form is it's perfect for experimenting with form. You wouldn't want to try making an 109 minute upside-down documentary but as a short, anything is possible and you can push things to the maximum. The end result can make a film sound very distinctive when described, which is important when you want your film to stand out.

I'd really stress the importance of that final tip. What's going to make your film stand out? I used to run a short film strand on Channel 4 called Alt TV, which ran for a few years. We concentrated on films that tried to do things differently – they we're often quite concept driven ideas. Paul Berzceller's *This Is A True Story* was told in still photographs. Jamie Jay Johnson's *Holiday Around My Bedroom* was exactly that: Jamie used blue screen to shrink himself down to pencil size for his journey of discovery in the most familiar place. Both films were very original, neither might have worked at a longer length, and both were nominated for BAFTAs. The Channel 4 British Documentary Film Foundation which I work for now has continued to look for original short film ideas and I can highly recommend *Talk To Me* which we case study in this section. It's a 23 minute film by Mark Craig made up entirely of his answer machines messages kept over a 20 year period.

All in all short documentaries are a great place for a filmmaker to start work – even if they are ultimately going to end up making fiction films – or the hybrids between fact and fiction that are so interesting at the moment. You may actually have a big advantage over planning a fiction short; depending on your idea, documentary can be quite accessible, easy to shoot, suited to a small crew and forgiving of a low budget!

I had never made a film before and so I had nothing with which to compare my experience making this one, but I am pretty sure that no TV commissioner would have given me any money to make it in the first place. I would like to think I would have made it anyway, since I actually got the money from The Foundation in February 2006 and by that time I was so far into the process I would not have been able to drop it, but it would have been extremely difficult without their help. Once they had agreed to fund the project I was allowed to just get on with it; the Foundation were there with help and advice but never interfered. For example I decided I wanted to edit the film even though I had never really done any editing before, and the Foundation backed that decision. Similarly when I was close to the end I showed a rough cut on two or three occasions and the various people at the Foundation who saw it offered advice but I never felt under any pressure to do anything other than what I thought was right, in terms of the edit or making it a particular length.

So far nothing specifically has come out of me making the film, I have met quite a few people and hopefully in the long term it will lead to me being able to make more films. I have entered various film festivals and maybe it will have some sort of life in that area. I would love to carry on making films, so I am trying to figure out a balance between making films I want to make, and making some money.

SPECKY directed by Anne-Claire Pilley

Featuring director Anne-Claire and her extended 'specky' family, *Specky* is an autobiographical adventure quest that looks at how short-sighted people survived the stone age.

Anne-Claire: Working with the Foundation was excellent - they made their decision very quickly. The idea was with them for just over a month, I came to London for the pitch meeting and the idea was commissioned there and then. They put me in touch with a mentor who gave me great feedback in the edit and on the script. They helped on most questions of copyright and budget and also had comments in the edit which were very helpful. Money was set aside at the end of the production to help me fund entries to film festivals.

Working by myself was the main difference from the TV work I'd done myself. Although I didn't enjoy it much it was great experience to learn how to put together a budget and production manage the shoot. I think I have one up on production managers compared to most producers now! I think the realisation that I CAN make my own films and don't necessarily have to go to a channel or through a production company was very liberating. Working by myself was quite tiring at times, and I felt that I was finding difficult to be creative when I was overwhelmed with paperwork. But I think this was partly a function of the documentary – which included archive, props, lots of original music – I think if it had been more observational it would have required less prepping and might have been less hard work to put together. The highs were the edit, seeing it all come together. And coming to the realisation that the idea I'd had all those months ago, worked.

Making *Specky* gave me my first gig as a PD (Producer/Director). On the back of *Specky*, which TV people seem to like a lot, I was given four one hours for network daytime to direct. Right now, I'm PDing, self-shooting and self-editing a half-hour documentary for the Princes Trust at IWC media – on the Z1 I was able to buy thanks to the grant given to me by the Foundation. Once I've got more self-shooting experience under my belt, I would very much like to make more of my own films. I have a few ideas which are more TV than independent film in with Channel 4 new talent initiatives, but I also have some independent film ideas I'd like to make when I have time to get my head round them.

Treatment for *SPECKY*
Director: Anne-Claire Pilley

'The Pitch' in 50 words or less:

Specky is an autobiographical-adventure-quest which sets out to establish how short-sighted people like me survived the stone age. A month-long journey that begins with the plight of speckies in modern society and ends with a promise to get my 20/20 vision back. Out of focus POVs chart my progress.

The idea

Get a camera. Focus it on this paper. Now, look through the camera at a picture on the far wall without moving the focus ring.

Welcome. Now you see how I see the world.

I'm not alone. The world is a fuzz for 25% of the population, making short-sightedness the commonest disability to affect humankind.

But it can't always have been like this. Otherwise, speckies would have been naturally selected out of existence at a time when Specsavers didn't exist and sabretooth tigers did. So why are we still here?

Specky is an autobiographical-adventure-quest which sets out to establish how short-sighted people survived the stone age. A month-long journey that begins with the plight of the specky in modern society and ends with a challenge to get my 20/20 vision back. Out of focus POVs chart my progress.

My glasses are a prescription minus 6. Proper milk-bottle bottoms. I can hazard a guess where I got it from. My Mum's specky, my Dad's specky, my brother's specky; my uncle's specky. My Grandad's specky, my Granny was specky and my Cousins are also specky. A whole family of goggle-wearers.

And it's a right pain in the arse.

8 Things I Hate About Glasses

scenarios to be re-enacted for demonstration

1. When you loose your glasses you won't be able to find them again because you can't see anything without them.

2. You'll always forget your contact lens solution when you go on holiday. And there's never a mention in the phrasebook of how to say 'do you have contact lens solution?' in Greek.

3. When you don't forget your solution it leaks in your suitcase.

4. They get all steamed up when you open the dishwasher. (though this can be quite a handy if you don't want to empty)

5. Boys don't make passes at girls who wear glasses (depending on the company, this can also be quite handy)

6. Girls without glasses can't see boys who make passes (this is rarely useful)

7. Patronising non-speckies say things like, "they make you look so intelligent" and "they suit your face"

8. When I wear glasses, I can see my spots.

Most speckies will attest that wearing glasses from an early age marks you for life.

You are 35% more likely to be bullied if you wear glasses. And it is any wonder with Milhouse (The Simpsons), Horace (the Broons) or Velma (Scooby Doo) as our four-eyed icons?

Things I've Been Called On Account Of My Glasses

1. Four eyes
2. Specky
3. Specky four eyes
4. Geekso
5. Freakso
6. Blindy/blind-o
7. NHS glasses face
8. Double glazing face
9. Face furniture face
10. Joe 90

Scientists at Wolverhampton have also discovered that speckies are also four times less likely to pull in a nightclub. Having suffered the hard end of these statistics, a team of specwearers demonstrate to the drastic effects of spectacle wearing on your pulling power. Two nights out on the town, one with glasses on, the other with contacts in: we confirm that the definition of Specky in the popular lexicon is (feminine) uptight and ugly librarian (male) Clark Kent.

But if we think we have a bad time —think of what it must have been like in prehistorical times, in the times before glasses? To the tune of 'My eyes are dim I cannot see, I have not brought my specs with me', a team of speckies go re-enact prehistoric natural selection. They go paint-balling, without their glasses. The aim: evolutionary survival. The unequivocal verdict: Speckies should all be dead.

So what's it all about? Why are we still here? Did Darwin screw up?

Controversial ophthalmologist, Thomas R Quackenbush (real name honest!) author of 'Relearning to See', has the earth-shattering answer. There is no such thing as 'genetic myopia' and modern day optometry is just a money-making scam. We survived the Stone Age because those with a propensity for myopia usually never developed it. It's our modern lifestyle - education the main culprit- that makes us blind.

We don't need glasses, he proclaims, all we need is to train our eyes to see. 'Natural vision', he calls it. And I am sold.

Specky culminates with three weeks' rigorous adherence to the Quackenbush Method, running the gamut from complex brainscan visual feedback exercises - up and down and up and down and left and right - which are quite difficult to do if you are watching the eyerobic video at the same time.

Will my sight improve? Viewers will find out in the final frames of the show as out of focus POVs chart the progress.

Project Development Contacts & Resources

UK

Arista Development

 11 Wells Mews,
London W1T 3HD

 020-7323 1775

020-7323 1772

arista@aristotle.co.uk
www.aristadevelopment.co.uk

TAKE NOTE: Hosts courses in script development, primarily for feature film projects. Also runs a number of short courses

B3 Media

PO Box 41000,
London SW2 1HN

020-7274 2121

studio@b3media.net
www.b3media.net

BBC Writersroom

1 Mortimer Street,
London W1T 3JA

www.bbc.co.uk/writersroom

TAKE NOTE: While no BBC departments take unsolicited work, you can submit scripts through the writers' room on their website. Check out the site for details of submission initiatives – they will usually call for entries for different programmes.

Euroscript

P.O. Box 3117,
Gloucester GL4 0WW

(0780) 336 9414

enquiries@euroscript.co.uk
www.euroscript.co.uk

TAKE NOTE: Most courses are for feature development but they do offer script consultancy and reading feedback services for short film scripts.

NPA (New Producers' Alliance)

The NPA Film Centre,
Unit 10.7,
The Tea Building,
56 Shoreditch High Street,
London E1 6JJ

020-7613 0440

 queries@npa.org.uk
www.npa.org.uk

TAKE NOTE: Filmmakers' networking and event membership organisation.

Also see Raindance in our Resources contacts

Rocliffe

 PO Box 37344,
London N1 8YB

 scripts@rocliffe.com
www.rocliffe.com

TAKE NOTE: Rocliffe host a series of events where you can have an extract from your script read by actors and then get feedback from the audience and a panel of experts. They also have special short film events.

Shooting People's Screenwriters' Network

 www.shootingpeople.org

TAKE NOTE: Screenwriters' Network is a daily bulletin for news and exchange on short and feature screenwriting. Great place for finding a writer or co-writer.

The Script Factory

Welbeck House,
66-67 Wells Street,
London W1T 3PY

(020-7323 1414

general@scriptfactory.co.uk
www.scriptfactory.co.uk

TAKE NOTE: Screenwriter and script development organisation that has training courses for writers and developers, plus regular screenings and master-classes. Throughout the year, they offer a number of special training courses for short filmmakers, including hosting the UK Film Council's digi-shorts training schemes (for funded filmmakers).

Writers' Guild of Great Britain (WGGB)

 15 Britannia Street,
London WC1X 9JN

(020-7833 0777

admin@writersguild.org.uk
www.writersguild.org.uk

TAKE NOTE: Trade union for writers in all media (film, TV, radio, theatre, books, poetry, and video games)

USA

Filmmakers' Alliance

The American Cinematheque,
The Egyptian Theater,
6712 Hollywood Blvd,
Los Angeles,
CA 90028, USA

(+1 310 568 0633

info@filmmakersalliance.com
www.filmmakersalliance.com

TAKE NOTE: Organisation with monthly meetings and seminars. Encourages members to share resources and help each other out and has member-created writers' groups. Also host the L.A. Short Filmmaking Competition, which is an annual filmmaking comp open to FA members. Winner receives a package of cash, and services.

Sundance Institute

8530 Wilshire Blvd.,
3rd Floor,
Beverly Hills,
CA 90211-3114, USA

(+1 310 360 1981

la@sundance.org
www.sundance.org

TAKE NOTE: The Institute runs the famed fest, and their site has info about the year round programmes they run, such as their Screenwriters Lab which is held two times per year with 12 feature writers each time.

Writers' Guild of America, West

 7000 West Third Street,
Los Angeles,
CA 90048, USA

📞 +1 323 951 4000

💻 www.wga.org

TAKE NOTE: Trade org for writers in the west of US. Primarily caters to feature writers but useful website.

Writers' Guild of America, East

✉ 555 West 57th Street,
Suite 1230,
New York,
NY 10019, USA

📞 +1 212 767-7800

💻 www.wgaeast.org

TAKE NOTE: Trade org for writers in the east of US. Site has a page of useful links and competitions for US-based writers.

For additional information, and to download extra materials and clearance forms which are in this book, go to www.shootingpeople.org/shortsbook

Section Two:
Get it Funded

Budgets

The sound of money - short film funding and budgets

Christos Michaels and Andy Gordon, Sound Films

Getting the funds to make a short film is generally hard work and for good reason. As opposed to feature films, you will probably have little or no track record and short films are highly unlikely to make their money back - not the most promising investment opportunity! Still, with preparation, determination, resourcefulness and flexibility, you will succeed.

We should start by confessing that we did not get the money to make our last short film, *Hibernation*, through the normal public funding bodies. Luckily we weren't forced to rob any banks (except our own accounts), nor did we lie, cheat or steal (except sometimes to ourselves about our chances of raising the finance). But we eventually had to acknowledge that, whilst the crew and many suppliers got what we were trying to do, some of the more unique elements (*"are you really trying to tell me that the main characters are 9 year old kids in full animal costumes for the whole damn film and you never even see them talk? You must be having a laugh, you loon"*) seemed to put off traditional funding entities.

The themes of a film can also put off investors, because with only a script and the filmmaker's previous work to go on, they may think they have seen it before, or that it is not strong enough, or even that it's just not to their taste. When we approached at least one of the regional funding bodies, they were very battle weary of our story (*"every short film we get seems to be about children dealing with the bereavement of a close friend; it has been done to death"*).

These sorts of responses may mean that (a) you are not pitching it correctly to the investors, (b) these are not the right investors for your film, or (c) you really are a lunatic and should be wearing a jacket that does up at the back.

Getting your dirty little hands on it
Assuming you are not a dribbly maniac and you have a great script and short film you want to make, where does the money come from?

1) Public funds
Sometimes known as official funding, these generally come from either nationwide schemes (such as the UK Film Council or, more rarely nowadays, broadcasters) or run through the schemes via regional film offices

(all are listed in the contacts area of this section). Most of these funds either apply to writers or directors, and will then help set up teams by bringing together directors and other crew, or else they may encourage a group application.

They often give much more than just funding by means of development support and services in kind. For example, the talented script editor that worked on our film, went on to help successful applicants develop their scripts under B3 Media's Digital Shorts scheme.

For the first timer, local and regional schemes are generally more accessible, with a higher number of lower grants, and are designed for new filmmakers using cheaper digital methods of filming. It is certainly one of the first places to apply, as the competition will generally be less than for the national schemes.

When applying for funding you will generally speaking need to satisfy the relevant eligibility criteria although you may find that funds are more flexible if they love your project. Often, if you look carefully, with a bit of creativity and flexibility you can adapt to meet public funding criteria.

These funds will not only give you cash but also support, advice, resources and the benefit of their experience, which can be invaluable. Therefore, regional screen agencies can be a great resource even if they don't fund your film. The Screen South office based at Pinewood was fantastic in helping us scout for a tricky location; we needed a secluded huge Sleepy Hollow style tree in which to build a full tree house and a traditional sleepy Cornwall village shop all within easy reach of Pinewood. They then vouched for us when we had to seek the permission of the Lord of the manor.

National Schemes are generally, though not exclusively, for filmmakers with a little more experience. The level of the grants may be much larger than the regional funds (e.g. UK Film Council's Cinema Extreme scheme which has a £50,000 budget) but for which the funder may demand more control over the project. Other schemes, such as the Digital Shorts, offer lesser sums but also welcome a less experienced filmmaker. There are also schemes specified by genre; for minorities; ones which benefit the community; and ones that push the boundaries of filmmaking or story telling. You will need to see if your film is applicable, or can be made to be applicable for these schemes. Before you submit an application, it is worth contacting representatives of the funding body to have an initial chat about what they are looking for in an application in terms of style, back up materials and tastes. We also think it may be worth contacting successful applicants to find out more about their projects.

> **"Often, if you look carefully, with a bit of creativity and flexibility you can adapt to meet their criteria"**

Also useful are the completion funds available to finish or undertake the post production on a short. The UK Film Council operates a national fund, but many screen agencies also have smaller ones for filmmakers in their region. Obviously, you should always aim to manage your resources so that you not only have enough to be able to deliver the film, but also leave a little to market it or get it into festivals. Yet even with the best will, this may not always be the case.

There are also funds at many of the Regional Screen Agencies to help you with print costs which may be necessary, if you filmed on tape, as you will have to transfer the short from digital tape to film in order to get in shown in certain festivals. Although this is changing as more festivals and cinemas accept digital copies, a 35mm print will increase your exhibition options greatly. Most cinemas still only screen film prints. Expect to spend £5,000 for a 10 minute film to blow up to 35mm. Of course the film is already in the can and viewable by that point, so it is less of a gamble for any investor, whether public or private, to put money into the project.

2) Private investors

Some people may be lucky or resourceful enough to find a wealthy investor who believes in their potential or the potential of the project. Private finance could also come from a group of friends or acquaintances. Less likely, but not impossible, a private company may be willing to invest in a film if it happens to promote a theme, product or person they have a vested interest in.

Generally speaking, sending out your short pitch with a plea for money to the top 100 in the rich list is not going to work. Normally for private investment, there needs to be an emotional or personal connection to the subject matter or to the method of realising the film or a desire to invest in the individuals making the film.

This method provided the majority of the investment for our film, though I confess we did promise the unthinkable- that we would recoup the investor's money back. We are *extremely* fortunate that we will be able to do so given the success of our film. This investment came about partly due to an existing relationship we had and partly due to being very professional about our pitch, treatment and outlook in respect of the film (there is more information about our pitch materials below).

> **"Generally speaking, sending out your short pitch with a plea for money to the top 100 in the rich list is not going to work"**

Really thinking out of the box may bring rewards. Certain feature companies sometimes give small grants to filmmakers on an ad hoc basis or if they would like to try out a director's/writer's work. We managed to get this sort of investment which, whilst it only represented 5% of our cash budget, was a great connection to make for the future and their endorsement gave us kudos in the eyes of other investors and service providers.

Recently, a girl who was a runner on our film produced her own short by winning the entire budget from on line poker. Not the safest way to make money, but in her case it got her the budget and a great marketing hook in order to get further investment and publicity for the film.

If you do get private investment, the investors will probably want to feel part of the process. As you never know if they are going to be willing to help you at a later stage, or on the next film it is best to make them feel special and part of the process. If you can, keep them copied in or consulted. You might send them call sheets/schedules, rushes and reports, invite them down to the set, the wrap party, the cast and crew screenings, and give them credits or special thanks. Unless rich and very naïve (in which case, please send them our way), they will generally know that this may not be the best financial investment they have made of their own hard-earned money. They are doing it for other reasons and thus will appreciate being made to feel a part of the filmmaking process.

As with all investment, if people take a recoupment position from proceeds (and possibly a net profits position), make sure it takes into account all others also taking a share and takes account of all the expenses, costs, fees etc required to market, deliver materials and distribute the film. You don't want to be paying out before you get the money in.

3) In kind support

Whatever your budget or your sources of funding, you can almost be certain that in real terms this will form the majority of your 'funding'.

The first type of 'in kind' support will be your crew who will be working for free in many cases. Treat them as well and professionally as you can. A crew that feels valued, and that this is a professional production, will give you their best. These people are not working for free; instead they are donating their time and might as well be putting hard cash into your film. More experienced crew will know what to expect and have an effect on others and you should make sure they are well fed and that your schedules are realistic and as near to union guidelines as you can. Even if crews are working for free, no one is going to thank you for saving a day by trying to cram it in; take an extra day rather than working dangerously long hours. If you have a shoot with many set ups and different locations, make sure you spend the time scheduling the shoot so that the locations are close by and avoid any unit move during the middle of the day as that is just a waste of time (and money, whether cash or in-kind resources).

On *Hibernation*, we wanted to show the crew that we were totally committed to the project and make everyone feel special. Instead of the same catering or food tokens all the time, for a few days our folks and partners took it in turn to come in with specially prepared foods for a bit of variety. Some believe we only got the crew truly on side after the stuffed vine leaves.

> **"Whatever your budget or your sources of funding, you can almost be certain that in real terms in kind support will form the majority of your 'funding'"**

We also wanted to make sure that people were looked after properly, so we had a runner with a great positive and warm attitude who's only job was to meet and greet and offer refreshments. Whilst this may be unnecessary, we are sure it was one of the factors that helped the atmosphere to be so good on our shoot.

Facilities houses are fantastic regular supporters of short films; other than short film funders, they must get approached more than anyone else about getting freebies or deals so do not feed then a line or try to pull the wool over their eyes. Do not harp on about who might be attached to the film or where the film may play when finished. Much better is to show them evidence of a well planned, thought out and organised project for which you have enthusiasm and are committed. If you have agreed a deal and a time by which you will give back equipment or vacate an edit suite, do it. Treat them and their facilities/equipment professionally and with respect and you will not only get the best for the project but also help leave a good impression, which will help you in the future.

Whilst certainly not necessary, having a gaffer or DoP that has some experience and knows the facilities house will help reassure them that you will look after the equipment. The same is true for an editor and edit suites.

Hibernation

Whilst it is pretty difficult to get finance from product placement, many companies may be prepared to give you some of their products for free just to support you. For example, biscuit and soft drink manufacturers gave us boxes of their goods, which helped keep the crew happy, and bottles of whisky made very good thank you presents on our shoot. Think creatively about the companies you approach. Producer Quinny Sacks wrote a successful letter to B&Q headquarters to ask for paint donation for *Death of the Revolution* (Dirs. Chris and Ben Blaine). Every little bit saved helps! Her letter is reproduced on page 66 with the production and post-production budgets for the film.

> "We tended to over estimate in order to leave a cushion for unexpected expenses"

4) Self finance

If you want to self-finance, then there are further ways to cut down on costs without cutting down on professionalism. For example, arrange shared cars to pick up crew; use edit suites at less busy times; get to grips with software that can help with all aspects of post; and use short ends if you need to shoot on film.

Make sure you talk through the shoot and schedule with the Heads of Departments (HoDs) and director; there are often unexpected ways to achieve what the director wants with less time and money.

If you are part self-financing, make sure you take a recoupment position along with other funders, so as to put you in first position (i.e. your money should come out first if it can, given that you are also providing your services plus blood and tears on top).

Tips for funding and budgeting and not faffing and babbling

1) Know why you are making your film

It may sound bleedin' obvious but knowing why you are making a film, who you are targeting and what must be kept in the film could help you half (or double) your budget. Knowing this will allow you to understand which costs are unavoidable.

Length - You should take on board that one of the most common criticisms of short films are that they are too long. Do you want to create a calling card for show reel, target a specific group or win recognition at competitions? In all cases you should know what audience you are aiming for and how to reach them. For example, Venice Film Festival does not accept shorts over 10 minutes in length, and often the cut off for festivals such as Cannes is 15 minutes. It is hugely unlikely to get a theatrical release if a film is longer than 10 minutes and the longer the film, the more it will generally cost to make in terms of shoot and post production time. In a world where downloads are taking over as a viable distribution route, the longer the film, the less easy it is to stream or download.

Shorter *is* generally better, but obviously, you will have to make the film the right length for your story. We tried to cut *Hibernation* down to 10 minutes but realised that it would compromise the story too much. In the end, we made sure we kept it to 15 minutes, knowing that we might find it very hard to get certain TV sales and into certain festivals if it were any longer.

Tape or film? We have said how much it could cost to blow up to 35 mm if you do not shoot on film, but do you really need to shoot on film? There is more freedom shooting on tape in terms of mobility (including speed, equipment, manpower and focus pulling). On tape you will also have instant playback and the ability to grade it to look like film (if this is what you want). Most festivals need a DVD for the purposes of submission and a good film will always catch the selector's eye, irrelevant of what format it was shot in.

We shot on Super 16mm. Why? It was what the director wanted and it worked for us. Interestingly, I heard from a couple of the crew that the fact we had a bigger 'film' camera emphasised the fact we were making a 'proper' film and they were very attentive and careful when the film was rolling in order to preserve stock. Would they have been the same if shot on digital? Knowing the great crew we had… certainly.

2) Create a budget and stick to it

If you want money, you need to create a realistic budget. This budget will change depending on what money and deals you can get but you have to start somewhere. You will need to investigate the deals you can make with lighting, camera, grip equipment, catering, transport, deals on stock, edit houses, disposables. The list goes on, but the more you come up with a realistic budget, the less surprises you will have later on. We tended to over-estimate in order to leave a cushion for unexpected expenses (as well as our contingency) but you may not have this luxury.

For a short you don't need to go over the top, but the more you flesh out the budget the more it will make you think of other things you could require, so we would advise starting with more headings and cutting down/out the sections you do not require. Be realistic and appreciate that some corners simply cannot be cut, however little money you have.

We found it invaluable to have a format we could use which cross referenced more detailed sections to the top sheet on an Excel spreadsheet so that everything altered every time there was a change. There are examples of a short film budget in this section on page 64 and a variety of sources for further information. Shooting People provide their members with templates which can be adapted for each film (shootingpeople.org).

Whilst certainly not required, we decided to create a budget showing the estimated total budget when taking into account the time and services donated, the deals we had achieved and any other value brought to the project but not paid for with hard cash. It is not only a way of showing just how much it would cost without the support but helps people appreciate the efforts put into the film. We found this invaluable to show when pitching to investors, potential cast/crew and service providers.

3) Be as professional as you can

This is not just a bit of fun and most people that help you will not appreciate you thinking it is. We are not saying that you have to be militarily sombre at all times, but do your homework. Use the same attitude for your film and its funding as you would for a feature. Every funding application should be well prepared and presented. There is no excuse for bad formatting in scripts or applications, which will just give them an excuse to pass in favour of another project.

> "Be realistic and appreciate that some corners simply cannot be cut, however little money you have"

For most applications, there is no point sending in marketing, storyboards etc if they do not ask for them. If you do not succeed but do not know why, don't send a boiling bunny with "why?" engraved in its forehead. Take a deep breath (perhaps take some time to show it to friends) and try to work out why your project did not come across. If you are still convinced this is a great script and film, then work on it before sending it off again.

4) Think about pre-pitch marketing

Whilst not essential, we do believe that it is well worth making up a 'marketing or pitch document' for potential investors/collaborators who do not have limitations on what they want to see. It helped enormously for our film, in particular for busy and non-film business contacts, who did not want to read the script but wanted to get a feeling for what the project was about.

Documents like this also focus you on what audience you are trying to reach and helps you build materials and info which come in useful when promoting the film and putting together the marketing materials at the exhibition stage.

Our pack was a glossy bound document containing mood boards, background on our company and project, the key cast and crew, a director's filmography and vision, a script, and a breakdown of how the film was to be made and distributed. It certainly gave us the icebreaker we needed for persons who we wanted to meet with but for whom we had no previous contact.

Given the fact that you probably are asking for cash or services for a film nobody has heard of and a writer with no track record, consider trying to get a quote from someone they would have heard of. Perhaps a film industry bod, or a known TV or film writer or actor saying "This is amazing stuff, the script is red hot, it is the finest team I have ever come across and you would be fool not to get involved". Ok, maybe this unlikely and OTT, but you get our drift. This may at least take it to the next stage of getting them to read the script to see if it is any good and worth investing in.

5) Collaborate

As we have set out above it is well worth sitting down together to brainstorm about how to do things in a novel way to save on costs. Nobody knows everything but pooling experiences can help you to find realistic and resourceful short cuts.

There is often a misconception that only people eager to get into film or fresh out of film school will get involved in your film for free and you will not be able to secure the services of more experienced crew and cast. Not true. We discovered that a lot of the leading industry crew are prepared and indeed want to help out every now again with shorts. They do this not only to support up and coming filmmakers, but also because they are genuinely interested in exciting new talent. Short films may also give them more creative flexibility and input than a feature and they can be squeezed into down time from their feature work.

Same goes for cast, though in each case they can generally only really afford about one a year. Do not be afraid to ask. The more organised and professional you are, the easier it will be to get quality people on board. Approach them with as much info as you can give. If they are interested, make sure their reasonable requirements are met and that they are treated, as much as possible, as they would be on a fully paid job.

Two of the Heads of Department of our crew had worked on Hollywood blockbusters. They came on board as they believed in the project, director and team and believed we would follow through. They were amazingly generous with their time and services and it worked very well in the mix.

6) Schedule - make one and keep to it

If you make a realistic schedule, and it is all you can afford, make sure you keep to it. That last shot covered may not be necessary if you are running well over time. Other common reasons for running over can be over experimenting on set (this should be done before) and getting hung up on the minor things instead of getting what you need in the can. It is also not a great calling card to be known as the director or producer who was not on budget and/or on schedule.

7) Get the clearances

Avoid this scenario: You make your film, try to distribute it and find that after all your hard work, you are either being sued, restricted, having to cut pieces out or spend three times the budget on clearing rights. This is not pleasant and just not worth it, so make sure you know the basics of clearance and that you get full releases from your cast (including all persons not just incidentally in front of the cameras; take advice if unsure), key crew, locations, any artwork or other copyright pieces appearing on camera and any necessary product releases. A simple standard form assigning all rights will do the trick but get the right one (there is also a sample actors' clearance in this book on page 108). This may need more work if the person wants more rights in respect of remuneration, approvals or controls.

In all cases, you should be clearing for all rights and exploitation of the film in all media whether now or in the future invented. Sounds technical, but agreements did not even allow or envisage internet streaming or downloading a few years ago. Now this is one of the main ways short films are seen. There should be no further payments (a full 'buy out' including a buy out of all mechanical royalties) except as you agree from net proceeds of the film. You will not be able to buy out the right to receive the royalties payable to the performing rights societies (which will be paid for by the venues which show the film publicly and have to buy a licence) but there should not be any others.

This is even more important in respect of music clearance.

For each pre-recorded piece of music you generally need a licence from two different sources: the owner of the copyright in the actual music and lyrics (generally owned by the publishing company); and the owner of the copyright in the actual recording (usually owned by the record company).

Realistically, unless you are lucky or in the know, the chances are that you will not be able to licence in a pre-existing track from a record company for your short film. I would advise strongly against either ignoring the clearance or only clearing for festivals. If your film is as successful as you think it will be, you will find yourself paying dearly when you want to get wider exposure.

The most straightforward way is to work with a composer on specially composed music for which you should acquire all rights for synchronising the music with the film (though if not paid, the composer may keep rights and income in respect of use in other media). On *Hibernation*, we were able to work with the composer to make the music fit the film like a glove. I still remember the first time we heard it put together with our film; it quite literally blew us away.

What does this all mean?

It boils down to deciding what you really need to make the film you want to make. You need to look closely at all the elements of production and post-production, and figure out the best way to do it using the resources you have to hand. You will also need to be very honest and ruthless with yourself (no whips please). Compromises are fine and absolutely necessary if you want to succeed, but make sure don't throw your baby out with the developing fluid. No one wants to see a bad film however cheap or expensive it was.

On the other hand, if you believe in your film, are prepared to be realistic, professional, resourceful and keep an almost insane determination, you will get the finance and resources you need to make the film.

> "It is also not a great calling card to be known as the director or producer who was not on budget and/or on schedule"

Chris and Ben Blaine, interview

Part 2 – budgets and finance

Chris and Ben Blaine have written and directed more than ten short films. This is the second part in an in-depth interview, which runs throughout this book.

Are there certain costs you can't, and shouldn't, scrimp on?

CHRIS: Food. If you don't eat well you get testy and argumentative and annoyed with everything that goes wrong. Everyone does. Feed people well and give them a decent-length break and they'll work better.

BEN: Absolutely. Good food, preferably good hot food, with a vegetarian option, is the one thing you really can't do without. I'd rather make a film without a camera than without lunch. OK I haven't thought that through but I'm probably going to stick by it.

What's your cheapest film? What were there unavoidable costs on this?

BEN: *Danny's Found Jesus.* I don't have an actual budgetary figure for it but I think it cost about £50, all of which went on beer. It's a film about our mate Keith, who's a passionate atheist, finding out from the angel Gabriel that he is actually the second coming of Christ. We shot it in Keith's local pub, which let us film all night for free. They even provided hot buttered toast at three in the morning.

All the camera, sound and lighting kit was borrowed for the night from the camera hire company where Chris was working and the stock may have been 'borrowed' from there too. The cast, including Keith, all donated their services for free, as did the extras. We shot on DVCAM and then edited at home on our G4. So I guess it's a bit of a cheek to say it only cost us £50 because we had to have the computer and Final Cut Pro and everything; but we didn't buy those things for this film so it sort of works out.

Excluding the costs of running your own home edit suite, the unavoidable cost was beer. It was St. Patrick's night and the pub stayed open 'til midnight so we had to do something to fill the time.

What are some of the different ways you have raised finance for your short films?

CHRIS: We started our filmmaking on money won by cheating at poker. I've worked. Paper-round, newsagents, data entry, temping, in a casino, a plug factory, a carpet factory, telemarketing, a camera hire company (making full use of their equipment and staff). Most essentially, I've gotten into a huge big load of debt, which I've continually refinanced and made larger and larger as we've continued to not make it big and get paid!

BEN: Yeah, neither of us are really what you'd call producers. Before we started working with Quinny Sacks and Barrington Paul Robinson, who between them have produced all of our last three films, it was all down to luck and hard work. Not sure which category the poker falls into, but after leaving school we were very lucky in that an aunt we never knew we had dropped dead and left us £10k. That disappeared with the first few shorts we made and after that it was just down to saving what was left.

The two most important things were saving enough for the G4 edit suite and Chris working for the camera hire company. Once we could get hold of lights, grips, cameras and stuff for free, and could then edit in our own time, the actual cash costs of film-making become just a burden rather a than a physical impossibility. Still it wasn't until we got involved with people who have the proper producer's gift that things started to really fall into place.

Finding good producers is hard, and they're few and far between. I think though, that one of the things that really helped us was that by the time we met Barrington we'd already made a lot of films. First, this meant that we had a better idea when someone was bullshitting us. More importantly though it meant we weren't so totally hung up on making a particular film. I've heard a lot of horror stories of writers and directors who get hooked up with a producer who's no good and it ends up seeming that the producer holds all the cards, like they're the only person who can make that film a reality. When we made *Free Speech* with Barrington we weren't desperate to make the film, we were just desperate to make a film that we felt had no compromises in it. This meant we were able to draw a line in the sand... either Barrington could get us what we needed by this date or the film didn't happen, and if it didn't that wasn't the end of the world for us.

It's the good thing about auditioning producers. If you're working with a new DoP you can often not find out that they're not up to the job until after the shoot. With a producer one of the best signs is if the shoot happens at all.

Free Speech
Photo by Jessica Thomas

Sample Budgets

QS Productions

Production Budget Summary

As at 29th March 2006

Title:	Death of the Revolution
Producer:	Quinny Sacks & Paul Barrington Robinson
Director:	Ben Blaine & Chris Blaine
Shoot Period:	14/02/05 to 18/02/05
Post Period:	21/02/05 to current
Stock:	Kodak 500T 7279 (13 reels)
Format:	16mm

ITEM	SUPPLIER	NET COST	VAT	TOTAL	PAID BY
EXPENDITURE					
Lighting Equipment	Nimbus	1064.75	186.32	1251.07	
Lights	Nimbus	0.00	0.00	0.00	
Film Stock (test)	Kodak	126.00	22.04	148.04	
Film Stock	Kodak	796.00	139.30	935.29	
Film Processing	Technicolor	709.61	124.20	833.82	
Sound Equipment	Richmond Film Services	18.00	3.16	21.16	
Catering Equipment	ABC Hire	203.19	35.56	238.75	
Art Department	Various	138.00	24.14	162.15	
Crew Travel Expenses	Various	44.89	0.00	44.89	
Insurance	AON	0.00	0.00	0.00	
General Equipment	Cruet	0.00	0.00	0.00	
Dat Machine	Personal Contact	50.00	0.00	50.00	
Food	Various	472.56	0.00	472.56	
Camera Kit	Panavision	750.00	131.25	881.25	
TOTAL		**4373.03**	**666.00**	**5039.03**	
INCOME					
Q.S. Friend	Donation			500.00	
Q.S. Friend	Donation			500.00	
Q.S. Friend	Donation			500.00	
Q.S. Friend	Donation			250.00	
BPR Friend	Donation			100.00	
BPR Friend	Donation			125.00	
BPR Friend	Donation			125.00	
QS Personal	Loan			1000.00	
QS Personal	Loan			1843.71	
TOTAL				**4943.72**	

QS Productions
Post Production Budget

As at March 29th 2006

Title:	Death of the Revolution
Producer:	Quinny Sacks & Paul Barrington Robinson
Director:	Ben Blaine & Chris Blaine
Shoot Period:	14/02/05 to 18/02/05
Post Period:	21/02/05 to current
Stock:	Kodak 500T 7279 (13 reels)
Format:	16mm

ITEM	SUPPLIER	COST
EXPENDITURE		
Music studio	Air Edel	241.00
x4 Musicians	As per Composer	400.00
Sound mix studio	Berwick st Post	450.00
Sound designer	Jules McDonald	250.00
Sound engineer	Sam Matthews	300.00
Film wash	Technicolor	96.00
Grading	Molinare	800.00
Processing//final cut	Technicolor	2600.00
T shirts for kids		451.77
Marc Bolan license		500.00
TOTAL		**6088.77**
INCOME		
Wandsworth film council	Post production grant	3000.00
Donation		300.00
Donation		1000.00
Donation		100.00
Donation		250.00
Credit	From Production	570.67
TOTAL		**5220.68**
TOTAL PRODUCTION COSTS		**10461.81**
TOTAL EXPENDITURE		**10461.81**
TOTAL INCOME		**10164.39**
Shortfall		**297.41**

Sample Letter for
In Kind Support

Q S PRODUCTIONS
39 EVERYROAD LANE
LONDON E8 8KP
+4420 123 4567
email@website.co.uk

To: Paula Shrimpton
B&Q
Court Road
Sutton
Surrey

19th January 2005

Dear Paula Shrimpton,

I am writing on behalf of my co Producer, Paul Barrington Robinson, with whom you had a conversation about the possibility of supporting our community film project. We appreciate your support and enthusiasm.

The project will take place at Camden Junior School during the week of 14th February where we shall be making a short film.

Our aim is to create a half term play scheme that gives them a real insight into filmmaking. As well as performing, they will be involved in designing the credits and a number of related projects. We will also be giving workshops, talks about the film process and hope to make it a fun, worthwhile experience for them.

Everybody is working on an entirely voluntary basis and although we have had generous offers of equipment loan we would like to ask B&Q for the possibility of a donation of paint in order to decorate the film set.

In return, the store will be given a film credit and exposure in our mail-out that will go to at least one hundred parents who live in the local area.

Your support would make an enormous difference to us and I thank you in advance for your time and hope that this proposal will justify your consideration.

Please do not hesitate to contact me if you should require any more information.

Yours sincerely

Quinny Sacks

(Producer)

Rebecca Mark-Lawson, interview

www.ukfilmcouncil.org.uk/filmmaking/shorts

Is there an overall ethos behind UK Film Council New Cinema Fund's short film funding?

RM-L: The UK Film Council's shorts programme seeks out and nurtures dynamic new creative talent with the potential to move into feature films.

We are looking for stories that reflect the rich social and cultural diversity of UK, bold visions and original voices.

Rebecca Mark-Lawson is Managing Executive at **Life-size Pictures** in charge of all of the short film schemes they manage on behalf of the **UK Film Council**.

How is the UK Film Council's short film funding distributed?

RM-L: The UK Film Council supports filmmakers through four different schemes.

Digital Shorts gives emerging filmmakers the opportunity to showcase their talent Digital Shorts are under 10 minutes in length, shot on dv and have a maximum budget of £10, 000.

Digital Shorts is co-financed with and managed by regional and national strategic partners.

Previous Digital Shorts include Pete Mackie Burns' *Milk*, winner of the Golden Bear at Berlinale, Matthew Thompson's *Gone*, winner of BBC New Talent Awards, and Tom Harper's *Cubs*, winner of BIFA Best British Short.

Digital Shorts Plus offers a progression route for filmmakers that have been supported through Digital Shorts or are of an equivalent level of experience. The scheme gives filmmakers the freedom to explore stories that don't fit within the Digital Shorts budget and length frameworks. The film must have the potential to provide a clear route within the directors career and illustrate their approach more fully.

Digital Shorts Plus are shot on DV and have a maximum budget of £20,000. There are no length restrictions.

Digital Shorts is co-financed with and managed by regional and national strategic partners.

Cinema Extreme supports filmmakers with a distinctive directorial voice and cinematic flair who are a step away from making the next outstanding, ground breaking new British feature film.

Cinema Extreme films have a maximum budget of £50,000. There are no format or length restrictions.

Cinema Extreme is managed by The Bureau and co-financed by Film4.

Cinema Extreme films include Duane Hopkins *Love Me Or Leave Me Alone*, winner of Best Short at EIFF and Andrea Arnold's Oscar® winning *Wasp*.

The **Completion Fund** supports short films that have already been shot but lack the funds to finish. It is not solely a print fund.

The Completion Fund is managed by Maya Vision International.

Films funded by the Completion Fund include D Hood's *The Other Man*, winner of Best British short at EIFF and Daniel Mulloy's *Antonio's Breakfast*, winner of the BAFTA for Best Short Film.

Each of the short film schemes has individually tailored training and after care in order to ensure maximum support and benefit to the filmmakers selected.

"We are looking for stories that reflect the rich social and cultural diversity of UK, bold visions and original voices"

Together the schemes provide support to emerging filmmakers at different points in their careers and the filmmaking process ensuring equality of access and an effective development structure for fresh new talent.

How much is allocated to each scheme by the UK Film Council?

RM-L: The UK Film Council's short film investment is made by the New Cinema Fund. Digital Shorts, £480,000; Digital Shorts Plus, £60,000; Completion Fund, £50,000; Cinema Extreme £175,000. The Total of £765,000 does not include management organisation fees.

How many short films were made under each scheme in 2005-06?

RM-L: In 2005/06 UK Film Council co-financed:129 Digital Shorts with our 12 partners in the scheme; 6 Digital Shorts Plus films with 6 of the partners mentioned above; 10 films through the Completion Fund; and 5 films through Cinema Extreme co-financed by Film4.

Who should I apply to?

RM-L: You should apply to the appropriate strategic partner or managing organisation for each scheme, full details of which are at www.ukfilmcouncil.org.uk/filmmaking/shorts

What are the managing organisations' responsibilities?

RM-L: The managing organisations are responsible for delivering all aspects of the schemes in consultation and partnership with Lifesize Pictures. This includes the submission, selection, development, training, production and post production stages of the process and physical and contractual delivery to Lifesize Pictures.

How does Lifesize work with the managing organisations?

RM-L: Lifesize Pictures oversees all of the UK Film Council's short film schemes on behalf of the New Cinema Fund. We work in partnership with the managing organisations, co-financiers and filmmakers to realise the short film schemes to their fullest potential.

We also work hard to ensure films and filmmakers are given an appropriate level of marketing and promotional support. This can range from producing DVDs to market talent to buyers to organising guest screenings at festivals such as Edinburgh International Film Festival and Encounters Short Film Festival.

What are your duties at Lifesize?

RM-L: I executive produce all of the short film schemes.

I am creatively involved in every part of the process. including working with the managing organisations to write guidelines for the schemes, assessing short-listed projects, advising on the selection of short film projects for funding, providing script notes during the development process, working with talent to ready their project for production, giving editorial feedback on rough and fine cuts, devising and delivering marketing and distribution initiatives. My role is also strategic. I develop new initiatives to address gaps in provision, seek out, nurture and connect talent

Milk
by Peter Mackie Burns

Milk is on Best v Best Vol. One
(bestvbest.com)

with the industry. I work in collaboration with Shorts Executive Julia Caithness and Shorts Administrator Jude Goldrei.

Does the UK Film Council retain the rights to all of the films that receive Lottery funding? Or is it different from scheme to scheme?

RM-L: The only right UK Film Council retains is the right to use the films for promotional purposes.

Is there an exhibition strategy for films funded through the UK Film Council, or is exhibition/distribution the filmmaker's responsibility?

RM-L: Where appropriate in collaboration our strategic partners we offer a tailored exhibition strategy for filmmakers on exit from any of the schemes.

In addition the UK Film Council promotes talent and films to the industry through targeted screenings, including UKFC programmes within a number of festivals such as Encounters and Edinburgh. We are currently producing a DVD for buyers at Clermont Ferrand called Digital Generation.

Why are short films important?

RM-L: Short films are a vibrant, challenging, stimulating and entertaining art form in their own right. Arguably they allow a filmmaker to express their vision in its purest form. But they are also an immensely valuable for emerging filmmakers. More affordable digital filmmaking technology allows filmmakers to take risks, explore new and innovative ways of telling stories, break rules, to learn. Making a short film through one of these schemes also helps filmmakers to create relationships with funders and commissioners and brings their work to the attention of people who want to work with new talent.

Short films are also hugely important to a new filmmaker as consumer – if you want to make shorts then you must watch them.

You can view a selection of short films supported by the UK Film Council's New Cinema Fund at:

www.bbc.co.uk/dna/filmnetwork

> "Short films are also hugely important to a new filmmaker as consumer – if you want to make shorts then you must watch them".

Matthieu de Braconier, interview

www.thebureau.co.uk

Can you give us a little background on Cinema Extreme (for example, when did the fund start, how many films have been funded so far)?

MATTHIEU DE BRACONIER: The fund has been running since 2002. The first and second years four films were commissioned each time and, last year, the scheme commissioned five films. Submissions have just come in for the fourth year.

Cinema Extreme is a scheme that has developed quite a bit over the three years. It was originally exclusively a commissioning scheme started up by the UK Film Council and Film4. The Bureau was approached initially because of the track record of Bertrand Faivre, who spotted Lynne Ramsey (he co-produced *Ratcatcher*), and also because of his experience in France where he ran the short film section at Lazennec Tout Court for almost 10 years spotting people like Mathieu Kassovitz (*La Haine*).

Photo courtesy of Anna Leader

Matthieu de Braconier works at production company, The Bureau where he is a Development Executive for **Cinema Extreme**, the premiere short film scheme funded by the UK Film Council's New Cinema Fund and Film4 Lab. He is also the producer of the short film *The Sickie*, and a new feature *Cossacks* from the same team (Rupert Jones, music promos director and Neil Hunter, *The Lawless Heart*).

The first two years we had deadlines and people submitted packages. We'd shortlist, do interviews and, based on their scripts and on their previous work, people would get commissioned. It was felt that the scheme allowed almost no space to accompany the filmmakers through the process of developing the projects. Towards the end of the second year Caroline Cooper Charles (UK Film Council) and Peter Carlton (Film4) came back with the idea of building a development stage into the scheme, because that would allow to work with more risky projects and to push filmmakers' visions. Previously, we'd had some really exciting filmmakers coming in with projects that didn't feel fully developed, and we had exciting ideas coming from filmmakers who perhaps weren't yet ready for Cinema Extreme.

Cinema Extreme has now evolved to include a proper development stage. Obviously one of the points of Cinema Extreme for the UK Film Council and also for Film4 is to develop relationships with the talent, and to have the opportunity to go through the development process with the filmmakers. It is all about relationships in this industry. Even for those that don't get commissioned Cinema Extreme is an excellent opportunity.

What's the role of the scheme within the wider remit of the UKFC?

MB: It's really designed to be a bridge for filmmakers who are intending to make the jump from short films to features. In addition to developing the relationships with commissioners and The Bureau through development, the 'talent' also have the opportunity to develop some of the practical skills of filmmaking which they might lack, but which will help them in the future when making a feature. These films are doing quite well in exhibition terms, but the aim of the scheme is really about creating a bridge for filmmakers to make that transition.

What really becomes clear from a longer form short is what your strengths might be when you make a feature. It gives you the opportunity to showcase your abilities, and storytelling is a really important element of this. Cinema Extreme gives you the opportunity to show you can handle this in a longer form.

The other aim of the scheme is to identify visionary filmmakers; people who have a strong distinctive cinematic identity, which they will then take into feature filmmaking. This is obviously important when you are making a low budget feature, because you really need to make sure your film stands out at a crowded festival market.

Strange Little Girls
by Savina Dellicour

Is one of the aims of the scheme also about seeing how filmmakers respond to the development process?

MB: Yes, this development stage has two functions really. Because we select more filmmakers for the development phase (almost 50 last time) than will be commissioned, it allows the commissioners to be introduced to a wider range of filmmaking talent, not just the four or five who end up making a Cinema Extreme short. Also, this stage allows them to make more informed choices about which films, and about who they want to make the films with. You obviously get to know someone so much better through a 3-day workshop, than you would in a brief interview.

I also think it has allowed a different kind of project to be commissioned because the commissioners as well as ourselves at The Bureau were aware of the 'fashions' in short films. You tend to get lots of ideas that are very similar which get pitched. The same subjects tend to appear over and over again, and within this, you occasionally have a few which are distinctive. So you can have a very interesting filmmaker come in with an idea which is similar to many other things which have been submitted. In that case, you may have the filmmaker use the development process to try to make that idea more distinctive and unique.

We have funding from Skillset now [the UK body responsible for funds for film training], which will allow us to focus more on the training side as well. So if someone comes with a good project, and they have done very interesting visual work before, but they don't have a lot of experience working with actors, we will be able to create the opportunity for them to work with actors, and perhaps edit something. We might also have a filmmaker who is very good with actors, but not necessarily as good visually. In this case, we could give them the opportunity to do tests with a DoP to help define what they want their film to look like. So the training process can be tailored to each film-maker's needs.

> "What really becomes clear from a longer form short is what your strengths might be when you make a feature"

What is Film4's role in Cinema Extreme?

MB: The four aspects of this scheme are selection, development, training and commissioning. Film4 and UK Film Council are very active in all those stages.

For filmmakers this is important. When you come to a workshop, you are already aware that the commissioners want to see you there. You know you can develop that relationship.

Again this is true as you develop the projects. You aren't just developing something and hoping to be commissioned. You are actually developing something with the commissioners. It's good training for a career in the industry because that is often how it works.

The commissioning process is totally up to UK Film Council and Film4. It's Jo McClennan on the Film4 side and Becky Mark-Lawson on the UKFC side.

What do you look for in a successful application?

MB: ...something different, fresh, something coherent. We will perhaps find it easier to select and trust a filmmaker's vision when their previous films point in a particular direction, instead of their application project being a U-turn from previous work. The word 'auteur' comes up, but that doesn't mean we are only looking for writer/directors. If you think of Stephen Frears, I would consider him an auteur, but he doesn't write himself. It's about applying a strong vision and style, having something to say and feeling strongly about what you have to say. It's also about having a personal understanding of cinematic language and a desire to use it in relation to theme or story.

Are successful applicants filmmakers whose careers you are already aware of?

MB: Not at all. For example *Love Me or Leave Me Alone* is a film which got commissioned where the director had only made one film, *Field*, which was very beautiful. We really look carefully at every application we get. We don't want people to think "I won't get this because they don't know me already...". Though I think it's important also to have a good assessment of where you are at as a filmmaker. Obviously we don't accept first time director applications (this would be more appropriate for the UKFC's DV shorts scheme). We require previous work and obviously that work is going to be a big part of our assessment of the application.

> "someone who has a clear identity will stand out. Filmmakers should be aware of which are their good films and which are their 'misses'"

From my point a view, someone who has a clear identity will stand out. Filmmakers should be aware of which are their good films and which are their 'misses', and they don't necessarily need to submit the weaker ones. When they do, it's just because they put them all on the reel years ago. If that's the case, why not include a note telling us which ones to watch? What someone presents to us gives a good indication of who they are and what they want to say. Often you get reels where there is everything...and nothing, and you wonder why the filmmaker doesn't guide you through the different levels of quality. It makes it worrying because you get the feeling that people don't know what they have achieved, and where they have achieved it.

How many applications do you receive each year, and how many films do you make?

MB: We had only one deadline this time (2006-2007) and we had 450 applicants. And that figure is applicants, not applications because they can apply with more than one project.

The same thing I mentioned before about guiding us through your application, is true in terms of the ideas a filmmaker submits. When you get these applications with three different ideas which go in totally different directions, you really feel like this is an applicant who is telling you, 'listen if you are into comedies, then here is a comedy, and if you are into horror, this is a horror and if you are into one-trick ponies, here's the one with the twist...'. For Cinema Extreme, it's not very encouraging because you get a sense that this isn't a very strong vision talking.

Monsters
by Rob Morgan

From the application stage to the filmmakers turning in the finished film, how long is the process?

MB: It's about a year. The length of the development stage varies from project to project. We aren't going to keep working on something that the commissioners know they aren't going to commission.

Are the workshops for more than just the five filmmakers who get through to the final commissioning stage?

MB: Yes. The workshops are focussing on story. Then we develop a certain number of projects, it's among those that final choices will be made.

So you cast your net a little wider and then narrow it down through the development stages?

MB: Yes. We will go up to 30 projects. Our aim is to train more filmmakers than actually get commissioned. And the training is also geared towards the needs of the individual filmmakers.

Love Me or Leave Me Alone
by Duane Hopkin

Cinema Extreme green lit projects to 2006:

After The Rain
directed by Gaelle Denis and written
by Gaelle Denis and Sibel Armutcu.

Dog's Mercury
by Martin Radich

Hallo Panda
by the Blaine Brothers

Honeymoon
by Miranda Bowen

Soft
by Simon Ellis

Monsters
by Rob Morgan

Strange Little Girls
by Savina Dellicour

One Minute Past Midnight
by Celia Galan Julve

Get The Picture
by Rupert Wyatt

Floating
by Mark Walker

The Bypass
by Amit Kumar

Wasp
by Andrea Arnold

Love Me Or Leave Me Alone
by Duane Hopkins

A Changed Man
by Jens Jonsson

Short Film Funding Contacts

UK-wide

UK Film Council

✉ 10 Little Portland Street,
London W1W 7JG

☎ 020-7861 7861

📠 020-7861 7862

💻 newcinemafund@ukfilmcouncil.org.uk
www.ukfilmcouncil.org.uk

CINEMA EXTREME: The New Cinema Fund and Film4 jointly fund Cinema Extreme, a scheme designed to push the boundaries of cinematic storytelling, which gives experienced short filmmakers the opportunity to work on a more developed and longer short form film with a budget of up to £50,000. The Bureau, an independent film production company, manages the submission, selection and development process and executive produces the commissioned films.

For 2006 the scheme will operate as a development programme for a number of filmmakers. From this selected group, a minimum of four fims will be commissioned by the New Cinema Fund and Film4 and be produced with a maximum budget of £50,000. The scheme is for writer/directors or teams of filmmakers as well as for individual writers or directors who may be put together in teams by the commissioners. Filmmakers must be nationals or residents from the UK or another EU country, or must be attached to a UK production company. Also see our interview about this fund with Matthieu de Braconier on the preceding pages.

SHORT FILM COMPLETION FUND: The UK Film Council's New Cinema Fund (NCF) invites individual filmmakers and production companies to apply for Completion Funds. The fund is designed to aid productions which have been shot but which may not have the funds to complete post-production. Maya Vision International are the managing company responsible for short-listing and selecting the films in consultation with the New Cinema Fund. There is a pot of £50,000 available in total for this fund (to be split between all awards). Films should be under 12 minutes and already be edited into a rough cut. The films should have main elements (e.g. producer, writer, director, location, story) which are substantially British in nature.

DIGITAL SHORTS: See information on all of the regionally managed digital shorts schemes under the listings for Regional Screen Agencies in this section and under B3 Media's Blank Slate scheme below.

B3 Media Blank Slate

✉ PO BOX 41000,
Brixton,
London SW2 1HN

☎ 020-7274 2121

💻 shorts@b3media.net
www.b3media.net/digitalshorts

SHORT FILM FUNDS? Blank Slate is a digital shorts film scheme, produced by B3 media, and aimed at supporting the next generation of black and minority ethnic filmmakers (African, Caribbean, Asian, Chinese or mixed). Funded by the UK Film Council and Arts Council England, Blank Slate, is UK-wide digital shorts scheme that funds up to 8 short films per year of less than 10 minutes including credits. They will be shot digitally and with a budget of under £9000 each. Selected projects will receive development support before they begin shooting. The scheme is not for film-makers who have previously been commissioned to make a film on the UK Film Council's other Digital Short schemes. You will need to submit a first draft of your script with the application and a directors' showreel, plus supporting materials which are detailed on their website.

England

EM-Media

📧 35-37 St Mary's Gate,
Nottingham NG1 1PU

📞 0115-934 9090

📠 0115-950 0988

💻 info@em-media.org.uk
www.em-media.org.uk

WHERE? Derbyshire, Leicestershire, Lincolnshire, Northamptonshire, Nottinghamshire, Rutland.

SHORT FILM FUNDS? EM-Media operate a DV Shorts scheme with funding through the UK Film Council. See their website for more details about this scheme. They also have individual production awards which are open with a rolling application process. Awards for short films range from £500 to £5000, and are unlikely to exceed £10,000. Before submitting an application, filmmakers should call their offices to discuss the project and they will advise you on whether you are eligible.

Film London

📧 Suite 6.10,
The Tea Building,
56 Shoreditch High Street,
London E1 6JJ

📞 020-7613 7676

📠 020-7613 7677

💻 info@filmlondon.org.uk
www.filmlondon.org.uk

WHERE? Greater London

SHORT FILM FUNDS?

PULSE: *PULSE* is a low-budget digital shorts scheme run with funding from UK Film Council. The scheme is for short digital films of 1-10 minutes and funding ranges from £2000 and £10,000.

LONDON ARTISTS' FILM AND VIDEO AWARDS: *London Artists' Film and Video Awards* (LAFVA) is an open-submission awards for artists making media work. Though be aware that this is really for visual artists rather than narrative filmmakers! If your film is intended for exhibition in galleries, festivals, specialist venues and as site-specific installations you may be eligible. Awards range from £2000 up to a maximum of £20,000.

Newer filmmakers may want to check out the London Borough Funds, which are intended to be a 'first step on the ladder'.

North West Vision

📧 233 Tea Factory,
82 Wood Street,
Liverpool L1 4DQ

📞 0151-708 2967

📠 0151-708 2984

💻 info@northwestvision.co.uk
www.northwestvision.co.uk

WHERE? Cumbria, Cheshire, Greater Manchester, Lancashire, Merseyside

SHORT FILM FUNDS? NWV have several schemes listed below.

VIRGIN SHORTS: *Virgin Shorts* is for filmmakers who haven't yet been funded by North West Vision but have have made a film on their own initiative or at school/college. The max award is £1000.

DIGITAL SHORTS: *Digital Shorts* is produced with the UK Film Council, and has two tiers - Mini Digital and Maxi Digital. Both are appropriate for filmmakers wanting to make short documentary, drama or animation. *Mini Digital Shorts* has a maximum budget of £3000 for a film of up to 6 minutes. *Maxi Digital Shorts* awards are for a max of £9000 for a film of no more than 10 mins. This second tier is for filmmakers with some track record and the film should be aimed at international fest screenings. They also have an additional scheme *Digital Shorts Plus* for filmmakers who aren't quite ready for Cinema Extreme, but are ready for a bigger challenge. You have to have experience on one of their other digishorts schemes but awards can be to a tasty £18,000!

Northern Film & Media

✉ Central Square,
Forth Street,
Newcastle-upon-Tyne NE1 3PJ

📞 0191-269 9200

📠 0191-269 9213

💻 info@northernmedia.org
www.northernmedia.org

WHERE? Durham, Tees Valley, Tyne & Wear, Northumberland.

SHORT FILM FUNDS? Northern Film & Media run a two-tied digi shorts scheme in conjunction with the UK Film Council. All schemes are run on a call for applications basis so watch their website for details. *Mini Stingers* scheme is open to new and emerging filmmakers and funds 2-5 minute screenplays that have the potential to become micro budget, interesting potentially experimental short films (drama, doc and animation). Successful applicants get to develop their scripts further with individual support from a professional script editor and training via the Short Course unit of the National Film & Television School before going into production. Each production will have an inclusive budget of not more than £2750. *Stingers 5* is geared towards newer filmmakers with a track record of making shorts or related projects for another medium. They fund 10 minute screenplays that have the potential to become original, imaginative short films aimed at an international festival audience (again, animation, doc and drama considered). These filmmakers also receive development support and training through the NFTS. Each production will have an inclusive budget of not more than £10k.

OTHER OPTIONS: If you want a little extra support before you make or write your short film, Northern Film & Media also offer other more open-ended funding options for training and development –

courses, specialist training courses or programmes, project development for new media, special animation schemes. Available funding varies depending on what type of programme or work you are looking to support so it's best to read the web guidelines carefully. You also must speak with the fund manager before submitting any application!

Screen East

✉ 2 Millenium Plain,
Norwich NR1 3JG

📞 (01603) 776920

💻 info@screeneast.co.uk
www.screeneast.co.uk

WHERE? Bedfordshire, Essex, Cambridgeshire, Hertfordshire, Norfolk, Suffolk.

SHORT FILM FUNDS? Screen East supports short film through its Digital Shorts scheme in partnership with the UK Film Council. Details on the scheme weren't available at the time of press so please refer to their site.

TAKE NOTE: There is no short film production funding outside of these schemes, but they may consider completion funding on a case-by-case basis.

Screen South

✉ Folkestone Enterprise Centre,
Shearway Road,
Folkestone,
Kent CT19 4RH

📞 (01303) 298222

💻 info@screensouth.org
www.screensouth.org

WHERE? Berkshire, Buckinghamshire, Oxfordshire, Hampshire, Isle of Wight, Kent, Surrey, Sussex, Channel Islands.

SHORT FILM FUNDS? Screen South and the UK Film Council's Digital Shorts Scheme has 2 tiers in the region – both are suitable for drama, doc and animation. *Close Ups* is geared towards new filmmakers making 1-3 minute shorts with a cash budget of £2250. *Long Shots* is for shorts of 5-10 minutes with a cash budget of £7250 and for filmmakers with a little more experience. For commissioned films and filmmakers, Screen South will also meet the costs of basic production insurance, training workshops, a script development executive, a production executive and an executive producer.

Screen West Midlands

 9 Regent Place,
Birmingham B1 3NJ

(📞) 0121-265 7120

💻 info@screenwm.co.uk
www.screenwm.co.uk

WHERE? Birmingham and The Black Country, Herefordshire, Shropshire, Staffordshire, Warwickshire and Worcestershire

SHORT FILM FUNDS? *Digital Shorts* fund is for films which are under 10 minutes and made for a maximum of £9000. Filmmaker should have some experience and will be expected to submit previous work with the application. *Digital Shorts Extreme* is a next tier scheme designed to give further experience and development to filmmakers who have made a film through the digital shorts scheme already. One film per year will receive a max budget of £20,000 and also needs to be under 10 minutes' (including all credits).

If you are a brand new and inexperienced filmmaker in this region, don't despair... SWM also regularly support entry level funding schemes and production programmes in the region. Contact them for further info.

Screen Yorkshire

✉️ Studio 22,
46 The Calls,
Leeds LS2 7EY

(📞) 0113-294 4410

📠 0113-294 4989

💻 info@screenyorkshire.co.uk
www.screenyorkshire.co.uk

WHERE? Yorkshire, Humberside

SHORT FILM FUNDS? Check out the website for full details on the short schemes below.

LOW BUDGET LOTTERY SHORTS: This fund is for first- and second-time filmmakers only and will support up to 12 short films per year of under 10 minutes (max funding available is £2000). This scheme primarily supports writer/directors

UP SHORT: This fund is for one short film per year with up to a maximum of £20,000 contribution. . This scheme is to support the career of directors who have preivoulst been commissioned by Screen Yorkshire, the UK Film Council, FilmFour or the BBC.

DIGITAL SHORTS (CAUGHT SHORT): *Caught Short* is a UK Film Council supported scheme, run in partnership with Screen Yorkshire. This year's scheme has commissioned 8 short films, up to a maximum of ten minutes duration, on budgets of approximately £9,000.

South West Screen

✉️ St Bartholomews,
Lewins Mead,
Bristol BS1 5BT

(📞) 0117-952 9982

📠 0117-952 9988

💻 www.swscreen.co.uk

SHORT FILM FUNDS? South West Screen's *Digital Shorts* programme commissioned 11 short films for 2006/07, all under 10 minutes and with budgets of up to £8000 each. The also fund one *Digital Shorts Plus* film per year which is open to filmmakers who have made a short through the Digital Shorts scheme. See their website for further details and to apply for alerts when new deadlines are announced.

Arts Council England

✉️ 14 Great Peter Street,
London SW1P 3NQ

(📞) 0845-300 6200

📠 020-7973 6590

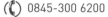

enquiries@artscouncil.org.uk
www.artscouncil.org.uk

SHORT FILM FUNDS? The Arts Council will only fund film projects in support of an artists' work in the moving image. So for example, they may fund a moving image/media work which is part of a piece from of visual artist or gallery-based media projects. No conventional film and video work is eligible. If you think your work may qualify, be sure to check the regulations on the website thoroughly, and even call to make sure you don't waste your time.

Scotland

Scottish Screen

 249 West George Street,
Glasgow G2 4QE

(📞) 0141-302 1700

📠 0141-302 1711

 info@scottishscreen.com
www.scottishscreen.com

SHORT FILM FUNDS? Scottish Screen's short production funds is a 'second-tier' fund: producers and directors should have already completed at least one short film, through schemes listed under GMAC (Glasgow Media access Centre) in this section such as Cineworks, Digicult, Little Pictures (or they will consider applications from filmmakers who have had a previous short screened in a number of international festivals). Their funds cover animation, live action and doc. Maximum investment is £50,000 and 25% of the budget must be partnership funding (10% of this can be deferred fees or in-kind sponsorship). These costs are recoupable against film revenue. Download the full guidelines from their website.

Glasgow Media Access Centre (GMAC)

📧 GMAC Shorts,
3ʳᵈ Floor,
34 Albion St,

Glasgow G1 1LH

📠 0141-553 2620

💻 info@g-mac.co.uk
www.g-mac.co.uk

SHORT FILM FUNDS? GMAC has three main funding schemes for filmmakers based in Scotland. Both Cineworks and DigiCult have pre-commissioning stages of training and project development before the final shorts commissions are awarded. We've listed the basics for each of the schemes below; check out their website for full details and eligibility.

LITTLE PICTURES: Little Pictures is for brand new filmmakers with little or no experience of filmmaking in Scotland. The scheme doesn't require experience but you must have an idea written on 1 page of A4 paper: "Little Pictures is simply looking for strong stories and ideas that can be realised on a very low budget".

It has a rolling commissioning process with a themed round every 4 months (deadlines and themes are announced on GMAC's website) and if successful, it offers a cash budget of up to £1,000 and *free* access to GMAC production and post resources.

CINEWORKS: Cineworks is short film funding programme for *emerging* drama scriptwriters, documentary filmmakers and animators in Scotland. Filmmakers should have some experience but not be 'established' in the industry. While the call for applications asks for scripts and treatments from writers or writer/director and writer/producer teams, it's also open to directors and producers who want to apply without a project (filmmaking teams may be created by the commissioners).

Commissioned teams will receive between £7,000 and £10,000 (VAT inclusive) to make their film. Budgets will be determined for each film by the GMAC Short Film Coordinator at commissioning stage and are for all all production and post production costs and delivery materials.

DIGICULT: DigiCult is also looking for emerging writer/directors with an emphasis on strong visual sensibility. Unlike Cineworks, you won't need a script or developed treatment to apply to the programme, only a basic story outline; the scheme includes training and development time to help ready scripts and ideas for production.

Commissioned teams will receive between £7,000 and £10,000 (VAT inclusive) to make their film. Budgets will be determined for each film by the GMAC Short Film Coordinator at commissioning stage and are for all all production and post production costs and delivery materials.

Scottish Arts Council

 12 Manor Place,
Edinburgh EH3 7DD

(☎) 0131-226 6051

(📠) 0131-225 9833

(💻) help.desk@scottisharts.org.uk
www.scottisharts.org.uk

SHORT FILM FUNDS? Scottish Arts Council gives grants in areas that Scottish Screen doesn't fund so filmmakers are only eligible for support if their project has a benefit to one of the other art forms that Scottish Arts Council funds

Northern Ireland

Northern Ireland Film and Television Commission (NIFTC)

 Alfred House,
21 Alfred Street,
Belfast BT2 8ED

(☎) 028-9023 2444

(📠) 028-9023 9918

(💻) info@niftc.co.uk
www.niftc.co.uk

TAKE NOTE: like all national and regional funds in the UK and listed below, NIFTC schemes are aimed at either filmmakers working in Northern Ireland or on projects that benefit the media industries in the area's film, TV and other media industries.

SHORT FILM FUNDS? *MINI Individuals* are for short, inexpensive narrative, experimental, doc and animations. Productions should be for a total budget

under £2500 and NIFTC may give up to 90% of the budget which would be a max of £2250.

MINI Small Awards are a next stage short fund for filmmaking teams, rather than individuals. Max you can apply for is £4500 and productions must have a total budget of under £5001. The costs are not usually recoupable.

Arts Council of Northern Ireland

 MacNeice House,
77 Malone Road,
Belfast BT9 5JW

(☎) 028-9038 5200

(📠) 028-9066 1715

(💻) www.artscouncil-ni.org

SHORT FILM FUNDS? General Art Awards grants are open-ended and are for individuals working in any art form in Northern Ireland. Priority goes to artists whose work is challenging and innovative, and explores new technology.

Wales

Arts Council of Wales

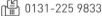 9 Museum Place,
Cardiff CF10 3NX

(☎) 029-20 376500

(📠) 029-20 221447

(💻) www.artswales.org.uk

SHORT FILM FUNDS? Grants for individuals are project based and range from £250-25,000 with all grants geared towards artists working in Wales with a partner organisation on board to show the work you produce. Deadlines for grants under £5000 are quarterly. Applications that meet several of ACW's funding priorities have best chances of success so check out their website very carefully before you apply.

Other schemes, competitions and awards

We've included awards and competitions in this section, because increasingly competition cash prizes work as retrospective 'funding' awards. Many of the organisations who might have once run regular funding schemes have now switched those resources into recognising and rewarding talent and good ideas once the shorts are already made. The major downside? This obviously, won't help you avoid maxing out your credit card!

This list doesn't include awards which we felt were just trying to scam filmmakers out of much needed money. You know the ones: dodgy website, requests for entry fees. Nor does it include the myriad of festival and national academy awards. Instead, see our Festivals' contacts section for more info on some of the fests that give special awards for shorts.

UK-based filmmakers may also want to keep their eye on the BAFTA/Orange 60 Seconds of Fame short award which was piloted in 2007 (www.orange.co.uk/bafta). Details will be posted on the BAFTA site if it is repeated in 2008 and beyond.

BBC New Talent
www.bbc.co.uk/newtalent

TAKE NOTE: The Beeb annually run awards schemes to find new talent in filmmaking – most recently in live action short film and music video of all genres. Call for entries is via their website and may change slightly from year to year so be sure to check regulations carefully.

NEW FILM MAKERS AWARD: For this award, they look for accessible, visually exciting films, which will appeal to a younger BBC Three audience. The winning film is considered for a screening slot on BBC Three as the Best British Short Film and receives £5,000. Two runners-up receive £2,500. All short-listed films will be broadcast on the channel, screened at the Encounters Short Film Festival and online.

NEW MUSIC SHORTS: This award calls for ideas for music shorts with the winning five applications

given up to £5000 and commissioned to make their film which would then be screened at BBC's Electric Proms at the Roundhouse. They look for an idea inspired by the tracks supplied by Domino Records, 679 Recordings, Ninja Tune and Warp Records. Ideas could be in any genre: documentary, animation, drama, experimental or even a straight promo. They could be for films running anywhere from 30 seconds to a maximum of 10 minutes. Films are also screened on the BBC's website.

British Short Screenplay Competition
www.kaosfilms.co.uk

TAKE NOTE: BSSC is run by Kaos films in association with the National Film and Television School and is a competitive international short screenplay competition that undertakes to produce the winning screenplay. Screenplays must not have been produced or optioned previously and should be original works by the screenwriter, not based on another work. They should also be for films between 5 and 15 minutes. The winner will have their film produced by Kaos and will receive a prize at the British Independent Film Awards. The runner up will receive a full suite of Movie Magic Screenplay Writing software.

CobraVision
PO Box 50653, London SW6 3ZA

www.cobrabeer.com/cobravision

TAKE NOTE: The CobraVision competition invites filmmakers to make and submit their own 50-second films to be shown on national television. Growing from its previous five-second incarnation, each month the winning 50-second films will be aired in their entirety before blockbuster movies on iTV4, and entered into a competition to win cash prizes at the annual CobraVision Awards. There are monthly prizes too, with past prizes including an Xbox 360 and trips to the Edinburgh International Film Festival. The competition is backed by Film London, the NFTS, Adobe and Sony PSP, and is judged by film critics from The Times, Little White Lies, Film Review magazine and Shooting People.

All films must have proper clearances for actors and crew and any music licenses where music is used. All films must be shot in widescreen or letterboxed. You can enter as many times as you like. See www.cobrabeer.com/cobravision to download full regulations.

DepicT!

✉ Watershed,
1 Canon's Road,
Bristol BS1 5TX

💻 maddy@watershed.co.uk
www.depict.org

TAKE NOTE: DepicT! is a micro-movies comp for films under 90 seconds. The award runs as part of Encounters Short Film Festival. A winner in Live Action and one in Animation each receive £2000, a screening at the festival and a membership to LOVEFiLM.

Filmaka

✉ Filmaka,
LLC,
7955 W. 3rd St.,
Los Angeles,
CA 90048, U.S.A.

💻 www.filmaka.com

TAKE NOTE: FILMAKA is a twice-monthly subscription-based worldwide short film competition that offers the chance to enter your film for possible cash prizes of USD$3,000, plus the chance of making a feature film. It's a new concept in short film – a regular short film prize judged by a panel of established industry insiders and filmmakers including Werner Herzog, John Madden, Neil LaBute and Paul Schrader, and it's the brainchild of Deepak Nayar who produced *Bend it Like Beckham*.

It's a new project, so it remains to be seen exactly how well it will work, but right now it looks pretty hot! Contests are divided into three levels, ENTRY, JURY and FINAL. You can only enter a contest at Entry level. *Entry Level* contest occurs twice monthly, up to 15 winners are selected and each is given $500 cash prize. They then move into the jury level contest. At the *Jury Level* contest, all winners

from the Entry Level are given a $1000 to make a second clip on the same subject. Two winners are selected. The first winner is given $3000 cash prize and a runner-up is given a $2000 cash prize. The winner and runner-up move into the final level. *Final Level* contest happens yearly. The winners and the runners up from each jury level contests compete for the grand feature film contract and the runner up wins a $5000 cash.

First Light

✉ Progress Works,
Heath Mill Lane,
Birmingham B9 4AL

📞 0121-693 2091

📠 0121-693 2096

💻 www.firstlightmovies.com

TAKE NOTE: …well yes, if you are aged 5-18 or want facilitate a film by makers in this age group. This is the Lottery-funded body set up to support films made by young people in the UK. First Light will fund films of any genre of 5-10 minutes' duration (depending on the scheme) where young people take a very active role in all aspects of the production process. Films must be mainly digital productions, should be geared towards increasing and understanding about heritage and community. Full guidelines are available on their website.

Pocket Shorts

✉ c/o BLINK,
The Old Caretakers House,
JL Brierley Mill,
Quay Street,
Huddersfield,
West Yorkshire HD1 6QT

📞 01484 301 805

💻 info@pocketshorts.co.uk
www.pocketshorts.co.uk

TAKE NOTE: This mini-scheme gives serious new filmmakers the funding to make shorts for mobile phones with a budget of up to £2000. The shorts are distributed at film festivals through 'Bluevend'

– Pocket Film's bluetooth 'vending machine'. You should have graduated from school no more than 5 years previously and you must live in the North East, North West or Yorkshire. Scottish applicants can apply to a separate scheme with £3000 support per film.

Reel Experience Talent Award

www.reeltalentaward.co.uk

TAKE NOTE: *The Reel Talent Award* is an annual short production award created by The Hospital together with The Script Factory, designed to provide a genuine opportunity for aspiring filmmakers to develop their skills and networks by producing a five-minute film on a given theme. Three winning teams are given budgets of up to £10,000 in cash plus in-kind sponsorship, as well as an intensive 3-day script development course run by The Script Factory before they shoot their films. In its first year (2005/06), completed films included the BAFTA-nominated *Heavy Metal Drummer* (dirs Toby MacDonald & Luke Morris). The second series is sponsored by the Audi Channel and is underway throughout 2007. For details on future call for entries, join The Script Factory's mailing list at www.scriptfactory.co.uk

Shooting People Film Competitions

www.shootingpeople.org

TAKE NOTE: Shooting People host monthly short film competitions for members (prize money for previous comps has been up to £15K). Also see the interview with Shooting People Film's Penny Nagle in the Get it Seen section of this book for more on previous competitions.

Straight8

ed@straight8.net
www.straight8.net

TAKE NOTE: Annual short film competition where filmmakers shoot a film on a single cartridge of super 8mm film (approximately 3 minutes) which is included in the £65 entry fee. You can only edit in-camera, and you send back your un-developed film to Straight8 for processing, together with an original soundtrack. Winners are screened at festivals and venues around the world (including Cannes in 2007).

Turner Classic Movies Short Film Competition

Turner House,
16 Great Marlborough Street,
London W1F 7HS

www.tcmonline.co.uk

TCM Classic Shorts is the UK's most prestigious shorts prize with awards totalling £10,000 in cash and subsequent screenings on the TCM channel. The award ceremony is each October at the London Film Festival. Past winners include Brian Percival's *About a Girl* which won a BAFTA as well as Alicia Duffy's *The Most Beautiful Man* in the World and Toby MacDonald *Je T'aime John Wayne*.

Training funds for filmmakers

Skillset

Prospect House,
80-110 New Oxford Street,
London WC1A 1HB

020-7520 5757

020-7520 5758

info@skillset.org
www.skillset.org

TAKE NOTE: Skillset supports training programmes for filmmakers – and in some cases offer bursaries for training courses through the Skillset Film Futures scheme.

Go to www.shootingpeople.org/shortsbook

Section Three:
Get it Ready

Preproduction Tips

Preproduction planning covers everything from lining up locations and organising catering for your shoot to rehearsing with your actors; advice on this stage of making your film could fill a book on its own. Every filmmaker will handle preproduction differently; much of this is down to common sense and simply doing the things you know you need to do make your shoot run smoothly.

It's almost inevitable that things will come up which you haven't thought about or planned for, but assuming you are working as your own line producer on your short, here is a list of general questions to get you started on preproduction planning. This isn't exhaustive. Each question may, and probably should, yield a host of other sub-questions in your own mind.

How many setups can we do each day

How many shots can we do within each setup? (What might our shoot ratio be? 4:1? 6:1?)

How long will I allow to prepare for each setup?

Is the scene already blocked or do I need to allow time for this too?

What is the schedule going to be and have I allowed enough time for breaks and lunch?

Where will we shoot each scene and how long will it take to move from one location to another?

What camera, lighting, stock and additional equipment will we need for each shot, and on which days?

What props will we need for each shot/ day, and who is responsible for getting these to the location?

Do I have all the necessary permissions to use the locations?

Are there likely to be problems with sound at any of the locations?

Do I have a one sheet (CALL SHEET) with contacts for cast and crew and with important shoot information like location addresses, directions and start times? Has it been circulated to all cast and crew?

Do we have sufficient transportation?

Do we need parking permits?

Do we need to get anyone to the locations or will they make their own way?

Have we lined up enough 'extras' where necessary?

Will cast and extras need make-up or costumes? If they need to bring their own costumes, have I briefed them properly?

If I am working with under 16's have I read up on the legal requirements regarding hours worked and guardians on set? Have I made their guardians aware of what is expected of them?

Is there someone available on set to run errands when necessary?

Do we need petty cash?

What will I feed my cast and crew and what drinks and refreshments will I make available on set?

Have I rehearsed my actors as well as I want to before the shoot? Do they know what is expected of them?

Do my crew know what we are trying to achieve creatively?

Have I thought about continuity issues from shot to shot and will there be someone on set to keep an eye on this?

What happens if we run over at night?

Have I thought through how everyone will be getting home?

Have I reminded crew to keep copies of all receipts (including travel cards, etc.)

Have we done a health/safety check?

Do we have our insurance papers with us?

Do I need a stills photographer to come on set to shoot stills for publicity afterwards (**Editor:** This is very, very useful if you can afford to do so)? And have I allowed for time to include this?

Chris and Ben Blaine, interview

Part 3: preproduction and rehearsals

When you shoot a film yourself, what kind of preproduction planning do you do?

CHRIS: Storyboards. In a full-on, properly planned shoot we always storyboard, it's imperative. We haven't shot a short film ourselves for quite some time though. I've shot a few music videos, but with shorts, we're very much of the opinion that if you're concentrating on the shot, then you're not looking at the performance.

There are times when I shoot stuff - usually something where I get to take the camera and run around, walk backwards, push a bike, a wheelchair, a skateboard, generally get to play with the camera. This is where the shot is about the shot, rather than the performance. That's just playtime. When you need to get a performance, you don't want to be concentrating on your framing.

BEN: There are exceptions, but we're both quite anal so we do tend to plan everything pretty obsessively. We were always able to organise our films back when we were largely making them alone, and in some ways that basic obsession with organisation is what makes our early films watchable. Ideas that should have been un-filmable on our resources became possible because we were so on top of the schedule.

I can't really stress it enough, actually - if you plan things right, you can achieve a hell of a lot on next to nothing. The more you rush headlong into production, the more expensive it will be. Like with kit, if you know what you want in advance, you can usually find it for a good rate (like free). If it's only on the morning of the shoot that you realise you need a crane then that's going to cost. You can only know what you want if you properly prepare yourself.

Not only does this include storyboarding, shotlisting and helping to draw up the schedule, but for the last two shorts we also put together animatics – putting the storyboard into Final Cut Pro and doing a rough cut of the entire film as a drawing. This is a brilliant resource and it enables you to start thinking about timing and pacing as well as shot sizes and positions.

What kind of prep work do you do with your Director of Photography?

CHRIS: Talking; drawing pictures; sharing pictures; 'recces' to sites; discussing shots; drawing storyboards; sharing storyboards; discussing format, lenses, lighting and jiggery pokery and bells and whistles. We also shoot tests and play with stuff in post to show the look we're trying to achieve before we shoot it.

All these things can happen and sometimes they don't. We did all of those for *Death of the Revolution* – although this doesn't mean it all went to plan – but we knew pretty much what we wanted anyway having done all this prep work.

> "We also shoot tests and play with stuff in post to show the look we're trying to achieve before we shoot it"

Can one afford to be more kamikaze on a short? Or do you still need the same careful daily schedules and shotlists as you would for a feature?

CHRIS: It depends on the scale of the thing. To be honest a short film needs as much planning as a feature: I read all about directors and actors taking on new ideas and changing the film as they carry on shooting but these are stories from feature film shoots. If you're shooting a short in a weekend you need to have had the discussions up front so you can get in and do the thing before your time runs out. Time always runs out.

One of the frustrating things about making shorts – and music videos as well - is that you're always starting. On a feature they say the first week is where everyone starts to get up to speed. On the first day you should expect to lose three hours just because when it's being done for the first time it takes longer. With short films, you get a lot of 'first days'.

Ideally you're really well planned so you can keep pushing the momentum of the shoot – you're always thinking ahead of the rest of the crew, so that any upcoming problems can be dealt with before shoot time. The director sets the tempo of the shoot, and chooses how much time the DoP and the rest of the crew get to set up on each shot. You may have a First AD to help you with this, but if *you* sit down and relax, then things will take longer. It's just the way it goes.

Do you need to have contracts with everyone who is working on the film, even if you aren't paying them?

CHRIS: Well, technically, yeah, you do.

BEN: I can't pretend that we *always* get everyone signed up to everything. So far it's not come back to bite us in the arse, but if you ask me what people should do then, yeah, you *should* get everyone on contract. Often seems a bit heavy-handed, especially if you're a bunch of mates. Yet mates fall out, and especially when no one is getting paid for their work, things can get very messy. It's always far and away the best policy to get everyone to agree to the terms and conditions of their work on your film, that way everyone knows where they stand.

Most short filmmakers can't afford to pay actors. How have you guys gotten around this and still made sure you get the quality you need?

CHRIS: Actors want to do good work. If you give them a good role in a good film they'll want to do it, regardless of the money. Nobody gets into acting believing they're definitely the next Tom Cruise, they just want to be able to express themselves with their craft and hone that craft with great roles.

BEN: Also, we really care about actors and we always have done. I mean, at the end of the day, the only way you can get quality is by *knowing what it is*. There are a lot of directors who come across as jumped-up camera operators, like the only important tool for a director to worry about is the camera. We've both always been interested in actors and acting.

We tend to know what we want from our cast and so we keep looking until we find it. Recently we've been very lucky to work with some recognised talents [like Danny Dyer and Benedict Wong] and that's been fantastic, but I think we've also done a pretty good job of finding brilliant people who no-one has heard of but who are perfect for the roles we write.

What's your casting process like?

BEN: It varies from film to film. Often we write with specific actors very much in mind, which is great if they can do it, less good if they can't because then you have to rethink your whole mental image of the character.

But if we are holding auditions, it's usually quite simple and just a case of exploring the character with the actor and also getting to know them as best as is possible. We never bother with prepared pieces: we just send a copy of the complete screenplay and then get them to run through the part or parts we're seeing them for. If, as sometimes happens, the part doesn't have enough actual dialogue to really work as a read-through, then we either get them to read a different part or just write something new for them to say.

Usually I like to do a run through without having said very much about what we're looking for, to see how they've responded to the text. Then, after we've been through it once and everyone is a little more relaxed, we try to give some direction and start again. It's not always direction we particularly *mean* for the film itself, it's just always good to see how people interpret what we say to them. As a director, you're job is always to get your ideas across to your collaborators as clearly as possible, but there's no getting away from the fact that some people really get us and some people don't.

We also like to have a chat to find out who they are. Of course *being* other people is what actors make their living from, but it's always good to try and get a handle on who someone is - what they bring to the part and, indeed, what working with them is going to be like. That's the hardest part about working with the more 'name' actor types who get offers, not auditions. The audition is actually a really nice place to start a working relationship because it's only a subtext not the main event. Meeting an actor for the first time after they've accepted an offer is a bit like how I imagine an arranged marriage would be.

Anyway, we always film the auditions, and this is vital because people are different on camera to how they are in real life. There are occasions when actors who you thought were brilliant come across very badly on camera and many, many more occasions when actors who felt quite weak in the flesh really come alive when you watch their tapes back. It is, therefore, of great importance that you do actually watch the tapes back, even if you were there when they were filmed.

Death of the Revolution
Photo by Jessica Thomas

CHRIS: For ages I tried to avoid going to the auditions. I much prefer seeing them onscreen and having that different perspective to Ben so we can make a rational judgement between the two of us. Nowadays I try to keep that distance by watching their performance through the viewfinder. It also means it'll stay in focus which was a problem when Ben set the camera to autofocus!

That's a big point actually. If you can, get someone to film the audition rather than setting it up on a tripod and pressing go. If you can get your DoP, then even better. They'll be able to point out any problems in lighting or shooting the actor you're thinking of, and may come up with some ideas simply by having seen them at the earliest point available. I do try to change angle and shot size between takes to see how they look.

BEN: Yeah, also, it's not only important how someone comes across on camera, but it's how they come across with the rest of your cast. Getting the right cast as a whole is as important as getting individual casting right and we're always happy to do recalls in order to get a sense of chemistry. You often do find that an actor may be perfect for the role as you'd imagined it, but actually, once the other parts have been cast, you need something a bit different. Also if you're having trouble choosing between a couple of actors, but you've got another role cast, a session which shows you how the different performers might work together, is a very good way of showing who is really right for the film.

> "we always film the auditions, and this is vital because people are different on camera to how they are in real life."

It's also important to hit the right tone. I never feel it's very useful to be too formal - the stereotype audition has a grim faced panel sat behind a desk whilst the actor nervously sits on a chair in the full beam of a spotlight. I've seen a lot of first time directors get a bit hung up on the power and authority thing. The only way you ever really get respect from your cast, and your crew, is by being honest and telling them what you want from them. This starts at the audition. It's not the *X-Factor*, you're not deciding who is or isn't a good actor, you're just trying to find the right person for the film.

With us there's only ever Chris and me and possibly a producer; at this stage you don't need anyone else. We always try to keep the atmosphere relaxed, friendly and most of all, secure. It's easy to forget how scary auditions can be, and the problem with scared people is that they don't give a fair account of their talents. You need to create a space where actors feel happy to give their best.

> **"I think it's important not to rehearse things to death. Film is very intimate and if something seems rehearsed it could seem fake"**

That said, it's equally important not to be too informal. Auditioning in your house is fine if there's nowhere else, but tidy up. Everyone likes to feel that they're auditioning for something worthwhile, something serious that will be interesting to be involved with. Equally the actor is not the only person who is being auditioned - they are well within their rights to turn you down so (for God's sake) be prepared: know their names, have spare copies of the script, if possible know your shoot dates and don't be afraid of discussing money, even if there isn't any. Relaxed is good, but professional is essential.

Lastly, but importantly, no-one ever needs to get naked in an audition. If you are thinking of exceptions to that rule, don't make films.

How important is rehearsal time with actors before the shoot?

BEN: It depends on the type of film, the type of shoot and indeed, how you like to work and how much rehearsing you think your cast need. I have to say that a lot of the time, because we're working with people who really understand our work, and a lot of our films have been pretty simple, there isn't all that much we want to do in a rehearsal space. Rehearsals are great for exploring character, developing ideas and building important relationships between your cast. They're rubbish though for blocking moves or doing much towards the real physicality of the shoot.

A lot of the time we've been working with actors who not only know us, but know each other too. A great deal of that ground work is already in place and so we tend to have a read through with everybody and then leave a lot of the work until we're on set when a scene can really grow in relation to its actual setting. Of course this is only really possible if you've either got a relaxed shoot or you're shooting something fairly simple. For instance, *Free Speech* is a single short conversation. The bulk of the film took a day to shoot and for almost every take, certainly every set-up, we ran the entire script. This meant that we were able

> **"no-one ever needs to get naked in an audition"**

to explore and develop the ideas and the characters with Jacqui and Danny but in a real environment. It kept it fresh and meant we filmed all of their really inspired moments.

CHRIS: For *Death of the Revolution* we did rehearse with the lead boy Alastair the day before we recorded the version of his 'thoughts voice over' we used for him to act along to when we shot. We did have more planned but after he learnt what the trickier words like totalitarianism meant, he sailed through it and we thought it best to wait until we did the recording so as to keep it fresh. I know he did a lot of read-throughs with his family though. He really knew his script when it got to the recording. Then, having gone through that we felt he was pretty ready for the onscreen stuff although we did more rehearsals with all the main people whilst waiting for the first lighting setup to be ready on the first day.

BEN: I think it's important not to rehearse things to death. Film is very intimate and if something seems rehearsed it could seem fake. The best thing to do is to get you and your cast to the point where the scenes are almost ready, but you really want the actors to only nail it once the camera is rolling. On *Hallo Panda* our shooting schedule was almost impossible, and the rehearsals we did do were a vital resource for the actors when they had to suddenly leap from one part of the script to the next.

On the set of *Free Speech*
Photo by Jessica Thomas

Act like you mean it: casting and rehearsals

If your actors are shit, your film will be too. Ok, so that may be a bit harsh, but it's not far from the truth. Audiences will forgive and forget many technical imperfections, but they will almost never forgive bad acting. Along with a good script and decent sound, acting is certainly one of the most important elements in your short (assuming you are making a drama, of course). Why then do so many filmmakers spend so little time in getting this crucial element right?

The obvious answer to that is that on most shorts you are flat out doing most of the work by yourself or with a small team, *and* you are making it for very little money. Short film sets also often have reduced crews and demands can be overwhelming. It's understandable why actors are sometimes the last thing a director thinks about. That's all the more reason to make sure you spend time finding the right cast and work in adequate time for rehearsals beforehand.

You may also be worried about the cost of getting the best actors, and this is a worry that sometimes drives filmmakers to cast their friends, family, even themselves in their short films. While this may be the right thing if your family and friends can act, or if you are confident you can get a natural performance from them if the role doesn't require much difficult 'acting', but this can be absolutely disastrous if you are doing it just to save the dosh. In this case, there's no point even making the film unless your ambitions for the film stop at having a laugh. But don't think you have to spend lots of money to get the right actors. Like you, there are many talented actors who are just getting started and need to look for work to build their own portfolios and experience. They understand that short films are almost never a money-making venture, and if you are clear about what you are trying to do and professional, a good actor – like the crew – may feel you are worth taking a punt on for little or no pay.

> "if you are clear about what you are trying to do and professional, a good actor – like crew - may feel you are worth taking a punt on for little or no pay"

It's always worth banging home the point that if people *are* working for free or almost nothing – and really anytime for that matter – be as professional as possible and let them know what's expected of them. If you decide on a 5-day/ 8 hour shoot, don't then expect everyone to shoot 12 hour days when you discover that 5 days was unrealistic. Again, it's stating the obvious, but be aware that being on set can be tedious for actors until they are called on. Plan your schedule sensitively to make sure you don't have people hanging around unnecessarily. If it's clear you've done your preparation properly, people will be more likely to work with you and offer flexibility if genuine unforeseen problems do arise which demand some schedule changes.

Where can I find actors for my short?

Shooting People's Casting Network (**www.shootingpeople.org**) is the first place to start advertising when you put out a call for actors (the Casting Network has over 8000 actors members Shooting People members can reach through daily bulletins. You can also search through actor profiles on the website). You might also want to spread the work to actors' groups and courses in your area. These are the places you'll be most likely to hook up with actors who are at a similar career stage to you. A&C Black publishes an annual *Actors'*

Yearbook that lists many of these along with acting classes and courses. It also includes a list casting directors and actors' agents (as does their *Filmmakers' Yearbook* which also notes where an agent actively encourages short film work for their clients). Be aware though that most agents will expect their client to be paid something (union minimum, at least) unless you are an unusually fêted emerging superstar or have someone famous already on board! With agents, there is even more of an need to be professional; they won't put you in touch with their client unless they think you are serious.

Short film sales agents all say that a famous, or semi-famous face can help to sell a film, but while that is true, it's probably not worth spending ages trying to track down Cate Blanchett or Ralph Fiennes via their agents. We're not going to say NEVER do this, but typically, unless you have a personal connection, this approach can take months and it rarely comes off. A better strategy might be to think about up-and-coming new actors from an indie feature you've seen, or from TV, or even people who have worked

> **"Non-professional actors may work best for you. You may get a surprising freshness and credibility that a trained actor may not have"**

extensively in theatre. They may want to get more film experience too. Try to make contact via friends and other filmmaker colleagues. You may also find this easier if you can work with a casting agent who can use their connections.

Non-professional actors may work best for you. Depending on what kind of film you are making, they can be even more appropriate because you may get a surprising freshness and credibility that a trained actor may not have. In this case, instead of casting family and friends, why not look for the right faces in markets, shops or schools? In addition to getting the look you are after, you may also be less distracted and feel more at ease if you are purely the 'director' to the cast (rather than their pesky little brother or a mate who they can take the piss out of – these family and friend dynamics are surprisingly hard to shake). If you decide on a community search, weeks before your casting days, make some flyers with details and go out with your filmmaking team to talk to interesting people. Obviously this approach has its own inherent problems, but

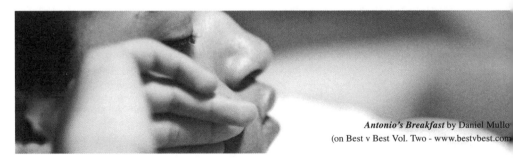

Antonio's Breakfast by Daniel Mullo
(on Best v Best Vol. Two - www.bestvbest.com

many a good film has been cast in this way. Make sure you approach people in non-threatening places and be prepared to enthuse them on the spot about the project always being honest about the scope and potential of the film. If they are someone you are generally interested in and they seem keen, get a name and a phone number or email address. You can then follow up the meeting with more information to show that you are serious and to confirm that they are indeed interested in attending the casting sessions, and give them a time to attend. It's so obvious as to be laughable, but don't bullshit people and make them think this is their 'big break'. It's an interesting experience and a chance to see how a film is made - and have a video copy of the film for themselves - but, it's not a star search! Some schools may also be willing to let a serious, impressive team of filmmakers pitch the project to students (it's a learning experience for their students too), as might youth and after-school groups if you need younger actors. In these cases, you'll have to take your case to the Head/Principal or Youth Group Leader first. Daniel Mulloy cast his BAFTA winning short film *Antonio's Breakfast* through schools in Brixton in South London where more than 100 kids turned up in some of the schools for the audition.

In all cases with non-professional actors, make them aware of what you'll expect from them in pre-shoot rehearsals and on set. Again, schedule their time on set to avoid boredom.

Casting and rehearsals

Find an accessible and appropriate place to hold your casting sessions and host these in as organised a manner as you can muster. This is the first real impression many of the actors/performers will have of your team. Actors on Shooting People often make the point that they don't like it when a filmmaker holds a casting session in their own home. They find it awkward and say it can be very disconcerting. Local churches, leisure centres and community centres often offer inexpensive, or even free, hire in their downtime. And no: the pub is not a good place to hold your casting session!

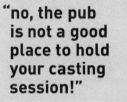

"no, the pub is not a good place to hold your casting session!"

You don't have to spend a lot of money, but borrow flasks (or buy them: you'll need them for the shoot!) to have coffee and tea and jugs of water. Biscuits if you can stretch. Give people a time to arrive and as much as possible stick to the schedule you set. While it's not the end of the world to make people wait for 15 minutes, don't waste their morning. Make sure there is a place for people to sit while they wait. For bigger roles, you'll obviously want to spend a little more time with that person than you will for other bit performers (you may find that speaking with your additional performers is enough without a formal session).

There are many different ways to handle the session itself. In what will probably be 15-20 minutes, you'll need to find out a little about their temperament and why they want to be in it the film if they are non-professionals. Find out how they look on film/tape; and discover if they are flexible as an actor. This is the best time to get them to try a line in more than one way.

Depending on how much information you have given them before the session, you might want to give them a pitch for the film to set the tone and relax them and tell them just a little about the part. Don't over elaborate or waste too much time on this; give them crucial details only. It's their time to impress you, not the other way around really. Some directors prefer to have actors come armed with a reading or even a little story to tell – maybe a memorable birthday or date. If you take this approach, make it something relevant for the role they are going for. It's not really going to do you any good to tape someone who has to play a jerk in your film telling you the story of their most delightful birthday memory.

Some filmmakers like to use this first open call to narrow down their choices to a smaller pool of actors who they can then spend more time with in a second, extended session. This extra investment of time is well worth the effort; casting the right person is one of the most important decisions you will make on your film.

Tips for rehearsal

1) Rehearse as much as schedules will allow.

Don't waste people's time, but make sure they are well prepared and know the role. Obviously, if you are working with an in-demand actor, this many only be one rehearsal for a few hours, but it's better than nothing. **Rehearsal is the time to let the actors to experiment with the role, not on set.**

2) Listen to your actors.

If they tell you that they don't understand something in the script, don't assume they are stupid. It may be that this part of the script isn't working. If it chimes with what other readers have pointed out to you already, then they are almost certainly right, and you aren't getting across what you wanted to. By the same token, if a line repeatedly sounds awkward and they have a problem with it, let them try something else that feels more natural as long as it communicates what needs to be communicated. It's even more important in a short film than a feature to be economical so don't let them go off the point, but actors often have a better ear for believable dialogue than many writers.

> "nothing destroys an actor's confidence like having their director constantly change their mind for no apparent reason"

3) Be clear about what you want before you start to work with them

This is not to say 'be inflexible', but nothing destroys an actor's confidence like having their director constantly change their mind for no apparent reason. Inevitably, it will seem like you are making it up as you go along, and you probably are if this is the case.

4) Know what that actor can and can't do and work with this.

If you are working with non-professionals, don't keep trying to get them to do something that isn't working. Keep them relaxed and natural. It's that quality you cast them for. Find a different way to communicate and get what you need, or compromise slightly. If you've cast wisely and well, you should be able to make small compromises without changing things, which will turn this into a different film. *Antonio's Breakfast* is a brilliant example of how to play to a non-actor's strengths. There is very little dialogue in the film and most of the takes are short.

5) If you can afford to, roll tape/film during your on set rehearsals

With non-professionals especially, you may get some of your best takes this way.

Lee Kern, On Documentary Preproduction

Documentary pre-production? All my stuff's kind of an 'internal', local world you can make on a whim so I don't really have to plot big adventures – that's only finding my shoes (if I'm meeting someone important). I made one thing in the Shetland Isles, so I guess that required 'pre-production', although I wasn't thinking at the time, "I'm doing pre-production", it was just kind of doing what I needed to do to make the film. Okay...what is there? There's organising boring, logistical stuff like car journeys or ferries or

Lee Kern's films include *The Edgware Walker, The House of Memory, Tales of the Creepy Crooked, Lee Kern's A-Z* and *October Mumbling.* You can watch several of Lee's short films on four docs (www.channel4.com/fourdocs).

Lee is also the editor of Shooting People's Filmmakers' Network.

making sure you haven't left your camera under some pants in your room. That's easy (don't get someone else to do that – do it yourself so you can keep as much money as possible). Then there's co-ordinating with your contributors, arranging to meet people. That's easy too (if you're rubbish at speaking to people or not very charming, get someone else to do it - but try and do it yourself so you can keep as much money as possible and buy your girlfriend necklaces so she doesn't leave you). I don't know...what else is there? Make sure you have release forms (and take them with you); there's also insurance and stuff that people go on about, and I guess you should check there are no legal problems with anything you're doing...that's something that people moan about. Oh yeah, make sure you organise things so you have enough time to cover yourself if everything goes tits up. Plan things so you have 'magic space' before your delivery. Actually you know what? When I went to the Shetlands, I was a total pre-production wizard – I drew up a timetable AND I put contact numbers on it. Do that because that's what real TV companies do when they make films. They're organised so they can get all the money whilst you scrabble around like an amateur looking for peanuts. Get organised...that's what pre-production is: getting shit in place so you can go out and make your film.

So to conclude, Britain and America mobilised three million troops for the Normandy landings in order to save the world from Nazi occupation, and what have you got to organise? Getting a camera somewhere so some schmuck can moan about something or other? It's easy. Go and make a film. Stop moaning.

James Fabricant, on sharing ideas and work with other filmmakers through MySpace

www.myspace.com

MySpace started as a place for unsigned bands to get heard. How does this work for filmmakers?

James Fabricant is Head of Marketing and Content for the UK & Ireland at **MySpace**

In late 2006, MySpace launched the MySpace UK Film Channel - an online community destination for filmmakers and film industry professionals. MySpace sets out to revolutionise the film industry as it has for music, by bridging the gap between artists, industry influencers and fans through the world's largest online community (160 million members and counting). With learning from the US experience, MySpace has built the premiere destination for independent directors, crews, emerging talent and enthusiasts in the UK. Our next generation Channel focuses on not only connecting film professionals who share work, but also in giving them the tools to help them learn the craft of filmmaking, facilitate the process, and allow them to promote themselves to a film community. With over 5000 UK filmmaker profiles already on the site (and another 40,000 in the US), MySpace provides an unparalleled suite of free networking tools (blogs, instant messaging, e-mail, streaming video, download options, photo uploads, voting, and networking/fan groups) that provide a powerful way to bring filmmakers together.

When you sign up for a MySpace filmmaker profile you essentially get a free website with a built in audience over 160 million. Uploading your film to your MySpace profile is easy, and doesn't require any technical knowledge of streaming video. Once uploaded, your film trailer or short film is 'viral'. This means it is easy for you, your friends or fans of your film to copy the html code and paste it to another MySpace profile or to anywhere on the internet. MySpace accelerates the 'word of mouth' process and helps independent filmmakers find the audience for their film and show this audience to potential distributors interested in taking on their project.

How is MyMovie Mashup going to work?

MySpace users in the UK submit short films. 12 films are shortlisted and a panel of leading filmmakers will choose three for MySpace users to vote on. The winner directs a feature film with a budget of £1 million. The MySpace community can watch the process of the film being made and are invited to take part in the creative process at key stages in the film.

Sample Clearance Forms

As has been said elsewhere in this book, it's extremely important that you have the correct clearances and permissions for your film. If you don't, then you may not even have the right to show it in public, much less, sell it to a broadcaster. Just as it would be unwise to use your favourite White Stripes song and hope you could clear it later when they see how fabulous your film is, so too would it be silly to not get the people in your documentary to sign a release form when you make the film. Save yourself much hassle later by being legit and organised now.

The following contracts and clearance forms were created by Shooting People (shootingpeople.org) for the reference of its members (the website also includes other important clearance forms and legal reference documents). They are reprinted here by permission and for your information and education only. As with all documents in this book, these are no substitute for talking to your own solicitor to come up with clearances which are right for your film. You are not authorised to use them for reference unless you have read and agreed to the disclaimer below:

These forms and other materials are provided on an 'as is' basis and Shooting People accepts no liability for any loss or damage arising out of or in connection with the use of such materials or reliance on any information available in this book. This is a comprehensive limitation of liability that applies to all damages of any kind, including (without limitation) compensatory, direct, indirect or consequential damages, loss of income, profit, revenue or goodwill, loss of or damage to property and claims of third parties. Shooting People gives no advice or guidance as to the suitability for any purpose of the forms or other materials below and, should you rely on any information or materials on our website or in this book, you agree to do so entirely at your own risk.

Nothing in the forms or other materials provided herein is intended to, nor shall it, confer any benefit on a third party whether under the Contracts (Rights of Third Parties) Act 1999 or otherwise.

The forms and other materials provided herein shall be governed by and construed in accordance with English law. Any dispute arising out of the accessing or use of our website, book or the forms and other materials provided herein shall be subject to the exclusive jurisdiction of the English courts].

Notes on the Copyright Waiver Form

This form for unpaid contributors is intended for people who are genuine collaborators in the project. Employees (other than genuine freelancers recognised by the Inland Revenue) must be paid minimum wage. Join Shooting People to read up on employment legislation and for advice on how much to pay film workers.

Notes on the Documentary Release Form

You need a Release Form for anyone who either gives you an interview or who speaks on camera. You do not need a Release Form for people on the street as long as your camera is not concealed.

You will need Release Forms for people who are identifiable in sensitive places even if they are not speaking e.g. hospital waiting rooms, gay clubs, law court corridors.

You should warn your interviewee that you will need a Release Form signed after the interview and get it signed straight away. Try not to leave it until the next day or the next week by which time they may have changed their mind.

Anyone under the age of 16 needs to have their Release Form signed by one of their parents.

It is crucial that the Release Form is not signed under any misapprehension or false pretences. Whilst you do not need to share all your plans or thoughts for the film with the contributors, what you do say must not be misleading. It is best to communicate with your interviewees in writing before the interview so that you have proof that you were clear about the nature of the film.

Most documentary interviews are given for no fee (if that is the case simply remove the clause which refers to the fee). However, many people do now ask for a fee – particularly if the whole film revolves around their contribution. There are no guidelines as to how much this amount should be although it is common for expert commentators such as historians or scientists to receive between £100-£200.

In recent years, documentary hoaxing has become more common – you are advised to double check your contributor's story. You should ask to see a passport to check they are giving you their real name and request appropriate evidence of their qualifications, if you are in any doubt.

Many release forms also contain a clause warning interviewees that they are liable for any libel case that might result from their contribution to the documentary.

That clause has not been included here for two reasons. Firstly, it will not protect the documentary filmmaker (and the TV channel that broadcasts it) from being sued if the interviewee has libelled someone. Secondly this clause can frighten off interviewees from taking part to begin with. Remember that the responsibility for good journalism lies with you not with the contributor.

These forms can also be downloaded from www.shootingpeople.org/shortsbook

Documentary Release Form

[Headed paper or Name and address of film company or producer]

Date:

The Name of the Documentary (working title)

I agree to the inclusion of my contribution in this documentary, the nature of which has been explained to me. I understand that my contribution will be edited and there is no guarantee that my contribution will appear in the final film. I agree that my contribution may be used to publicise the documentary.

I have agreed to accept £X for the use of my contribution. This fee is payable on completion of the interview.

I understand that this documentary (or part of it) may be distributed in any medium in any part of the world.

My contribution has, to the best of my knowledge, been truthful and honest. I have not deliberately sought to conceal any relevant facts from the makers of this film.

Signed

Copyright Waiver Form

[Headed paper or Name and address of film company or producer]

Date:

[NAME OF THE FILM] (working title)

[ROLE OF CONTRIBUTOR ON FILM]

I agree to collaborate on this short film and to assign to [NAME OF THE ASSIGNEE], with full title guarantee, the following:

> i) all of my rights, title, interest and property in [NAME OF THE FILM] (the "Intellectual Property Rights");

> ii) the full and exclusive benefit of all the Intellectual Property Rights including all forms of protection and all rights, privileges and advantages appertaining thereto;

> iii) the right to recover and to bring proceedings to recover damages and/or to obtain other remedies in respect of infringement of the Intellectual Property Rights whether committed before or after the date of this Agreement.

AND to hold the same unto [NAME OF THE ASSIGNEE] absolutely.

Further, I hereby agree to waive all moral rights in the Intellectual Property Rights.

The nature of the project and my role in it has been explained to me and I have agreed to collaborate on this project for [NO FEE/ FEE OF £X].

I understand that this film (or part of it) may be distributed by the producer in any medium in any part of the world.

I shall, at the request of [NAME OF THE ASSIGNEE], sign all instruments, applications or other documents and to do all such acts as shall be reasonably required by [NAME OF THE ASSIGNEE] to enable [NAME OF THE ASSIGNEE] or its nominee to enjoy the full and exclusive benefit of the Intellectual Property Rights and to fully and effectively vest the same in [NAME OF THE ASSIGNEE] including, where necessary, the registration of [NAME OF THE ASSIGNEE]'s title in the Intellectual Property Rights in the appropriate intellectual property office at which the Intellectual Property Rights are (or at the nomination of the [NAME OF THE ASSIGNEE] shall be) registered.

Signed ....

Print ....

Actors Agreement

[Headed paper or Name and address of film company or producer]

Date:

RE: [NAME OF THE FILM] (working title of 'the film')

[NAME, ADDRESS OF ACTOR]

The above named actor agrees to take part in 'the film'.

1.   Start Date:

2.   Period of Engagement: to
     (These dates may vary from time to time).

3.   Rate of pay: £   per hour/day/month

4.   Agreed Expenses:

5.   Conditions: Producer agrees to obtain standard cast insurance for the Artist

6.   The Artist knows of no reason why he cannot freely enter this agreement

7.   The Artist gives all consents required under the Copyright Designs and Patents Act
     1988 or any re-enactment consolidation or amendment thereof in order that the Pro-
     ducer may make full use of the Artist's services and any other moral rights to which
     the Artist may be entitled under any existing or future legislation.

8.   The Artist agrees that the Artist shall:
     8.1.   perform and record the Artist's part to the best of the Artist's skill and ability;
     8.2.   attend for fittings rehearsals and the taking of still photographs;
     8.3.   dress, make up and wear the Artist's hair (subject to prior consultation with
            the Artist) as directed by the Director;
     8.4.   comply with all reasonable and notified directions given by the Producer or
            the Director;
     8.5.   keep the Producer informed of the Artist's whereabouts and telephone
            number at all material times; and
     8.6.   not pledge the credit of the Producer nor incur or purport to incur any liability
            on its behalf or in its name.

9.   All rights in any way attaching to the Film and all photographs and sound recordings
     shall belong absolutely to the Producer throughout all periods to the extent permit-
     ted by the law. The Artist waives the right to receive any further remuneration in
     relation to the exploitation of the rights.

10. The Producer shall be entitled by written notice to the Artist given at any time to
     suspend the engagement of the Artist if:
     10.1.   the film is prevented suspended interrupted or postponed by reasons not
             within the control of the Producer;

10.2. the voice of the Artist shall become unsatisfactory;

10.3. the Artist shall by reason of any illness or physical or mental incapacity or disability be unable to perform his duties; or

10.4. the Artist's full services shall fail material obligations under this Agreement.

11. Any suspension shall be effective from the date of the event giving rise to such suspension and shall continue for the duration of such event.

11.1. the Producer shall during the period of suspension cease to be liable to make payments to the Artist save such instalments of remuneration which have become due.

12. The Producer shall be entitled by written notice to the Artist given at any time to terminate the engagement of the Artist hereunder if:

12.1. suspension under clause 13 continues for 28 (twenty-eight) days consecutively or in the aggregate;

12.2. circumstances under Clause 12.1 continue for at least 2 (two) consecutive days or 3 (three) days in the aggregate;

12.3. circumstances in Clauses 12.2-12.4 occur subject to the Producer giving notice of such default; or

12.4. any suspension under the provisions of Clause 12.1 shall continue for six weeks or more then the Artist shall be entitled to terminate this engagement by seven days' written notice.

13. In the event of termination of the engagement or death of the Artist:

13.1. any claim which the Producer may have shall not be affected or prejudiced;

13.2. the Producer's title to and ownership of all copyrights and all other rights in or in connection with the services rendered shall be or remain vested in the Producer; and

13.3. payment of the instalments of remuneration due and payable to the Artist shall operate as payment in full and final discharge and settlement of all claims.

14. All consents granted hereunder to the Producer are irrevocable.

15. Credit will be given only if the Artist appears recognisably in the Film as released if this Agreement has not been terminated for the default of the Artist.

16. The Artist shall keep as confidential the provisions of and any information which may come to the Artist's attention in connection with this agreement.

17. This agreement is governed by and construed in accordance with the laws of England and subject to the exclusive jurisdiction of the Courts of England

Signed ....   Dated ....
    [Artist]

Signed ....   Dated ....
    [Producer]

Casting Resources

Shooting People Casting Network

 www.shootingpeople.org.uk

TAKE NOTE: SP's Casting Network has over 8000 actor members, and sends a daily bulletin to actors looking for work. Become a SP member to post notices about your film.

The Actors' Centre

✉ The Actors Centre,
1a Tower Street,
London WC2H 9NP

☎ 020-7240 3940

📠 020 7240 3896

 admin@actorscentre.co.uk
www.actorscentre.co.uk

TAKE NOTE: This is a resource for actors which hosts workshops and classes. Its good place to post flyers.

Actors' Yearbook

 www.acblack.com

TAKE NOTE: Annual UK directory for actors which has extensive listings for casting agents and actors agents throughout the UK.

CastNet ✎

 www.castnet.co.uk

TAKE NOTE: Website with a database of actors looking for work. Free use for people who are employing actors.

The Casting Directors' Guild

 www.thecdg.co.uk

TAKE NOTE: Good place for finding a casting director - website includes a complete list of members with credits so you can see what kind of work they do.

CastWeb

💻 www.castweb.co.uk

TAKE NOTE: Casting information network with daily bulletins.

Conference of Drama Schools

💻 www.drama.ac.uk

TAKE NOTE: Website has links to 22 member schools across the UK.

Equity

✉ London Office,
Guild House,
Upper St Martins Lane,
London WC2H 9EG

☎ 020-7670 0247

💻 www.equity.org.uk

TAKE NOTE: Trade union for all performers for stage, screen and radio, and they publish a Job Information Service for their members. Will advertise unpaid work.

National Association of Youth Theatres

 www.nayt.org.uk

TAKE NOTE: The website includes a search function which allows you to find member groups by town.

Northern Actors Centre

21-31 Oldham Street, Manchester M1 1JG

(📞) 0161-819 2513

 info@northernactorscentre.co.uk
www.northernactorscentre.co.uk

TAKE NOTE: Publish casting calls on their website.

Production and Casting Report (P.C.R.)

www.pcrnewsletter.com

TAKE NOTE: Weekly production newsletter with lists of cast and crew jobs. Will run casting notices for student and short film productions (see site for details).

Spotlight

www.spotlightcd.com

TAKE NOTE: Casting publication with more than 30,000 listings for actors and performers in the UK with pictures and CVs. Three month access for the online version of the book costs £60.

Youngblood

 The Rag Factory,
16-18 Heneage St,
London E1 5LJ

(📞) 020-7193 3207

info@youngblood.co.uk
www.youngblood.co.uk

TAKE NOTE: Not a casting resource, but they provide fight directors and trainers for film production. May consider special deals for worthy low budget productions.

Section Four:

Get it Made

No Banana Skins:
A Director On Common Production Cock-ups
Cath Le Couteur, Award-winning filmmaker and Shooting People Founder

Let's be honest. Directing a film is closer to crisis management. In fact it's not just close, it's often well and truly in your face, full blown disaster avoidance. But for every mistake that is made on set, there is also, sometimes - when your heart is impaled by the bloody stick of the clock - a serendipitous moment that emerges too. This is one of the wonders of cinema. Out of disasters, mistakes and things outside of our control, moments of cinematic brilliance can and do emerge. This guide however, is an attempt to help steer you clear of basic hassles, stresses and common mistakes that tend not to facilitate these moments of wonder, but instead, can make your life hell!

Production starts in Preproduction – the buck stops here.

No discussion of production can start without taking account of preproduction basics. Making a low budget short often means you start out as the Director, Producer, Writer, Location Scout, Production Manager, Casting Director, Assistant Director, Runner and everything else in between. If you are lucky enough to already be collaborating with other people then you will already know how important this process is.

Collaboration is what sets the film medium apart from its literary/art counterparts, and the critical question is, how can YOU create an inspiring environment that facilitates the creative process. If you can (and planning is often crucial to this), you will elevate the film way beyond what any of you as individuals have imagined.

1. WORK WITH PEOPLE YOU LOVE

I stole this from Danny Boyle. And it's true. Working with people you love is just the best place to start. And this doesn't *just* mean 'mates rates' (pulling your flatmate in to work for free, although you will also do this repeatedly) but can also mean finding new collaborators you jive with.

> **QUICK TIP:** *A great place to find crew is Shooting People (www.shootingpeople.org). Meet collaborators, talk through the film together, be open to new ideas, see if you have a common vibe and discuss upfront and honestly what you hope to achieve within the budget.*

2. PLANNING PLANNING PLANNING

The more work you do in preproduction, the million, trillion, zillion times better your film will be. Making the days of the shoot work is your biggest responsibility. Where possible, team up with a production manager (or producer) who will production manage the shoot. This is one of the most valuable people on your team and you want a person who is incredibly organised, a great communicator and a lovely problem solver. If they are inexperienced, work with them to help ensure they have everything before the shoot. Your basics are: a shooting schedule, a contact sheet of everyone participating, a location sheet that tells everyone where to be at what time, a health and safety check list (including closest hospitals), equipment supplier information and insurance details. Get these sorted properly before the shoot and you can then just concentrate on making the film fly.

Ben Crowe, on getting a noir-ish film look on a micro budget short.

Ben Crowe is the director of the short film *The Man Who Met Himself,* which screened in competition at Cannes Film Festival, and which he made for just £400 and shot on Canon 10-14 XLS.

I had never worked with Super 8 before and I went out and picked up a cheap camera. I chose it because I wanted to make a film where the sound and the pictures didn't have to be in sync all the time and I wanted a filmic look. I wanted it to be grainy, I wanted it to hark back to film noir-ish urban thrillers. Super 8 is the cheapest format probably to be able to do that particularly if you want to re-create something and then tweak it later on, because digital's got its own qualities and characteristics which can be used to do their own thing. So if I wanted to shoot it in a film medium, Super 8 was the choice. And then the idea of non-synchronous music and dialogue, that was also informed by the choice of using Super 8. That also meant that when shooting, I could really focus on the images. Sound was to be dubbed later.

Interviewed here by James MacGregor. Read the interview in full:

www.shootingpeople.org/shooterfilms/

3. COMMUNICATION – YOUR DOP AND OTHERS

> "It goes without saying that EVERY shoot runs out of time!"

Meet with your DOP to discuss the aesthetics of your shoot and a style you both feel will best serve the film. Also decide what you want to shoot on, and make a kit list. Make sure you also meet well in advance to discuss a realistic shot list. If you shoot loose, and prefer not to plan your shots, then it can still be vital to prepare an outline shooting schedule. It is often at these meetings that you may find you need to adapt/change your script or schedule to work within your money and time constraints. It goes without saying that EVERY shoot runs out of time; set-ups always take longer than everyone thinks. So discuss this with your DOP and see what suggestions they have. When making my short *Spin*, I worked a much slower day into the schedule with my DOP, so that we had some latitude later on if we fell behind – which we inevitably did. We were so grateful for the extra time. The same applies to anyone else on your particular team (art direction, costume designer, catering, etc). Plan, be open, agree on what can be achieved within the budget and try and anticipate problems beforehand.

Live On Set – the buck bites here

1. CREATIVITY AND MANAGING YOUR TEAM

Apologies for using the 'management' analogy again because hey, we are all making 'art'. But if you have a good plan, and people know what to expect each day, you are setting yourselves up for a dream shoot. Some of the most exciting aspects of making a film can be in the moments when you make a mistake and it looks great, or when you decide to try something new, or even grab totally different shots on a whim. But finding the space and confidence to allow that creativity and spontaneous collaboration to emerge, paradoxically often comes out of giving your team a clear sense of where you are going each day. If everything is chaotic all the time, it can be hard to stay focussed, inspired and open to new possibilities.

Joe Lawlor, on camera action in a single take film

Joe Lawlor with co-director Christine Molloy

Joe Lawlor was co-director with Christine Molloy of *Who Killed Brown Owl?* which was the joint winner at Edinburgh in 2004. The film is also included on Best v Best Vol One (www.bestvbest.com)

People will see a single take, lasting nine and a half minutes, shot with the camera moving at a slow speed. It is very much influenced by Englishness and the sort of representations we see from artists of village scenes. There's no centre, but up in the corner you've got this happening, over there you have got that happening, so the eye kind of rambles through a visual narrative. We wanted the film to represent that kind of village scene, of the village green on a lazy Sunday afternoon, the public park, the village square and so on, but the only thing that connects these different happenings is the social setting, the geography, the sight, if you will. It begins randomly, but what we have got in this case is the Mayor of Enfield cutting a ribbon. I asked him what he could do in the film for us and he said he could cut a ribbon, that's what he does best, so we said brilliant, you can open the film then. It is a civically engaged film and there you have a mayor cutting a ribbon in the first frame of the film, opening it. After that the camera just ambles its way through this scene, sometimes hovering, but not making anything more significant than anything else, making no particular judgements.

Interviewed here by James MacGregor. Read the interview in full:

www.shootingpeople.org/shooterfilms/

2. FOOD WONDERFUL FOOD

Low-budget shoots often mean you have begged your crew to work for a nominal fee, sometimes unpaid. So make sure (*at the very least!*) that you have delegated someone to look after decent food/drink throughout the shoot. Good food makes for a very happy crew and a happy crew is the lifeblood of your film.

3. GIVE GOOD SOUND

I really wanted to make this my first point. SOUND IS SO SO SO IMPORTANT. If shooting DV, NEVER EVER use on the on board mics unless you have the proper XLR inputs and a quality mic. The most horrible lesson in the world is when you go back to review the footage from a day's shoot to find bad audio. Sometimes it sounds hollow and you think, 'I'll just bring up the levels in post.' It won't work! Because when you do bring up the levels, up comes everything else - the ambient level of the room, the reverberant echo, the slight wind outdoors, the hum of the refrigerator, or the air conditioning... There is also an old saying in film. When the sound is GOOD, people come out of a film saying 'Wow... the lighting was great in that film!'. The importance of sound is remarkably underrated because it is often subliminal to the direct experience of a film. And yet it is one of the most important technical aspects to get right on the day.

4. WORKING WITH YOUR ACTORS

Everybody works differently (actors and directors), but I want to quickly emphasise here the importance of getting good performances on set. Much of this will be down to spending the time to find a great cast, but if you want to rehearse the film or key sequences, don't ever assume you can do this on set – there will be no time!

Check out the Get it Ready section of this book for additional casting and rehearsal advice.

QUICK TIP: *Also check out the wonderful book **Directing Actors** by Judith Weston. The author understands that directors, actors, writers, and technicians are all involved in the collaborative process. She explains in practical steps, how you can learn to share a language and a method of exchange that fosters creative cooperation so that together you all have the best shot at creating something true and meaningful. Working through these steps at rehearsals will also increase your confidence.*

Spin, by Cath Le Couteur

Without sounding mawkish, my final tip is to also really try and enjoy the experience of shooting. There is no question that there will be huge amounts of pressure on any shoot. And things will always come up that will throw you. On *Starched*, I remember the hotel we were shooting in suddenly told us we couldn't use the top floor (our planned set) because a new important guest had arrived. On *Spin*, I was using a scalectrix set for shots of the cars with a lipstick camera and WISH I'd shot the close-ups first before the set broke (after we were all playing with it at lunch!). On the *Normski Talking Pictures* series of shorts, I wish I'd tested a glue we were using on a piece of glass beforehand so that I didn't find out on set that it destroyed the glass... which meant we lost precious time sourcing a different variety. At the end of the day, staying flexible and open under pressure can be the most important attributes you've got in your backpocket, and they will help you make the best film of your life.

QUICK TIP: *And finally, remember that all this planning is meant to help you enjoy the shoot!*

119

Sample Shot List
SPIN

Directed by Cath Le Couteur

(view film at www.youtube.com/cathlecouteur)

ACT 1. OPENING

MASTER A.
Tilt up from bottle to Emily -> Fiz takes over

MASTER B.
Travelling with Group to Staircase

MASTER C.
Travelling back to table (Fizz/Ellie -> JAD)

Ai. Brad being a lech
ii. Ellie playing with Bar
iii. Watch Boy
iv. Watch ECU
v. Misc Girl/Boy reactions - touch shirt/skirt
vi. JAD POV longshot

Bi. Jad retrieving cap
ii. Cover action from Behind crowd
iii. Version where Brad/Emily travel out of view
iv. Misc crowd - behind glass

Ci. Ellie/Fizz -> ends on Jad
ii. Kitchen 'Who's that Guy' / 'I'll have a go soon'
iii. Jad longshot - (foreground blocking)
iv. Tighter Jad (misc action)
v. Tight Fiz 'Come on Everyone' -> end on clocking JAD

ACT 2. SOME TIME LATER

MASTER A
Party Misc -> Reveal FIZZ/ELLIE (Arguing re rules)
(crying girl, snogging couple, beer boys, dancing queens)

MASTER B
Party Misc -> Reveal JAD -> Hand on Glass
(Ross/George, funnel alcohol, Jad playing with Bottle)

MASTER C
BRAD comes down staircase - > squares up to JAD

Ai. Barbie Car whizzing around track
Aii. Barbie/Head cutoff – Scaletrix Boys laugh (incl J?)
iii. Fizz/Ellie argue over Brad's cheating

Bi. CU Bottle to Jad(keeping to himself)
ii. CU hand on glass (from inside, we see J from behind)
iii. LS argument taking place, rest of party scene bkgrnd

Ci. Cover Jad watching Brad and Caro
ii. Cover Brad spotting Jad watching
iii. Cover Caro's brush off Brad
iv. Reverse Angle (1+2) square off
v. Cover Elly fiddling with bar, eyes open 'everyone has
to play'
vi. CU JAD (cut pt to table)

Chris & Ben Blaine, interview

Part 4: Production

What are some of the 'secrets' to ensuring a successful shoot?

CHRIS: It really does come down to pre-planning. Even the stuff we've done off-the-cuff. It's sitting in your head - how it's going to happen, all the shots, the cuts - we can usually see the film before we make it.

BEN: Yeah, I think the important thing is to know what you want. When you start getting into all the nuances of lens size, perform-ance style, colour theory, narrative pacing and key changes it can be a little dizzying. But none of these things are actually your job as the director. Understanding them, mastering them, makes your job easier and more enjoyable and enables you to achieve more. But fundamentally the director's job is just to know what they want. If you surround yourself with supremely talented pro-fessionals, then you can actually get by without knowing any-thing except your own mind. No matter how well you understand the process, if you don't know what you want, then everything you do will be a waste of time and everyone will hate you. You can think about it on set. Just not for too long.

For me the other secrets to a successful shoot are good food and good friends. If you can answer every question, including what's for dinner, and not behave like you're god's gift, then it might just turn out all right.

Are there things which you have learned over the course of making your shorts that you wish someone, had told you from the start?

Hallo Panda
Photo by Jessica Thomas

BEN: Well there is all sorts of stuff, but people probably *did* say it and I just didn't really listen, or quite understand the significance. Shooting a film is always such a mammoth task - no matter what size it is - and I don't think anyone can ever really prepare you for it. Some lessons I think you only learn the hard way.

I guess therefore the important thing is not to worry about fuck-ing up. And not necessarily to shoot your best idea first. Shoot something you think is achievable, and then find out how wrong you were. Once you've done that you've got a good grounding to start making a film that's worth watching...

What kind of set design did you have for *Death of the Revolution*?

CHRIS: We redid the classroom it was set in, which was a first for us. We chose it because it was on the ground floor, and so easier to light, rather than for the look. We painted it orange and did new displays on the walls, plus we took out all the green and blue objects - trays, pens, pencils, posters, books, chairs. Actually, we swapped all the chairs with a different room - because we wanted the whole palette of the film to be warm and autumnal - browns, reds, yellows, golden sunshine.

I had seen some Russian Propaganda posters by Gustav Klutsis down at the Tate, and we wanted to rip them off, basically. There's one which has four red flags with the founding fathers of communism on it and we wanted to kind of replicate that. In the dream sequence you can see it looking pretty much the same, except it's been made by kids and we've stuck Che on there rather than Engels, I think. In the 'reality' bits of the film, the flags are flags of the world, keeping it nice and educational - although there are less red flags without blue or green in them than you'd think so we had to go for fairly obscure countries.

> "If you can answer every question, including what's for dinner, and not behave like you're God's gift, then it might just turn out all right."

On a short, does it become even more important to find the right location to keep dressing/production design costs down?

CHRIS: Yes, very much so. Even when you've got a budget, it all costs money and time. That said, if you can find yourself a good art director, then they really add a whole other layer to your film. They're always looking at the empty spaces in the frame, trying to make sure every shot looks interesting, leaving you to concentrate on what's important.

BEN: Good art direction doesn't have to cost anything either; good art directors are like Wombles.

How important is location sound? Can you fix problems later?

CHRIS: Location sound is incredibly important. You can have a bad picture, and it looks arty. Bad sound hurts your ears and makes you switch off. I hate pirate DVDS because I can't hear what the hell's going on. And no you can't fix problems later - badly recorded sound can't be polished so the bad sounds in the background go away. You can either re-record anything that is screwed up, or you can live with it, using yet more background sound to hide the joins in the stuff that's poorly recorded.

> **"It's very good practise to get your sound recordist to record silence after each set-up"**

It's very good practise to get your sound recordist to record silence after each set-up. If you've got background noise it will sound the same only if the mic is in exactly the same position it was for the shot, so if you need to hide the joins between your dialogue, you will need silence that sounds the same as the silence after they've finished speaking. It's no good getting random room tone after the scene is shot - it never matches. Leave the mic where it was. Leave everyone where they were so the sound is exactly the same, except there's no movement or speaking.

Obviously you'll always forget to record this sound but the more you remember, the better-equipped you'll be to put your sound together in post.

BEN: Yeah, good sound recordists are gold dust and they can be quite hard to spot. Good cameramen are easy to see; you watch them do it and it looks great on the monitor, and you know you're sailing home. Good sound recordists are only revealed once you get into the edit, by which time it's too late.

Until you get into the edit, the only way to tell if a sound recordist is good or not is if they demand you do another take - but not too often. If the sound recordist says nothing all morning and then suddenly comes out with, "I'm sorry, there was plane noise all over that. We'll have to go again", and you say, "What plane? I didn't hear a plane", then you've got a good one. Marry them.

Which camera should I choose? A comparison chart

Chris Blaine

It's not fair. A few reasons the professionals have it easy:

1) Shooting on 35mm is easier to light. Film has a larger latitude for light, meaning it'll capture more information where a lesser video camera will see only white or black – thus you have to work harder with bringing the contrast in front of you down, using more lights to 'fill' the shadows or gels and filters to bring the highlights down.

2) Shooting on 35mm looks more beautiful. It has a greater resolution than video both in pixel and colour space, and most importantly it has a shallower depth of field, making things in the background more out of focus and creating big and beautiful circles of confusion (a good illustration: points of light become big circles when they're out of focus).

3) Shooting on 35mm means you'll have a Focus Puller, someone whose only job is to make sure what is *supposed* to be in focus *is* in focus. Indeed, shooting on 35mm means you're more likely to have Gaffers and Sparks to look after the lights; a Camera Operator whose only job is framing; and Grips with big steel dollies which make the camera glide through the air, and with arms which can rise or descend gracefully, smoothly taking you from one position in the scene to another. You're also more likely to have money to invest in the art direction, so you'll have people fussing over every part of the frame to make colours, design, lines, perspective, light, shadows, clothes, make-up, props... hell, *everything*, look as good as it possibly can. I mean, when they hit autumn whilst shooting the Errol Flynn *Robin Hood*, they simply painted the forest green again...

So you're making a short film? You're likely be making it on a DV Camera. Maybe HDV if you're lucky, with a few mates to help out, a wheelchair for a dolly, a dodgy tripod for everything else and a couple of desklamps for lighting. Most of the money spent on the film will go on travel expenses and food. You'll work until God knows when, because there is no, "we'll come back tomorrow", only, "we have to get it done now". But as far as I'm concerned, this is the perfect place to learn your craft. After all, if you can make your film look beautiful using a camcorder, well... film is easy.

Anyway. To the camera guide. Every different format, and in the case of many digital cameras, every different camera, will give a different look and feel to your pictures. There is no 'golden rule' for the look of a film; it depends entirely upon the aesthetic and way of shooting which you choose. *All* of the formats and cameras mentioned here can give amazing results that will look great on the big screen (as long as the projectionist is paying attention *and* you have good sound. This is incredibly important. After all, fucked-up images are all part of the art, right? But fucked up sound…). My brother, Ben and I have shot on many of the formats listed in the camera chart on the following pages, and screened them in cinemas using both digital and film projectors, so hopefully I can be some sort of guide to choosing the right camera for your production.

As the big electrical manufacturers push hard for the coming of digital cinema, with true 16:9 chips and progressive scan to make it look more film-like than interlace scan, it seems ever-easier to forgo the farrago of shooting on film. But please bear in mind that using the latest in digital cameras can cause headaches; once you've shot your film you'll need to edit it, and the more exotic the format (i.e. if it isn't Digibeta) the less likely post houses will have the deck ready to hand. This will mean additional costs when they have to hire them in. And if it doesn't have a firewire output, it's going to cost a lot more for that home editing system than you thought it would. Much of the time, it makes sense to wait for the problems involved in a new format to be ironed out before using it. With so many websites and forums online – www.cinematography. com and .net, www.dv.com, www.creativecow.net, www.adamwilt.com, www.pixelmonger.com, plus www. wikipedia.org for 'the basics' and history – you can learn a lot and solve problems sooner, rather than later.

Another benefit of manufacturers' push for digital is that has also become easier to pick up good deals on *film* camera packages, which could be a good thing if you're going for a more classical style for your short. There are few other bonuses to shooting on film. As the complexity of camera kit increases, so too does the number of crew needed, and the amount of care and attention required (and crew who really know their film cameras tend to be incredibly careful and thorough in their working practices). The costs of film stock mean that you don't just keep the camera rolling; you have to think a lot more carefully before shouting "action!". These things, in turn, mean a more considered end-product. On a technical note, film kits are also far more likely to have a set of prime lenses with them; with digital, you'll often get zoom lenses which won't be of quite as good quality. On the downside of shooting on film, if you're looking to shoot on the run, then there's nothing more freeing than a small camera and a tiny crew, which allow you to change your mind easily. And if you want to know exactly what you're getting, shot by shot as you shoot, the video assist of film also can't compare with the perfect reproduction on a high-resolution colour monitor that video can provide.

To help you get a better sense of the images these cameras produce, I've included many stills in the camera guide from the actual film and video images shot by Ben and me. They are all in proportionate size to one another in terms of picture resolution you'll get from the format – and I've tried hard to get the image sensor pictures exactly the same size as they are in real life. The guide will be biased towards our own preferences; I'm sure there are thousands who'll disagree with me about the various qualitative judgements I make. I'm also afraid I haven't been able to put in EVERY camera out there (it seems like there's a new one out every week and I'm sure it will continue in this vein for some time).

This leads me finally to money. It's entirely possible to get an amazing deal on, or borrow, all of the cameras listed on the following pages, but this usually requires that a) you're a big client who spends a lot of money with the camera hire firm on other projects, like commercials and dramas, or b) you work for the company, or c) your DoP is a big client or an employee of the hire company…

Thanks to The Cruet Company (www.cruet.com) for assistance in compiling images for this chart.

View the Super8mm film stills on the colour pages

Super8mm

Mainly 2nd-Hand
Pro8mm Classic Pro

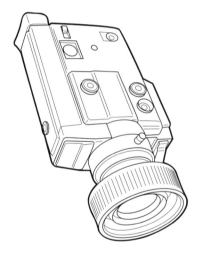

TECH SPECS

1.36:1 Aspect Ratio.

8mm wide, actual space used is smaller than that because of the sprocket holes. It's Super 8 because they made the sprocket holes smaller to give more area over to the image than was managed for standard 8.

With the film size being effectively the same sort of size as MiniDV camera chips, the picture quality could be thought of as similar to those cameras. It probably won't look quite as sharp though due to the digital cameras 'enhancing' their picture's sharpness.

Traditionally super8mm runs at 18fps but the more advanced cameras have options to change the frame rate – bear in mind that using a faster frame rate will use the cartridge up faster.

PROS

➤ Film Grain. Lots and lots of lovely film grain

➤ On some cameras (including the Pro8mm which you can hire or purchase new) you can use C-Mount film lenses, meaning more possibilities with different lens lengths and also the possibility of improving the quality of the picture with better quality lenses

➤ On some cameras you can do slow-motion

➤ Easy to load super8mm cartridges which you can post off to get processed

➤ Usually small, fairly easy to operate, fun cameras

CONS

➤ Resolution isn't always the best, depending upon lenses and how much you have to crop into the image to get your correct aspect ratio

➤ To get best resolution you need higher cost camera with inter-changeable lenses

➤ Running time on cartridge not much more than three minutes

➤ Not many places to get profes-sional processing or transfer to tape. If you need that then www.widescreen-centre.co.uk or www.todd-ao.co.uk are good places to go

➤ Old cameras can be loud causing problems for sound

CHRIS' BIAS

We've shot on super8 for a couple of short films and nearly for a couple of music videos and it's a great format to play with. You can pick up second-hand cameras really cheaply (ebay always has a few) so if you want to trash them it's a good option (as long as you keep the film cartridge safe!). The glory of the grain is lovely. There's a fantastic competition www.straight8. net which I still want to enter despite having made a vow to never make another short film again.

COSTS

You can buy second hand cameras from £10–£50 and they go into the thousands.

Stock starts at about £11 for a cartridge (running for approx 3mins).

Processing starts at about £15 per cartridge, telecine to miniDV about the same. If you need it quicker it'll cost more.

View the MiniDV film stills on the colour pages

MiniDV

Canon XL1, XL1s, XL2
Panasonic DVX100

TECH SPECS

4:3 or 16:9 (1.33:1 or 1.77:1) Aspect Ratios.

3x 1/3" CCDs** (measured diagonally).

720x576 pixels.

8-BIT

5:1 Compression.

4:2:0 Colour Space

25Mbps Data Rate

The real harbinger of change, the MiniDV camcorder has made thousands of short movies since it's inception towards the end of the last century. Coupled with affordable editing systems, MiniDV revolutionised film-making, putting it into the hands of those with modest resources as well as the extremely rich or lucky.

** CCD is the 'charge-coupled device' - the image sensor, a little rectangle made up of tiny light-sensitive electronics, as opposed to the light-sensitive chemicals of film.

PROS

➤ Availability and ease of use. It's easy to get cameras and tapes (which are dead cheap), every home editing system supports the format using firewire, most cameras are easy to pick up and shoot with, and they are compact and therefore easy to transport

➤ Possibility of using better-quality lenses on Canon XL range

➤ Smaller cameras are camcorders and are treated as such by the public, who can be less of a pain than with larger cameras, also subjects can feel a lot more at ease with a smaller camera pointing at them, and the usual LCD screen makes it easier to look at your subject whilst continuing to shoot

➤ Canon XL2 and Panasonic HVX100 can both shoot progressive. XL2 is 16:9 native too

CONS

➤ Except when using optional manual lenses for Canon cameras, can be a bit of a bugger finding focus (servo rings not helped by usually fairly poor viewfinders and LCD screens)

➤ Always look soft under bright red lighting (a lack of green and blue really affects the sharpness).

➤ Can add nasty detail (increased contrast on the edges of objects in focus designed to add sharpness), which is very noticeable on a big screen, putting halos round the subject. This option can usually be turned down in user menus

➤ Poor compression and colour space means it's not great for doing greenscreen. That said, we've found it is possible to do passable stuff

➤ Most of the cameras are 4:3 native

➤ Worries over how long before tapes begin to degrade (not a good archiving format!)

➤ Looks good on the big screen with close-ups, but you notice the lack of resolution on wide shots

CHRIS' BIAS

Ever since we bought a Canon XL1 years and years ago I've loved the Canon XL range and we've made loads of films and videos using all the different models. The CCDs they use give you a really wonderful image and the XL2 has a great progressive scan mode, which for me gives the best picture you can get on a MiniDV camera, without even thinking of using something other than the standard lens. Bugbears are that getting focus is sometimes tricky. There's no pull-out LCD screen and it's bigger than the others and therefore more of a pain to lug around.

COSTS

You can buy these cameras second hand for between £500-£2500.

Rental of a full camera kit is approx £50-70 a day.

Stock can be bought for as little as £2 for a 63minute tape.

You can usually use the camera as a deck.

View the DVCAM film stills on the colour pages

DVCAM

Sony PD150, PD170
Sony DSR-450, 500
Ikegami HL-DV7

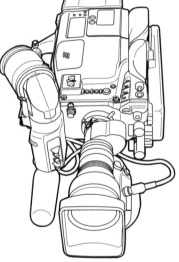

TECH SPECS

4:3 or 16:9 (1.33:1 or 1.77:1) Aspect Ratios.

1/3" CCDs for the smaller cameras, 2/3" chips for the larger ones…

720x576 pixels.

8-BIT

5:1 Compression.

4:2:0 Colour Space

25Mbps Data Rate

For the professional version of MiniDV, the tape runs a third faster and therefore more information is written to tape, meaning it's that bit more stable than MiniDV. It doesn't improve the picture or the sound quality on it's own though, it simply means a lot less likelihood of dropout or timecode problems.

PROS

➤ Much the same format as MiniDV, will work easily with all home-editing systems using firewire

➤ Can use MiniDV tapes if you get stuck without DVCAM stock

➤ With the 450, 500, HL-DV7 you're in the world of using proper manual lenses and decent viewfinders and the effect is startling. Suddenly it's easy to get things in focus!

➤ Progressive frame rate with the 450, means it captures only 25 solid frames per second rather than "interlaced" (50 half-frames per second which are interwoven to make up a full picture)

CONS

➤ Pretty much the same downsides as MiniDV

➤ It's a lot more cumbersome to be working with the larger cameras. They're heavy, meant for the shoulder rather than in front of you. Tri-pods, steadicams, everything has to be larger. Batteries are bigger, tapes are bigger, and it all means more thought needs to go into the logistics of everything you do – (usually a good thing, actually). One-man-banding this is a pain in the arse, you need helping hands

➤ Looks good on the big screen with close-ups, but you can notice the lack of resolution on wide shots

CHRIS' BIAS

The Sony DSR-450 is a good camera in that it can do progressive frame rates. The Ikegami feels a little tougher than the rest but the 450 will give the best pictures, with the added benefit of a small flip-out LCD screen, which is always useful for quickly checking colours when you're working at speed. The PD150 and 170 were the workponies of the TV industry for years, always there for a keen researcher to shoot that slightly dodgy second-camera stuff or the video diaries you see on reality tv.

COSTS

You can buy the smaller cameras second hand for between £1000-£2500.

Rental of a full camera kit is approx £200-250 a day for the larger cameras, £50-£100 for the smaller ones.

DVCAM stock starts at about £12 for a large 64min tape or £8 for a small 40min.

You can usually use the camera as a deck.

HDV 1080i (interlace)

Sony HVR-Z1, HVR-A1, HVR-V1

Canon XL H1

TECH SPECS

16:9 (1.77:1) Aspect Ratio.

1/3" CCDs.

1440x1080 pixels

8-BIT

40:1 Inter-Frame Compression.

4:2:0 Colour Space

25Mbps Data Rate

The new pro-consumer choice launched not so long ago, the Sony Z1 has quickly become the new TV industry favourite for handing to the researcher for some top quality second camera work. The format manages to squeeze so many more pixels in by trying out a new way of compressing, much like that used with DVDs. Unlike most of the other digital formats mentioned here, in addition to comparing like-for-like within the frame and being able to discard information by saying "same here", HDV also does this between different frames.

The Sony V1 uses CMOS chips rather than CCDs, normally found in digital stills cameras. This may be a sign of the future.

PROS

▶ You can pretend you're shooting High Definition!

▶ In reality you're looking at a sort of "half HD" – these cameras can't compare to the larger professional cameras, but then when you think of the difference in price they get really rather closer than you'd expect

▶ All the benefits of having a small camera

▶ Uses cheap as chips miniDV tapes, although you can buy higher grade ones if you'd rather

▶ Most home editing systems can now handle the format

▶ 16:9 native

▶ Supposedly a more stable format than DV as there is a larger danger if you get dropout because of the inter-frame compression, so it's been designed with more safety measures in place. That said if you do get dropout it will affect a much larger amount of frames than on other formats

▶ XLH1 has HD-SDI output so you can bypass the HDV compression for greater quality (means you need a deck or a capture system onset though)

▶ HVR-V1 can do 1080p resolution! This should mean it can compete with the 720p cameras at the same level

CONS

▶ Have a look at that compression rate! There's been a serious amount of jiggery-pokery to get such a bigger picture out of exactly the same tapes and data rate as MiniDV

▶ Interlace cameras with pseudo-progressive modes which lose resolution

▶ Same problems with colour as the DV formats, making greenscreen harder

▶ The LCD viewfinders and pull-out screens still make it hard to get focus, although the XLH1 has a fairly decent viewfinder

▶ Audio is compressed, down to 384kbps

▶ In the early days people were having trouble editing the format because of the inter-frame compression and indeed some broadcasters are wary of the format for that same reason. That said, we've used it since and it's working ok

▶ Can look good on the big screen but feels a little soft compared to HD, S16 or 35mm

CHRIS' BIAS

I work a lot with a director called Adam Brown who is always keen as mustard to use the latest formats. This means I get to watch him find all the pitfalls of the format before I have to touch it. We've shot stuff with the Z1 and XLH1 and personally I'm taking the curmudgeon's route to being persuaded. The Z1 to me is large and plasticky, hard to handhold for any length of time and it's unbalanced, heavier at the front so it naturally wants to drop away from you – you had better want to focus manually... Once the problems have all been ironed out I expect I'll be looking at the XLH1 because of the ability to use better lenses and the joy of using Canon CCDs. Also the V1 is especially intriguing because of it's unique progressive frame abilities (it's doing things HDV isn't supposed to do – the standards were set at 1080i or 720p but Sony have done something clever). All that said, right now I'm most intrigued about the Panasonic HVX200.

COSTS

New, these cameras cost upwards of £3000.

Rental of a full camera kit is approx £80–150 a day.

HDV stock starts at about £7 for a 63min tape.

You can usually use the camera as a deck.

HDV 720p (progressive)

JVC GY-HD100U

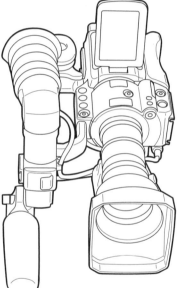

TECH SPECS	PROS	CONS	CHRIS' BIAS	COSTS
16:9 (1.77:1) Aspect Ratio.	▶ Chance to use different lenses and a proper manual focus	▶ Same thing with compression (video and audio) and green screen as the other HDV cameras	I haven't had a chance to use this camera but it's one where JVC have really upped the ante with a progressive rival to the XLH1 and it sounds like it's the real deal. However, I've always had quite a few niggles with miniDV JVC equipment which makes me a little nervous. Guess I need to try it out.	New, upwards of £3000.
1/3" CCDs.	▶ 16:9 native. Progressive pictures	▶ Not as much pixel acreage as the interlace cameras		Rental of a full camera kit is approx £120-200 a day.
1280x720 pixels	▶ Doing well in tests, compares well to the other pro-consumer HD cameras on the market	▶ Can look good on the big screen but feels a little soft compared to HD, S16 or 35mm		HDV stock is approx £7 for a 63min tape.
8-BIT				
40:1 Inter-Frame Compression.				
4:2:0 Colour Space				
19.5Mbps Data Rate				

TECH SPECS

16:9 (1.77:1) Aspect Ratio.

1/3" CCDs

960x720 pixels

8-BIT

7:1 Compression

4:2:2 Colour Space

100Mbps

This could be the first of a new step in the digital revolution. There's still a tape deck but much more importantly, there's the chance of putting it to P2 solid-state memory cards, or hard drive, for the best quality pictures, meaning it's recording at exactly the same quality as the fully-grown Varicam. Obviously it's not as good; it uses smaller chips and lesser-quality lenses. But it's not far off.

PROS

➤ You can do Slow Motion and using P2 you can watch it back straight away! On the Varicam you need a whole extra box to do that

➤ 16:9 native, progressive

➤ Using P2 cards or a hard drive you can get full-quality DVCPRO HD pictures (which is now becoming supported by home editing systems), whilst still backing up to a lesser format on tape

➤ Still a small camera so has all of those benefits

➤ Better colour space means it should be better for greenscreen than HDV or miniDV

➤ Final Cut Pro up-resses it to 1280x720 pixels

➤ No audio compression like in HDV,nor inter-frame compression so less worry with post

CONS

➤ Only records miniDV to tape and the P2 cards are very expensive. That said, given time they may get cheaper and there are small portable hard drives you can connect via firewire to record in top quality DVCPRO HD

➤ Using P2 in post may still be a little painful, given time it'll all be ironed out

➤ Compression is still pretty high and can cause problems in grading when you try and push the image

➤ Not as much pixel acreage as the interlace cameras

➤ Can look good on the big screen but feels a little soft compared to HD, S16 or 35mm

CHRIS' BIAS

I haven't had a chance to use this yet. I was going to use it for a music video but the hire company warned me that there were no edit systems capable of using the P2 format so we spent more money and used the full-size Varicam, which was a bit of a pain in the arse (the video was all about rolling around in bed which is much easier with a small camera). Anyway, it's now changing and I'm keen to get my hands on one and try it out.

COSTS

New, these cameras cost upwards of £4000.

Rental of a full camera kit is approx £120-200 a day.

P2 cards are reusable but rather expensive - £800 for 8GB (8mins of DVC-ProHD). Hard Drives start at £1600 for 100GB.

You can use the camera as a deck but bear in mind you may have to spend time on the shoot capturing so you can shoot some more.

Digibeta

Sony DVW970, DVW790, DVW700

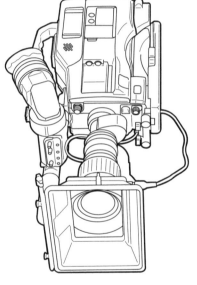

View the Digibeta film stills on the colour pages

TECH SPECS

4:3 or 16:9 (1.33:1 or 1.77:1) Aspect Ratios.

2/3" CCDs

720x576 pixels

10-BIT

3:1 Compression

4:2:2 Colour Space

90Mbps

The true TV industry workhorse, Digibeta is still the choice of most producers making TV and is pretty much always the tape format you'll be required to deliver for tv and a lot of digital cinema screenings. The 970 is a progressive frame update to the 790, now discontinued because it doesn't meet new European regulations.

PROS

▶ Ok we're now into the proper world of the professionals and all these cameras have mounted lenses so you can use anything in front of the camera – using HD lenses WILL give you better quality pictures

▶ Better compression rates and colour space means this is a better choice for greenscreen.

▶ A solid format, very little worries about dropout

CONS

▶ Bigger, heavier, more expensive, you want people who have used this stuff before to be operating and carrying it around

▶ All said and told, it's still only standard definition. Pictures are the best you can get in SD, but on a big screen they will look softer than HD, S16mm or 35mm

▶ Higher bit rate and no firewire connection means you're looking at editing in a post house and then you're getting into a world of offline/online which takes a little while to get used to if you've always edited at full resolution at home. Alternatively you can get the tapes dubbed down or get someone to put all your rushes onto hard drive

CHRIS' BIAS

We've used the 790 for short films and TV and the 970 for a couple of corporate videos. Both work well and the 970 looks great with its progressive images. In many ways Digi is a great choice because of the ubiquity of the format; you can pretty much guarantee that there will be a dozen cameras per hire house and that post houses will all have Digi decks. This could save you money; people can give you stuff for free if they own it, but not if they have to hire it in themselves.

COSTS

Rental of a full camera kit is approx £250-350 a day.

Digibeta stock is approx £14 for a 40min tape.

Most post houses will have Digi decks but there'll be a cost if you're trying to get it onto hard drive for editing at home.

DVCProHD

Panasonic AJHDC27 (Varicam)

View the DVCProHD film stills, on the colour pages

TECH SPECS

16:9 (1.77:1) Aspect Ratio.

2/3" CCDs

960x720 pixels

8-BIT

7:1 Compression

4:2:2 Colour Space

100Mbps

The Varicam works in mysterious ways. It ALWAYS records 60 frames a second to tape (or 59.94 frames if you're using American formats) no matter what frame rate you record at. It simply doubles or triples up frames and 'flags' them so that your edit system will recognise this and take them out, leaving only the frames that should be there.

PROS

➤ Slow Motion! This can't be over-emphasised. Video has always fallen down compared to film due to the lack of this function and it really adds something special to your footage to be able to mess around with frame rates

➤ You can edit at home! Using Final Cut Pro and a firewire cable you can edit everything at home in full resolution (although you really do need a recent-decent spec Mac to contemplate it. It does - just - work on G4s and indeed my little G4 iMac but it takes a LONG time)

➤ Progressive frame rate

➤ Ok for greenscreen but higher compression and lower bit rate mean it's not necessarily better than Digibeta

➤ Good looking pictures. If it's for TV, in some ways it's comparative lack of resolution means that it can look more 'film-like' than the sharper HDCAM

CONS

➤ Ah the pain of variable frame rate. Unlike film, which simply speeds up the amount of film going through the gate to get slow-motion (why it's called 'high speed'), videotape always runs at the same pace. The Varicam jumps through hoops which the P2 (no tape) HVX200 doesn't have to. It's a shame there is no P2/hard drive option with the camera. This can cause problems in the edit and it's probably wisest to use Panasonic's frame rate converter as well as their deck to capture your footage at the correct rate – there is a frame rate converter within Final Cut Pro, but it's sometimes erratic. Likewise we've had problems where sometimes FCP has decided footage has been shot at a different frame rate to the one we've shot it at, a confusion we haven't worked out a solution to yet

➤ The camera doesn't have a firewire port so you have to hire a deck for post. This is obviously how it's supposed to be - the camera is for capturing stuff not playback - but it's still that bit harder

➤ Looks good on the big screen but feels a little soft compared to HD, S16 or 35mm

CHRIS' BIAS

I really like the Varicam despite its foibles and once you've learnt enough about it, it's fantastic to be able to edit at full quality on a home editing system, opening up a world of high def, slow-motion and fx work which makes your end product that much better. We have shot music videos and our last short film, Hallo Panda, on this format, and will continue to use it for music videos.

COSTS

Rental of a full camera kit is approx £450-550 a day.

DVCProHD stock is approx £16 for a '126' tape which'll last for a quarter of that time due to the faster speed of the Varicam tape mechanism.

You will most likely have to hire a deck to capture footage, and the Panasonic Variable Frame Rate Converter will help if you've shot at different frame rates too – these are approx £150-250 and £150-300 a day respectively.

16mm / Super 16mm

Arri SRI, SRII, SRIII
Aaton Xtera, Minima

View the Super 16mm film stills on the colour pages

TECH SPECS

1.34:1 or 1.67:1 Aspect Ratios (16 or S16).

The Film is 16mm wide. Standard 16 has space on one side of the film for sound. This is mainly useful in projection rather than capture though, which is where Super 16 comes in, using that space for picture instead to get more resolution, with the knowledge that it will be used only for telecine to video or blow-up to 35mm. We once made a short film and got a super 16 print made, meaning we had to have sound running on magnetic tape – at the screening it was, of course, out of sync!

To get widescreen aspect ratios you have to crop the image or use anamorphic lenses.

PROS

> Film grain. It looks good

> Better latitude for lighting than video, can be pushed further in post

> Much better handling of highlights than video, there'll be a lot more information there which makes it easier to grade

> Slow Motion

> Cost of stock forces you to be a little bit more considered

> Super 16mm could be thought of as about the same as HDCAM. I know that the digital folk will be claiming HDCAM is as good as 35 but in my humble opinion, I'd put these alongside each other, with 16mm and DVC-ProHD looking similar onscreen

> A wide choice of high quality lenses

> TRUE Prime lenses (those for video are fixed-focal length with a lot more glass in them than Film Primes, meaning a better quality image with Film Primes)

> Aaton make small cameras

CONS

> All the paraphernalia that comes with film will make things slower

> Changing film is tricky and scary and requires someone who really knows what they are doing

> No full-quality monitors, only flickery stuff, means focus pull-ers want to take more time to get it right (which is also a plus point, means your film will look as good as it can do)

> Quite a bit of kit usually means quite a bit of crew

> That said, it's entirely possible for things to be simpler, just make sure you have someone who really knows what they're doing when it comes to loading the camera, sorting out focus and metering light to get the correct f-stop

CHRIS' BIAS

We've shot on both 16mm and Super 16mm in a variety of different short films. We have always loved the experience but been really rather scared at the cost. However with HD being pushed heavily, there'll be plenty of deals for 16mm cameras and with that you'll get all the benefits of shooting on film, of which there are many.

COSTS

Rental of a full camera kit is approx £150-300 a day.

16mm stock is approx £50–90 for a 400ft can (runs for approx 11mins). Kodak do good dis-counts for short films.

Processing is usually approx 8-15p per foot (£32-60 per can) and not something you can get for free.

Telecine depends a lot upon what process you choose to use – 2K, to tape, with an operator, one light (usually done at the time of processing and costing approx the same again), and at one extreme it's possible to get thrown in with the cost of the grade (which we managed on *Death of the Revolution*) or could be as much as £400 per hour.

View the HDCAM film stills on the colour pages

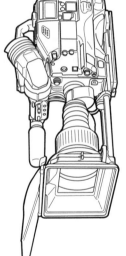

HDCAM

Sony HDW-F900, HDW-750

HDCAM SR

Sony HDW-F950

	TECH SPECS	PROS	CONS	CHRIS' BIAS	COSTS
HDCAM	16:9 (1.77:1) Aspect Ratio. 2/3" CCDs 1440x1080 pixels 8-BIT 5.5:1 Compression 3:1:1 Colour Space 140Mbps	▶ Looks good. As has been said a thousand times, old Greybeard Lucas shot Star Wars with the F900 (which was modified at the front end and may well have been modified at the back end as well, but what the hell. Star Wars!). It looks great on the big screen, much like Super 16 but with less grain ▶ Progressive frame rate ▶ Funnily enough the fact that HD hasn't quite taken off in the way it was thought it would has meant you can still get deals on these cameras – camera houses are still keen to have stuff to show off	▶ Not quite as wide-spread as it will be in a few years, meaning there's usually an added expense in post with the need to hire in decks for capture and putting it back to tape ▶ No slow motion ▶ Compression and poor colour space means, again, that green screen is trickier	We've used the 750 for a short film and a few music videos and it's always given great results and we were only persuaded away from it for Hallo Panda by the ability to use slow-motion on the Varicam. I'm sure we'll be using HDCAM again in the future.	Rental of a full camera kit is approx £450-550 a day. HDCAM stock is approx £25 for a 40min tape – which may last longer or shorter depending what format you shoot in. You will most likely have to hire a deck to capture footage and put it back to tape, these are approx £250-400 a day.
HDCAM SR	16:9 (1.77:1) Aspect Ratio. 2/3" CCDs 1920x1080 pixels 10-BIT 4.2:1 Compression 4:4:4 Colour Space 440Mbps To get 1.85 aspect ratio, image is usually cropped.	▶ All the benefits of using a professional video camera and at the best quality you can get without moving onto 4K			

Camera Stills

The 'Gate' images are all at actual size throughout these pages, and the 'Stills' are all at the correct pixel size for their resolution.

Super8mm

Actual size

Still taken from our short film *If Looks Could Kill*, shot on a £30 auto-everything second-hand camera by our mate Adam Waine. You can shoot on negative stock but the most common is reversal so you can project it without having to do any answer print.

Mini DV

Actual size

Still taken from our short film *Burnt Bernard*, shot on a Canon XL1 in 4:3 'Movie' mode by me. If you follow the light inside a video camera lens you'll come to a prism which separates the light into red, green and blue like you've got your very own miniature Isaac Newton hiding inside the plastic. These separate beams of light head off to their corresponding CCDs. One thing you'll notice because of this arrangement is that you can get strange red, or green blurring on high contrast edges – instead of a clean line between white and black you'll see red or green bleeding over. But before we decry video's RGB setup too much, this technology has all come from film. Technicolor used a prism to split the light and red/green/blue filters to record only one colour onto black and white film, and this was eventually surpassed by Kodak Eastman who managed to put separate layers of emulsion sensitive to red, green and blue onto one film strip. Anyway…

DVCam

Actual size

Still taken from our music video for *It's Easy* by Ian Wills & The Willing, shot on a Sony DSR-450 in 25p mode by Jonny Tyson.

HDV

Actual size

Still taken from Adam Brown's music video for *Slam* by Pendulum, shot on a Sony HVR-Z1 by Max Rijavec.

P2

Actual size

Still taken from our music video for *Stop and Remember* by The Immediate, shot by me on, well, this is a little bit of a cheat 'cos there weren't any editing systems which could cope with P2 footage at the time, so we shot on it's bigger brother the Varicam. The CCD sizes are correct for the HVX200 however and you can expect the same resolution and data rate from the two cameras – the main difference is obviously the Varicam's larger image sensors and superior lenses.

DigiBeta

Actual size

Still taken from our short film *Old Man Dies*, shot on a Sony DVW-790 by Oliver Russell. This has been down-graded to DVCAM so we could edit it, so there has been a generation loss and extra compression on the still.

DVCProHD

Actual size

Still taken from our short film *Hallo Panda*, shot on a Panasonic Varicam by Oliver Russell.

Super 16mm

Actual size

Still taken from our short film *Death Of The Revolution*, shot on an Arri SRIII by Oliver Russell. Super 16 (and 35 for that matter) is normally shot on negative stock as it offers better resolution than reversal. DOTR was taken in at 2K resolution and a print struck from the digital grade. This still is from a standard def downgrade so there's obviously a loss of resolution. I've kept the still at the correct size for Super 16mm in relation to the others.

HDCAM

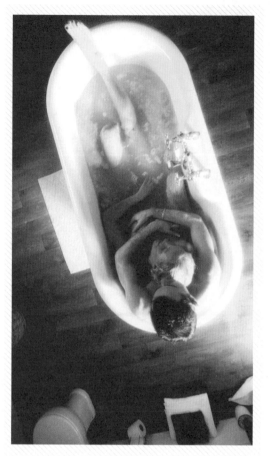

Actual size

Still taken from our short film *Free Speech*, shot on a Sony HDW-750 by Oliver Russell. Again this is a down-graded standard def version of the film but I've kept the still at the correct size in relation to the others.

Still taken from a promotional still for *Hallo Panda*, shot on a 35mm *stills* camera by Jessica Thomas. Ok, so this is the one still pretending to be a film still – but we haven't shot on 35, as much as I'd like to! I read somewhere that Stanley Kubrick insisted on using actual stills blown up from the film print for promotional purposes rather than using those from a promotional stills photographer – his reckoning being that if the photographer's stills were better, then that's where the film camera should be too. Which is something we've found in the past too, with Jess sometimes influencing our DoP Oli's decisions with what she is finding on the set. Anyway, the gap between the left hand sprockets and the film image is for sound (hell, when it comes to the projected prints, they use *between* the sprockets as well and outside them on all different Dolby DTS mixes you get these days). One last thing to point out here is that 35mm records an image kind of similar to 4:3 – this is incredibly handy if you're using a 1.85 aspect ratio as you can track the shot up or down to show exactly what you'd like in the frame. This is a trick we've used on video before by making the aspect ratio wider than 16:9, and putting black bars on top and bottom. This is also why you sometimes see the boom in shot in the cinema; the answer prints should have been matted so you only have the correct image and black top and bottom. If it isn't, and if the projectionist gets the tracking wrong, they can reveal parts of the image which aren't supposed to be seen....

Actual size

35mm

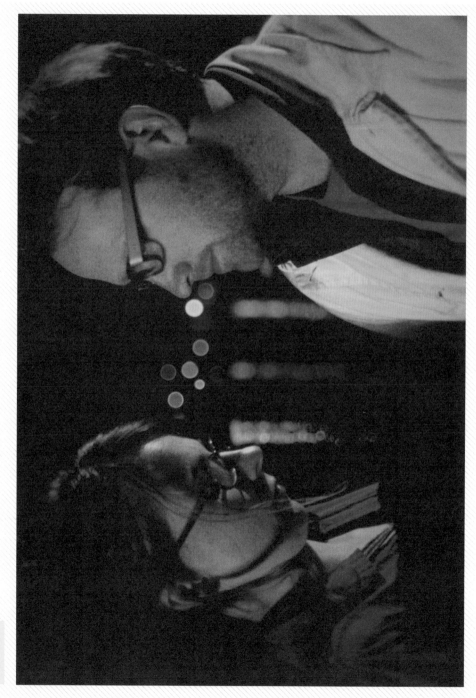

35mm

35mm

Panavision Millenium XL, XL2, Panaflex, etc.

Arricam, Arriflex 435 etc.

Aaton 35 III

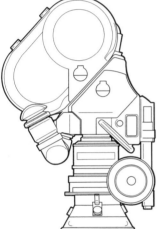

TECH SPECS

1.33 Aspect Ratio (4:3)

The film is 35mm wide with sprocket holes on both sides. The image is between those but with a space for optical stereo sound down one side. Usually for 1.85 aspect ratio, the image is cropped and Super 35mm uses the space for sound to record a 2.35:1 ratio image.

Anamorphic Lenses can be used (Panavision, Cinemascope, 'Scope') to achieve a 2.35 aspect ratio. This squashes the image in much the same way you see 16:9 being squashed into a 4:3 aspect ratio; it uses more of the height of the film and makes for a better resolution. You notice when things are shot in scope by the funny way things move when there's a focus pull.

PROS

➤ Better latitude for lighting than video, and can be pushed further in post

➤ Much better handling of highlights than video, there'll be a lot more information there which makes it easier to grade

➤ Slow Motion

➤ Cost of everything forces you to be very considered

➤ Best choice of high quality lenses

➤ TRUE Prime lenses (those for video are fixed-focal length with a lot more glass in them than Film Primes, meaning a better quality image with Film Primes)

➤ Unlike digital, there's no compression at capture so you've got the best quality original to mess about with in post

CONS

➤ Not as good in capturing information in the blacks, a reason for Michael Mann to be so keen on shooting his latest stuff on digital

➤ COST! This is prohibitively expensive, the main reason we've never used this format

CHRIS' BIAS

One day. One day we'll get the chance to use 35mm, which will be lovely.

COSTS

Rental of a full camera kit is approx £1000-1500 a day – but that is a full-on kit of everything including primes, zooms, dolly and track, not included with the previous cameras.

35mm stock is approx £90-150 for a 400ft can (runs for approx 4 and a bit minutes). Kodak do good discounts for short films.

Processing is usually approx 15-30p per foot (£60-120 per can) and not something you can get for free.

Telecine depends a lot upon what process you choose to use – 2K, 4K, to tape, with an operator, one light (usually done at the time of processing and costing approx the same again).

High-End Digital

Dalsa, Genesis, Viper, Red, Kinetta etc

TECH SPECS	PROS	CONS	CHRIS' BIAS	COSTS
These cameras are at the top of the scale or are merely hopes and dreams right now. Either way, you're looking to have to spend as much as you do with 35mm.	‣ Support of the manufacturers. Because they're so new, you'll get a lot of help in making it all work out, so everyone can boast about being at the forefront of new technology	‣ Problems. Because they're so new you'll encounter problems. ‣ COST! These are expensive machines, which cost a whole lot of money! ‣ They're IMAGINARY! Right now the Red and Kinettas are not workable cameras that you can use. Maybe by the time this goes to print, it will have all changed	The Kinetta floated my boat when I first read about it. I'd love to use the Viper. The Red sounds exciting. And it's all very much over there at the moment.	Camera kits are as dear, if not dearer, than 35mm. The Red is supposed to be coming in at an amazing price, so wait and see if we have another revolution in digital pictures coming round the corner.

Thoughts on Editing

Lisa Gunning, Editor, *Breaking and Entering*

Photo by Emma Innocenti

For me, editing is a beautiful and mysterious process. It has infuriated, delighted, maddened and rewarded me in equal measure over the years. I've had the opportunity to work on commercials and pop videos, short films, art installations, documentaries and, most recently, a feature film called *Breaking and Entering* (Dir. Anthony Minghella). I've learned something different every project and it seems that my learning curve never seems to level out. Working on commercials has challenged me to find ways to communicate ideas quickly, while promos are usually more about movement and music. More narrative pieces like short or feature films require a more structural approach to create an emotional response over time. The most mind-blowing and practical lessons I've learned have been on these longer form projects, so these are what I'll concentrate on when trying to give some tips to you as as a short filmmaker. The editing process a critical part of making your short film, so this collection of thoughts, both practical and theoretical, will hopefully shed some light on how you can make the most of your material. Bear in mind that I still have a lot to learn and these thoughts are by no means gospel, they've just helped me along the way!

It's essential to put on your editing hat before the shoot. Look at the script and try to think of things that you'll really need in the cutting room. For instance - and this may sound obvious - it's always good to have cutaways and establishing shots. These will give you options when constructing your scenes. More importantly, try to guide the focus of the shoot around the main moments in the story. It would seem that from an editing point of view, in the glorious realm of hindsight, the best advice to give directors when shooting a short film would be to think about the true moments in the film. What are the turning points? The seminal moments? The moments which tell the story in the most pure way? Identify them and work down the list of priority from them. When you end up in the cutting room, those will undoubtedly be the bits you play with the most!

Cutting the first frame of film is terrifying. It feels like being on the edge of a precipice. A number of takes multiplied by a number of setups can amount to several hours of material for any one scene. This means millions of possible ways to cut it, and is usually the moment to make a cup of tea, have a chat... or do ANYTHING other than start. It's a rude awakening to have the material for a well covered, dialogue heavy scene in front of you. However, there is one thing worse than having too much footage. That's not having enough of it.

> "There's nothing worse than wasting your time and energy looking for things. Sometimes a wallchart can help"

Every editor will have a different way of navigating and putting the material together. First and foremost, spend time organising your project so you can find things easily. While this is absolutely critical to cutting a feature, it's certainly important for short films too. There's nothing worse than wasting your time and energy looking for things. Sometimes a wallchart can help. If you can see the film in one piece somewhere, it helps you feel more in control of what you're doing. I hang strips of card on the wall to represent each scene and then update it when I move them around in the computer. It helps me think of the film as a whole. When I worked on a film version of Samuel Beckett's *Play* (Dir. Anthony Minghella) I found it really helpful to make a graph to help me plan the edit. *Play* is about a love triangle, the characters being stuck in the purgatory of self-analysis for 17 agonising minutes. Anthony covered the whole play on each character in close-up and extreme close-up, as well as doing a series of whip pans and pull focus shots between the characters. I remember feeling quite overwhelmed by the abstract nature of the piece and by how many ways I could cut it. So I read it over and over again trying to 'feel' which parts of the writing would suit the different shots. I made a kind of flow chart to group a certain style of shot to each act. This planning really helped me get my head around the whole thing.

When putting the material together, a methodical approach seems to help, although, being dyslexic this proves extremely hard for me. I seem approach the rushes a number of different ways each time and although I've tried very hard to find one, there is no secret way of doing it best. In fact the only secret is hard work. Fortunately, there are happy accidents; unfortunately there is no shortcut to knowing your material inside out.

> "It's very easy to get obsessed with the minutiae of a scene before you've put the whole thing together; that's like trying to put up wallpaper before you've built the house!"

I usually work out the main moments, the turning points in the scene and look at how they play out in the material. I choose my favourite take from each angle, plus some other pieces I liked here and there, then I go about constructing the scene in the simplest possible way. I try to make rough sketches first and add to them by reinvestigating the other takes. It's a bit like a painting, you start with the pencil so you can find your way and then add the paint. The main challenge is not to get caught up in detail. It's very easy to get obsessed with the minutiae of a scene before you've put the whole thing together. That's like trying to put up wallpaper before you've built the house! I always try to get to the end, sketch the whole thing out and then you know what you have. Now you can attend to the problems with some perspective. Trial and error, trying to be true to performance, narrative, and emotion (as much as one can at the assembly stage), is the infuriating but rewarding process of assembling a scene.

During the assembly stage you're cutting 'outside the film' (i.e. the film doesn't know itself yet). The individual scenes evolve as the film evolves. Essentially the goalposts for each scene change as the film reaches the final stages of editing. What you think is important in a scene at the beginning of the process may be very different towards the end. In fact, its possible to make a scene do a whole range of things it may not have done at the start. Watching a first assembly for the first time reveals a whole host of things which are clearly surplus to requirements, and usually the sequence is way too long. The process of boiling it down forces you to work out what is essential in the storytelling. It also forces you to be more economical within the scenes themselves. Pauses between the dialogue are a good example. If someone thinks too much before they speak not only does it become monotonous it also reduces the effect of a dramatic moment in a scene. A pause among many pauses means nothing. A pause on its own can really mean something. Likewise, on a larger scale, overly repeating themes can have a similar effect. Repetition and circularity in storytelling and technique can dilute the most important moments in any film.

The most common complaint at a test screening is that a film is too slow. If the audience feels the film 'drags in parts', interestingly it could be down to a lack of engagement in the emotional threads of the story. It's like a kind of 'Tardis' effect. If an audience is totally transfixed by the story and the characters they can sometimes withstand a more languid pace. When looking for places to speed up the story, usually areas of 'air' suffer the most. BUT sometimes these moments serve to let the audience melt into the predicaments of the characters. To simply speed everything up and subsequently take the air out of the emotional scenes sometimes give the illusion that the film is longer. Likewise adding these moments of air in exactly the right places also gives the illusion of a tighter cut.

Editing is all about falling in love with sequences, smashing them up, making them perfect, throwing them away and then sometimes putting them back again! What ends up in the cut is just as important as what you take out. Every scene must be given a chance before you reject it. Anthony often asks if a scene is 'wearing its best clothes' in other words, have we given it a fair trial? In *Breaking and Entering* there is a scene where Robin Wright Penn jumps out of a car and screams at Jude Law. We had an allergy to this scene and for a long time it wasn't in the movie. We reintroduced it because people felt Robin's character was too 'cold' and needed to become more 'earthy'. It had an enormous effect on the test audiences (especially the women) who felt they could now relate to her much more. It seems amazing that this scene was ever cut out in the first place. It's now essential to the film. I've learned a lesson from this. Towards the end of the process, even with a short film, it's a good idea to think about the scenes you cut out and wonder if any of them are useful with the benefit of hindsight.

I'm constantly amazed at how many times a scene can be smashed to pieces before it feels absolutely right. The pain of doing this is hard to bear but is an absolutely essential part of the process. If you get into a rut, leave the room. A small dose of fresh air can save a lot of time banging your head against the keyboard! Give your eyes and mind a break and they'll work better and faster when you go back to work.

> **"Editing is all about falling in love with sequences, smashing them up, making them perfect, throwing them away and then sometimes putting them back again!"**

It may seem like you're going round in circles but it is vital to be open to change. Sometimes I find myself clinging to a way of cutting a scene and being utterly convinced it is the best and only way of doing it. Once I've bitten the bullet and broken it apart, 7 times out of 10 the scene will improve. I'm working on getting better at not being so stubborn, and gradually it's coming, with experience. The other side of the coin however, is to recognise when something isn't getting better. The mind plays tricks. If you watch something 20 times it feels permanent. It feels preposterous to change it. And likewise, when you do change it, it takes another 20 times before you get used to it. Being a good editor is finding some balance between being open to change and being able to challenge change. Resistance is mostly a good thing. A healthy friction between the editor and director is essential. Anthony and I seem to have a fundamental similarity in the way we think about things, but we push and pull in different directions a lot of the time. Good things always come from this.

Screening your film as early on as possible is a painful but good idea. I've been amazed at the different 'goggles' you can watch the film through depending on who is in the room. I watched a cut of *Breaking and Entering* with Jude Law sitting next to me and it was almost like I watched it through his eyes. I tracked his performance and character much more closely than I did when I sat next to a friend of mine. With her, I found myself being very aware of pace and narrative issues. The film changed in ways I never knew possible when I watched it with a test audience. It literally feels like pulling your pants down in front of them! People are incredibly critical. They simply don't care that you put your heart and soul into every frame and the barrage of criticism you get afterwards is often excruciating. This is the whole point. There's no value in constantly screening your film to people who know and love you. They will never be completely objective. I've found the most useful thing to take away from the terror of the test screening is what you 'felt' in the room. It's very animal, you can easily feel people losing interest or becoming confused. They can fill in questionnaires and tick boxes as much as they like but at the end of the day, it's our job to diagnose what the problems are and how to fix them. Above all, it's our job to listen and be open to criticism and learn how it can help us make the film better. That is really all that matters. The film must get better and better. It's not about how much it hurts you, or the musician or the actor; it's about the film being everything.

"The treatment of sound is extremely delicate. I've found that sometimes the best sound is no sound."

It's important that the audience 'sees' the film in the right way. The beginning of the film sets up fundamental expectations for what kind of film it is. It seems that if the film presents itself as something it is not, it causes disappointment, confusion and a general lack of engagement. This may be part of the plan so I don't want to generalise too much about this. Sometimes unsettling the audience at the start is very effective. But in *Breaking and Entering* the way we started the movie was causing huge ripple effects later down the film. In the script, there was a lot of 'setting up' which we felt was delaying the 'meat and potatoes' of the story. We cut a lot of this out by starting the film at the first break in. This helped advance the story but it also created a general lack of focus. People were finding it hard to decide which character to get their teeth into. First Anthony and Sydney Pollock, one of the film's producers, suggested we make a title sequence out of the material we cut out. This was very effective and gave a lot of information about all the characters and the world they inhabit. But then Anthony came up with a brilliant idea to put a shot that was originally supposed to go near the end (which is, in fact, repeated to create a satisfying sense of circularity), at the beginning. The first shot of the movie is of Jude and Robin driving in silence in the car. This sets up that the film is about a relationship. This is the main thrust of the film and by putting this shot at the beginning puts the right 'goggles' on the audience. You know what to look for in the story and then track the main characters in the right way. The point of this is to settle people down, then it somehow gives us licence to throw a lot of confusing information at them which they can enjoy decoding. Anthony did a similar thing in *The Talented Mr Ripley* and it's one of many examples of how he's a brilliant writer, especially in the cutting room. He's taught me that editing **is** writing.

There is something weird and wonderful about the relationship between film and music. Both have a rhythm and a shape. A few times I've had the pleasure of laying up some temp score (ie. music that hasn't been composed for the film) on a cut and found it fit like a glove. I always take this as a sign that there must be something right with the edit. Somehow it reaffirms the edit choices because it suggests that the film has a pulse of its own. Ideally, the score has its own narrative. It should tell the story in parallel to the picture and help you feel the right thing about what you're watching. In fact it should go a long way to making you feel the right thing without the picture. BUT it should never tell you too much. Although generalising is dangerous, it seems that an audience feel patronised and manipulated if the music is saying more than the picture is.

In *Breaking and Entering,* Gabriel Yared and Underworld's score sampled certain sounds from the special FX tracks. They blended the elements together beautifully to create a kind of soundscape, taking on the rhythm of the picture and enhancing it with music. The treatment of sound is extremely delicate. I've found that sometimes the best sound is no sound. The absence of it can be louder than the sound itself. The 'normality' of production, sound, and FX, can make a scene too pinned in reality and can take away from the emotional drama. Removing the sound atmosphere in a scene can create a dream-like, surreal quality. In *Breaking and Entering* there is a shocking scene where Juliette Binoche and her friend take incriminating photos of Jude and her in bed. The love scene between them turns sour as the music stops and the shots of Jude sleeping and Juliette posing become jumpcut as the friend takes the pictures. I kept lowering sound atmos because I was worried that the audience would expect Jude to wake up with the noise going on around him. In the end I just removed it. This seemed to give an unsettling claustrophobic effect. It adds a surreal quality and works well to mark a turning point in the film. It feels as if the air has been sucked out of the cinema.

Anthony often says that "the IQ of the audience is much higher than the individual viewer". I'm amazed at the remarkable ability an audience has of filling in gaps in story. It's incredible what scenes you can cut and how the audience still knows exactly what's happening. Sometimes jumping from one scene to a much later scene can actually clarify and strengthen the storytelling. It may be that cutting a scene which tells a lot of story actually helps the audience track the emotion of a character better ie its much more satisfying for the audience to track the emotional journey of a character than being spoon fed plot. Gaps in the story can be strangely effective. If the audience engage emotionally with the character then the gaps are easy to fill.

Filling in the gaps in a story is fun. Encouraging an audience to do this creates a sense of additionality. Their imagination is far better than anything that you can put on a screen. This is like being in zero gravity with your characters - you can float around them, seeing them from all angles and know them like real people.

When plot rules it can lead to a feeling of being marched through an inflexible world. When emotion rules it seems that the sum of the whole equals much more than the parts. Ellipsis is a wonderful but dangerous thing. There is a biting point. The optimum balance comes when the film tells people enough to keep them engaged and confident they know what's happening, but withholds enough to make them wonder what happens next. Predictability can be very dangerous. An audience likes to work things out but they hate feeling lost.

A film usually ends up being true to a script in its essence but it undoubtedly has a life of its own. The script may work beautifully, but once the film is shot you can make the film do what you want it to: moving scenes around, cutting them down, adding to them, cheating them or even creating new ones by using additional dialogue recording (ADR). It's a beautiful creative process, almost like magic, essentially smoke and mirrors. My experience on this film has shown me that nothing is impossible if you think around it hard enough. This is the job of an editor, to find solutions, play tricks, use cheats. As long as the end result seems intended. It's a bit like cooking. You look at what ingredients you've got, sometimes they're fresh, ripe, and exactly what you need to cook the perfect recipe. Sometimes there are bits missing and you have to improvise. Sometimes there are happy mistakes,

> **"When plot rules it can lead to a feeling of being marched through an inflexible world. When emotion rules it seems that the sum of the whole equals much more than the parts"**

sometimes just bad mistakes but there's always room for experimentation, a little seasoning here, a little cheat there. The principle of less is more is essential. Ultimately, the most important thing to remember is that if you put your heart and soul into it, and a lot of love, the food tastes better. People can tell if it's been made with love, they can feel it.

Here are 12 things which have really helped me along the way.

If you have someone else editing your short, try to get them involved before the shoot. Help to concentrate the collective effort towards the seminal moments in the film, the turning points. Think of what may be useful in the cutting room before it's too late.

Be organised. Always know where everything is. Make a simple, well-labelled system that works for you. You'll need to find things on autopilot.

Watch the rushes with the pure intention of the scene in mind. It will help clarify what is important and what isn't. This may seem obvious but it's quite easy to go off into a tangent when selecting your material.

Push yourself. There are no shortcuts to knowing your material inside out.

Keep it simple. Initially assemble the scene in the most basic possible way. Try not to get caught up in detail. You probably won't know what details are important until you see the scene as a whole.

Walk out of the room. Sometimes you find yourself in a rut. Five minutes of fresh air can save you three hours banging your head against the keyboard.

Don't be afraid of change. Always save your versions along the way. Now you can experiment to your heart's content.

Think of the sound elements as a story-telling device. The music and sound effects can and should be telling a story in their own right.

Try to 'boil down' the scene to its most essential parts. A process of reduction usually helps to make a scene stronger.

Remember what you cut out. You may find that what you didn't think was important at the beginning of the process can be very useful at the end.

Be open. By the time you've cut the film you've lost your 'innocence'. Always listen to people who haven't seen it before and don't take what they say personally! Its all about the film not the individual.

Think radically. Make the film do what you want it to. Use tricks like Additional Dialogue Recording (ADR) to enhance ideas and moments. You don't have to have big budgets to do this – be creative! Never confine yourself to using the material as it was originally intended.

Project Profile:
Mike Figgis, A Portrait of London

As we mentioned in the introduction to this book, established filmmakers are turning to short films for creative expression, disproving the common idea that a short is *just* a stepping stone or a calling card for new filmmakers. In many cases, they are attracted to short films as a way to experiment with style and expression, even when the projects are hard to achieve and are not for commercial gain.

For the 50th anniversary of the London Film Festival, Mike Figgis (*Leaving Las Vegas*, *Timecode*) curated a free outdoor short film spectacular – part gallery piece, part cinema. Figgis designed a 45-minute show, which would be projected onto Nelson's Column in Trafalgar Square. The plan was to select a group of seasoned British filmmakers and artists like John Boorman (*Deliverance*), actor Simon McBurney, music vid creator Sophie Muller (Bjork, Mika, Gwen Stefani), rapper Plan B, and cinematographer Alwin Kuchler (*The Mother*), who would all make a five-minute 'movie-image of London' about the capital's diverse population, and which celebrated the city 'warts and all'.

The project was an exercise in guerrilla filmmaking; from conception to event was less than 2 months, and most of the films were shot in the three weeks prior to the screening. Figgis ended up shooting a number of the shorts himself. When Figgis made one of the films with Plan B and singer Killa Kela, they recorded a song in the evening, and then set out in East London to make a film based on that track: "We finished at 4 o'clock in the morning, after Hackney Council said they would arrest us if we made any more noise." Simon McBurney went one better. He had just 2 days and nights to shoot his short and *did* get arrested for filming outside St. Paul's Cathedral.

Yet despite the headaches, the night was a huge success – Trafalgar Square was packed as the films were projected onto a giant screen with a soundtrack from producers Roxbury (Goldfrapp).

Photo courtesy of Matthew Andrews

Chris and Ben Blaine, interview
Part 5: sound and post-production

How important is a creative approach to sound in post-production?

BEN: Sound is an amazingly powerful tool and one that is often overlooked. I watch a lot of short films and almost without fail when I enjoy something and go back and look at what makes it different from the others I've seen that day, it comes down to the quality of the acting and sound design. Everyone knows to think about what the camera is doing. Caring about what is happening in the audience's ears is the sign of someone who really cares about their film.

CHRIS: For us it's a brilliant chance to play. We love playing about with sound but, as with most of our films, we try to keep all the work underneath, not pushing things to the point where you'll notice it. The main thing is that you're setting the mood with everything you do, including sound. Some people only think about shot size, position of the camera and what the actors are doing. You can add so much to the mood of the piece with sound.

BEN: The best thing about sound is that, on the whole, you really have to go over the top before it becomes intrusive. It's almost like because it's not seen it doesn't enter the conscious mind, instead it slips in through the back door. The sound design of a scene is a brilliant way instantly to set the mood. As soon as you put that whine of fluorescent lighting into something everything always feels just that little bit more stressed; put distant bird song coming through the window and actually it's not so bad after-all...

Many short filmmakers may feel like sound design is beyond their budget. Do you have any stories about how you've achieved good results for little money?

BEN: Yeah, though I'd also like to stress that it's always worth spending money on a good sound mix. Actually, that's the thing I wish someone had told me before we started. Digital filmmaking and the power of home editing software means you really can do a superb edit without leaving your house. Increasingly, you can also do a decent job on the sound mix and the final picture grade, but it's only ever going to be *decent*. If you want real quality you have to grade with a broadcast monitor and you have to mix in a studio.

As with most things, it is possible to blag both of those things, but if I was spending your budget, I would spend it on Insurance, Food, Sound Mixing and Grading. Cover all of those and you give yourself a good chance of ending up with a good end result.

But, if there is no way you can afford a sound mix and none of your blags are working, then there are still things you can do. A lot simply comes down to thinking about sound and planning for it. One of the best 48hr Challenge Films we shot was in Paris [The 48 Hour Film Challenge asks filmmakers to script, shoot and edit a 5 minute DV film in 48 hours – there's currently no live website for the competition but sites like Shooting People and BBC Film Network will announce dead-lines, if and when it runs again]. By the end of the first day, we'd shot about two thirds of the story and had put together a rough edit. Realising that we needed to give each scene its own distinc-tive flavour, we took our sound recordist, Alex, and Cariad, our actress, out into Paris at dawn. She does a lot of running in the film so we re-recorded her foot-steps in different locations and also her breathing in the differ-ent parts of Paris we went to. It's a really simple little film but the different textures of sound really give it a depth. None of that cost us anything - except sleep and the threat of legal action from some guys at a park we weren't allowed to film in!

> **"If I was spending your budget, I would spend it on Insurance, Food, Sound Mixing and Grading. Cover all of those and you give yourself a good chance of ending up with a good end result"**

CHRIS: I think if you have no budget for a sound mix - and some-times even when you do - the best way of getting the right sound is to go to the right place. We couldn't use the original sound of Cariad running because I was pushing a bike with the camera taped to the seat to film her so we had lots of bike noise. Replac-ing it meant we could become a lot more atmospheric with it all.

For *Old Man Dies* we had quite a bit of dialogue that needed re-recording. This is normally done with your actor in a voiceover booth speaking along to the film. To get it sounding like it's been said in the same place as the other dialogue becomes very tricky and it's usually best to replace all the dialogue for that scene so you can make it all sound the same rather than try and match it. We didn't have a voiceover booth, and with no real clue about changing sound in post we decided the best way to make the atmospherics realistic was to record the dialogue in places that would sound right.

Your kit for dialogue replacement:
1 x sound recordist;
1 x sound kit and sound recording device;
1 x battery-powered playback machine with headphones;
1 x battery-powered monitor; and
1 x tape of your finished film with each line looped.

The way we've seen it done in post-houses is that they play back each line again and again and the actor gets closer and closer and the sound mixer clicks loads of buttons and gets it all in sync for you. Personally, I think the best way of getting lip-sync on the cheap is if you turn the dialogue into a song so it's simple to sing along. Every line we needed to record I looped as if it was a line from a song, keeping the tempo going and simply repeating the action again and again in a sing-song rhythm so that there weren't any pauses. It meant that our actor, Nick Simons, quickly got into the rhythm and was 'singing along', and there was no stopping and rewinding the tape and "ok shall we go again". It all becomes a little bit more automatic and means the actor can start placing nuances without having all the worry of keeping in sync.

We had an *Old Man Dies* scene outside a house at magic hour (rush hour!) on a busy road: beautiful shot, awful sound. So for the sound to feel right we went to Richmond Park and sat beneath some trees with birds singing away. Nick had the headphones on lipsyncing to the monitor. Ryan Chandler, our sound recordist did a fine job, and it was pretty simple!

In fact, we recorded all the sounds in the film again in an appro-priate location. For a boxing scene we needed some meaty punches, so Ryan told me to punch him in his (tensed) stomach again and again until we'd got the right stuff... which was rather fun for me. A sound recordist will go to extreme measures for perfect sound!

On set the of *Death of the Revolution*
Photo by Jessica Thomas

How you have approached music on your films? Have you had specific pieces composed and licensed tracks?

CHRIS: Composed, primarily. We've licensed a track for free from a band we did a couple of a music videos with, and also we licensed T Rex's *Children of the Revolution* for the kids to sing at the end of *Death of the Revolution*, but that cost us a substantial part of the budget. In the main we get people to compose for us. *DOTR* was done by the magnificent Paul Englishby, who was also doing *Confetti* at the time he was working with us. Our special favourite is Daniel Teper (aka. Danny Fromajio). Danny seems to be able to tap into our subconscious and give us what we were after without us ever really being able to explain it to him. We sort of ramble at him for a while and he comes back a couple of days later with something so much better than we'd been thinking of.

BEN: On the whole you're probably not going to be able to afford to license music so it's always best not to go down that route. If you edit with a track on the first edit, then it tends to get stuck and you really miss it when it's gone. If you use unlicensed music, then suddenly you can't show the film at festivals and no broadcaster will touch it. You may have a great sounding film, but no one can see it.

Finding the right composer is difficult, not least because there are so many out there. On the whole the only thing I found that worked was to listen to their reel. If their music makes you think of pictures, then they're worth talking to. Time after time, I get reels full of stuff that sounds really nice, really interesting, but it's just music; it's not film music. You put Danny's music on and instantly you can see something.

> "If you use unlicensed music, then suddenly you can't show the film at festivals and no broadcaster will touch it. You may have a great sounding film, but no one can see it"

Equipment Hire in the UK

Unless otherwise stated, these companies pretty much hire what it says in their name. Where it was unclear, we tried to make a note of what services and equipment they offer in *take note* and also whether 'wet hire' (equipment + experienced crew) is available.

Information on editing and post-production facilities in your area is available from most regional screen agencies (see Get it Funded contacts)

Greater London

Aimimage Camera Company

✉ Unit 5,
St Pancras Commercial Centre,
63 Pratt Street,
London NW1 0BY

📞 020-7482 4340

📠 020-7267 3972

🖥 www.aimimage.com

Alpha Grip

✉ The Matte Stage,
Pinewood Studios,
Iver Heath,
Iver,
Buckinghamshire SL0 0NH

📞 01753 656886

🖥 www.alphagrip.co.uk

ARRI Lighting Rental

✉ 4 Highbridge,
Oxford Road,
Uxbridge,
Middlesex UB8 1LX

📞 (01895) 457200

📠 (01895) 457201

🖥 sales@arrirental.com
www.arri.com

ARRI Media

✉ 3 Highbridge,
Oxford Rd,
Uxbridge,
Middlesex UB8 1LX

📞 (01895) 457100

📠 (01895) 457101

🖥 info@arrimedia.com
www.arrimedia.com

Awfully Nice Video Company Limited
✉ 30 Long Lane,
Ickenham,
London UB10 8TA

☎ (07000) 345678

📠 (07000) 345679

💻 www.awfullynicevideo.com

The Cruet Company
✉ 11 Ferrier Street,
London SW18 1SN

☎ 020-8874 2121

📠 020-8874 9850

💻 info@cruet.com
www.cruet.com

TAKE NOTE: good selection of digital cameras, kit and crew

Elstree Light and Power
✉ Millennium Studios,
Elstree Way,
Borehamwood,
Herts WD6 1SF

☎ 020-8236 1300

📠 020-8236 1333

💻 www.elstree-online.co.uk

Four Corners
✉ 121 Roman Road,
Bethnal Green,
London E2 0QN

☎ 020-8981 6111

📠 020 8983 7866

💻 info@fourcornersfilm.co.uk
www.fourcornersfilm.co.uk

TAKE NOTE: Film camera hire with Arri Super 16mm and 16mm and Bolexes, plus flat bed editing equipment plus sound and lighting equipment.

Fuel Film & Television Ltd
✉ 30 Kingsfield Road,
Watford WD19 4PS

☎ (01923) 233956

📠 (01923) 224289

💻 allen@fuelfilm.com
www.fuelfilm.com

TAKE NOTE: Complete 16mm packages

FX Rentals Ltd
✉ 38-40 Telford Way,
London W3 7XS

☎ 020-8746 2121

📠 020-8746 4100

💻 www.fxgroup.net

TAKE NOTE: Audio equipment, AV gear, backline, recorders, microphones and video equipment

Ice Film Equipment Ltd
✉ Unit 2,
Bridge Wharf,
London N1 9UU

☎ 020-7278 0908

📠 020-7278 4552

💻 hire@icefilm.com
www.icefilm.com

TAKE NOTE: 16mm and 35mm film equipment plus lenses and grip equipment

Kitroom Monkey Ltd

 Ealing Film Studios,
Ealing Green,
London W5 5EP

(☎) 0845-166 2597

📧 mail@kitroommonkey.co.uk
www.kitroommonkey.co.uk

Lee Film & TV Hire

✉ Unit 32 Sheraton Business Centre,
20 Wadsworth Road,
Perivale, London UB6 7JB

(☎) 020-8998 9977

📠 020-8998 2781

 info@leefilmhire.co.uk
www.leefilmhire.co.uk

Panavision

✉ Metropolitan Centre,
Bristol Road,
Greenford,
Middlesex UB6 8UQ

(☎) 020-8839 7333

📠 020-8578 1536

 enquiries@panavision.co.uk
www.panavision.co.uk

Richmond Film Services

✉ The Old School,
Park Lane,
Richmond,
Surrey TW9 2RA

(☎) 020-8940 6077

📠 020-8948 8326

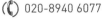 bookings@richmondfilmservices.co.uk
www.richmondfilmservices.co.uk

Super 8 Camera Company

✉ 10 Granville Gardens,
Ealing Common,
London W5 3PA

(☎) 020-8992 6451

📠 020-8992 6451

TAKE NOTE: Super 8 and 16mm specialists (including stock for each) and also offer crew

Take Two Films

✉ Rentals - Unit 10,
West Point Trading Estate,
Alliance Road,
Acton,
London W3 0RA

(☎) 020-8992 2224

📠 020-8992 2204

 services@take2films.co.uk

TAKE NOTE: 16mm and 35mm film cameras, grip equipment and camera cranes plus film and tape stock

Scotland

Axis Glasgow

 64-68 Brand St,
Glasgow,
Lanarkshire G51 1DW

(☎) 0141-427 9944

📠 0141-427 1199

📧 glasgow@axisfilms.co.uk
www.axisfilms.co.uk

TAKE NOTE: lights and camera hire

GB Audio

 Unit D,
51 Brunswick Rd,
Edinburgh EH7 5PD

 0131-661 0022

 hire@gbaudio.co.uk
www.gbaudio.co.uk

TAKE NOTE: Sound equipment rental as well as sound operators and technicians

Glasgow Media Access Centre (GMAC)

 3rd Floor,
34 Albion Street,
Glasgow G1 1LH

0141-553 2620

0141-553 2660

www.g-mac.co.uk

TAKE NOTE: Open-access facility for young filmmakers – light, camera and editing equipment

The Warehouse Sound Services

 23 Water Street,
Leith,
Edinburgh EH6 6SU

0131-555 6900

0131-555 6901

www.warehousesound.co.uk

TAKE NOTE: Can also supply sound crew

Other UK Hire

Acorn Film & Video

13 Fitzwilliam St,
Belfast,
Co Antrim BT9 6AW

028-9024 0977

028-9022 2309

info@acorntv.com
www.acorntv.com

Axis Leeds

Suite 7.3,
Joseph's Well Building,
Hanover Walk,
Leeds,
West Yorkshire LS3 1AB

0113-380 4862

0113-380 4863

leeds@axisfilms.co.uk
www.axisfilms.co.uk

Eye Film and Television

 Chamberlain House,
2 Dove Street,
Norwich NR2 1DE

(01603) 762 551

(01603) 762 420

production@eyefilmandtv.co.uk
www.eyefilmandtv.co.uk

Panavision Manchester

✉ Unit 3,
Littlers Point,
The Village,
Trafford Park,
Manchester M17 1LT

📞 0161-872 4766

📠 0161-872 6637

💻 mike.heaney@panavision.co.uk
www.panavision.co.uk

Procam North

✉ Unit 4,
Clayton Court,
The City Works,
Ashton Old Road,
Manchester M11 2NB

📞 0161-604 0701

📠 0161-220 9801

💻 info@procamnorth.com
www.procamnorth.com

ProVision

✉ 96 Kirkstall Road,
Leeds LS3 1HD

📞 0113-222 8222

📠 0113-222 8110

💻 provision@granadamedia.com
www.provisionequipment.tv

Sheffield Independent Film

✉ 5 Brown Street,
Sheffield S1 2BS

📞 0114-272 0304

📠 0114-279 5225

💻 admin.sif@workstation.org.uk
www.sheffieldindependentfilm.co.uk

TAKE NOTE: Facilities and equipment hire

Stock and Labs

Most of the following companies offer negative processing for film, and can also make prints of your film or trailer (though for this later service, many filmmakers are swearing by the less expensive Eastern European labs, so worth doing some research).

Bucks Laboratories Ltd

✉ 714 Banbury Avenue,
Slough,
Berks SL1 4LR

📞 (01753) 501500

💻 mail@bucks.co.uk
www.bucks.co.uk

Deluxe Laboratories Ltd

✉ North Orbital Road,
Denham,
Uxbridge,
Middlesex UB9 5HQ

📞 (01895) 823 323

💻 www.bydeluxe.com

Film and Photo Ltd

✉ 13 Colville Road,
South Acton Industrial Estate,
London W3 8BL

📞 020-8992 0037

📠 020-8993 2409

💻 info@film-photo.co.uk
www.film-photo.co.uk

Film Lab North

 96 Kirkstall Road,
Leeds LS3 1HD

(📞) 0113-222 8333

🖷 0113-222 8110

💻 www.filmlabnorth.tv

Soho Images

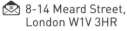 8-14 Meard Street,
London W1V 3HR

(📞) 020-7437 0831

🖷 020-7734 9471

💻 www.sohoimages.com

Technicolour Film Services

 Bath Road,
West Drayton,
Middlesex UB7 0DB

(📞) 020-8759 5432

🖷 020-8759 6270

💻 www.technicolor.com

Section Six:

Get it Seen

So you've finished your film – What next?

Méabh O'Donovan, Short Circuits Films Ltd.

Film is a shared experience, both in the making and viewing. If you make a film that no one ever gets to see then the reasons for making it have eluded you. With shorts, thought is only often given to the marketing and market once the film is made. It has been said that the only audience for a short is the three executives who will potentially fund your next film. But, throwing cynicism aside – and as true lovers of short film – we all know that there are now more opportunities than ever for screening shorts. It is important to understand the market for short films and to be realistic about your chances in that market. Remember that however many new technologies come into play and however a film is delivered to an audience, the content and quality of the films are still key.

The traditional route for a successful film used to be festivals, theatric, DVD and then terrestrial television. That has all changed and, whilst those routes still exist, there are also mobile phones, VOD (video on demand), cable and satellite dedicated channels for shorts and internet. Some of these areas are still in the early stages of development in the UK, and rapid changes will take place over the coming year.

Short film is very useful for companies wanting to test out their technologies, but they often do not offer money for screening the films. With their promises of profile and exposure, it is important that you understand the contracts you are being asked to sign. Never sign away all rights exclusively for no money or royalty over a long period of time. That said, short film is not about making money, it is about getting your work screened and moving on to make other films, so look carefully at each offer you are made to screen your work and select those that will be of most benefit to you.

It is good to remember that every avenue in the UK is replicated in almost every country around the world. There are festivals, television channels and DVDs for shorts on every continent. Do not satisfy yourself with just getting a local screening, use the internet to research worldwide opportunities. The strategic use of festivals can bring your film to a worldwide audience.

Never have there been more opportunities to screen short films, but with the numbers of films increasing rapidly, each slot has fierce competition. Rapidly changing and advancing technologies have meant that commissioners, programmers and buyers are always looking for content.

So: what to do next?

Festivals, the cornerstone of your exhibition strategy

Festivals are still the primary way of getting your short film screened before an audience and, let's face it, what's more important to a filmmaker than that? This is where you will undoubtedly put the most energy and time, but there are so many film festivals that you could spend your entire working life submitting your short to festivals. Not only will you have to fill in a lot of submission forms, but you could also pay submission costs, so it could end up being an expensive past-time. Spend time preparing for your festival approach.

Firstly, UK-based filmmakers may want to submit your film to the British Council's film and television department (see www.britfilms.com for contacts). If they take up your film, they will put it forward to festivals and they can assist with travel grants for the director. Even if your film is not selected, their website is a useful starting point in creating your festival strategy. Treat it as a business plan. Select a wish list of about

40 festivals over an 18 month period after your film is finished, then look at the entry criteria and deadlines and draw up a month-by-month submission list. Start by submitting to the first three months' worth of festivals and then work on a one month rolling programme. Treat this as a living document that you assess and revisit with each selection or rejection. If your film is not being selected time and time again, then maybe you need to look at why this is the case and not put yourself to further expense.

Top Tips:

> Use companies like www.withoutabox.com where you can submit your film to a number of festivals online.

> Get some high resolution stills in a digital format and compress them so that you can email them to the festivals.

> Spend time at the beginning reading festival criteria so that you don't submit to festivals for which your film is ineligible.

> Be creative with the festivals to which you are submitting – there are hundreds of niche festivals such as Gay & Lesbian, Jewish, Women's, Horror, Music etc. Is there a slant in your film that could fit their criteria?

There is a more comprehensive list of festivals at the end of this section, but here are a few key festivals for shorts:

UK, Encounters Festival	www.encounters-festival.org.uk
France, Clermont-Ferrand	www.clermont-filmfest.com
Canada, Worldwide Shorts Toronto	www.worldwideshortfilmfest.org.uk
Germany, Oberhausen	www.oberhausen.com
Finland, Tampere	www.tampere.com
USA, Aspen Shortsfest	www.aspenfilm.org

✱ Read our interviews with the curators behind **Sundance Film Festival** on page 179; **Aspen Shortsfest** on page 181; and **Halloween Short Film Festival** on page 183

What can a Sales Agent do for me?

You assign the rights of your film to an agent, who will then go out and represent your film in the market place. They generally operate on a commission basis, which can be up to 50%. You will need to deliver to them a broadcast quality master and all paperwork relating to the film. You must have signed agreements with every contributor to the film, from actors to crew. There must be a music clearance licence and a clean chain of title i.e. from the writer to the producer who will then have the rights to sign deals with agents, festivals and others. There are agents all over the world and the reality is it doesn't matter where your agent is as long as they like your film and see its potential.

When you sign with a sales agent, you will be agreeing to give them a significant commission on the exhibition and distribution income of your film and the most likely scenario is that you will sign an exclusive contract with them (they can't sell a film if another agent is trying to sell the same film to the same buyer). This relationship can be brilliant for many filmmakers; sales agents are paid to have contacts and resources that you probably won't have and many buyers will prefer to deal with agents rather than individual film-makers. Yet it's always worth doing your research. Find out all you can about the company and feel free to ask them what their plans are for your film. Get a sense of why they like it. Their enthusiasm for your film will certainly help them to sell it.

In the UK the key players are:

Shorts International: www.shortsinternational.com

Dazzle Films: www.dazzlefilms.co.uk

Future Shorts: www.futureshorts.com

One Dot Zero: www.onedotzero.com

British Film Institute: www.bfi.org.uk

Some international agents of repute are:

Holland, SND Films   www.sndfilms.com

Germany, Hamburg Short Film Agency www.kurzfilmtage.de

USA, Big Film Shorts   www.bigfilmshorts.com

France, Premium Films   www.premium-films.com

USA, Apollo Cinema   www.apollocinema.com

To find out about other sales agents around the world, it's worth checking out festivals that have markets attached such as Clermont-Ferrand or Cannes and seeing their buyers and sellers list – these are usually available on their website, though sometimes you may need to pay for access to online market resources. Alternatively, if you see a film that you feel is similar to yours in terms of style, see who is representing it.

---

* Find out more about short film sales in our interviews with **Simon Young** from **Shorts International** on page 194 and **Sydney Neter** from **SND Films** on page 198

Television sales

For many years, after midnight was the slot in which you were most likely to see a short. Unfortunately, even those days have gone. Whilst there are some short films screened on BBC or Channel 4 they are most likely to have been commissioned by the channels themselves. However, don't despair; there are lots of other avenues to explore. Also, internationally, there are still many TV stations that buy shorts such as IFC (USA), Sundance Channel (USA), Canal+ (France), SVT (Sweden) and VPRO (Holland). Rather than attempting to approach television channels around the world, get yourself a sales agent who can approach them on your behalf. They will have the relationship with the buyers, who in turn will trust their recommendations. They may also sell their films in small packages and pair your film with a bigger award-winner to help the sale.

Theatrical and non-theatrical screenings

Having a short screened in a cinema is a great ambition for many filmmakers. The advent of the Digital

Chris and Ben Blaine, interview
Part 6: Learning from the audience

CHRIS: It's incredibly important to watch your film with an audience; you learn where you've made mistakes simply by sitting in a room of people and feeling how they react to it. You also see where you've gone right as well, which is a wonderful feeling.

BEN: There is a really strange force within filmmaking that keeps the creators away from the audience. It's perverse, but the number of filmmakers I've met who don't feel obliged or responsible to go and watch their work when it's screened makes me really froth at the mouth. As a creative community no one whinges like filmmakers, just read Shooting People for a couple of months. The British film industry is dying on its arse and it's always the fault of the Film Council, or Hollywood, or the BBC, or Shooting People, or the Unions, or the non-unionised workers, or the press, or the public. Far as I'm concerned the real problem is that, somewhere along the line, filmmakers have lost touch with their audience, and that's our own fault, our own laziness and arrogant stupidity.

Hallo Panda
Photo by Jessica Thomas

The idea has grown up that film is either art or it's commerce. If it's art then the only person you are creatively responsible to is yourself as the divine artist and prime mover. If it's commerce then nothing matters but bums on seats for the opening weekend and you should throw everything you can at the screen until you feel people will come to look, if only out of horrified fascination. But, good art should always been a conversation between the artist and their audience and good business depends upon knowing your market. As an artist you have a moral duty to be at your screening to understand how your work effects your audience. As an entrepreneur you have a financial responsibility to be there as golden market research.

If you are lucky enough to get a public screening of your film - be there. It may be nerve-wracking, it may be painful, but it'll teach you more about good and bad filmmaking than anything else you can ever do. Ever.

Screen Network in the UK and the general (if slow) roll out of digital projectors around the world may also soon mean that you do not need to have prints for cinema screenings, which should open the door for lots of shorts to play. But, think carefully about how often you yourself pay to go and see a package of shorts in the cinema or when your local cinema last screened shorts. For a cinema to programme a short film before a feature is also a big investment of valuable screen time with no real commercial value for them (see our interview with Catharine Des Forges from the Independent Cinema Office in this section for more on this). When you assess this then you can understand the true picture. Apart from the committed few such as the Curzon Soho, London, most cinemas do not screen shorts.

Still, there are options. It is always worth approaching your local cinema to see if they will screen your film and a very small handful of filmmakers have also had luck getting a small distributor to send out a short film in front of one of their features (be aware this is rare and also only really appropriate for films under 10 minutes). Alternatively get together with a group of filmmakers and see if the cinema would screen a programme of shorts. You can also approach groups such as Bite Size Cinema, Birds Eye View (Films by Women) in the UK; Future Shorts in Europe and the UK; or Rooftop Films and Asbury Shorts in the US who put on short film nights.

In the UK, film societies are great for screening shorts. Your film will be screened to an audience of real enthusiasts. They sometimes will pay a fee to show your film or alternatively they will invite you to attend the screening and do a Q&A afterwards. You can find details of film societies on the ICO website www. independentcinemaoffice.org.uk

Internationally, there are also opportunities are within festivals' travelling programmes, should your film be selected.

✱ Check out our interviews with **Catharine Des Forges** from the **Independent Cinema Office** on page 175; **Fabien Riggall** from **Future Shorts** on page 201; and **Dan Nuxoll** from **Rooftop Films** on page 204

DVD

A number of organisations are doing compilations of short films. It is difficult to release a film yourself – though not impossible – so it's best to look at current compilations and approach the companies behind them and show them your film. Good compilations to view are:

Best v Best	www.bestvbest.com
Cinema 16	www.cinema16.co.uk
Big Stories Small Flashes	www.play.com
Specialten (monthly DVD magazine)	www.specialten.com
Wholphin (quarterly DVD magazine)	www.wholphindvd.com

If you do decide to go the route of making your own short available on DVD, look at on-demand DVD production sites as CustomFlix (www.customflix.com) or Short Film Central (www.shortfilmcentral.com). They have systems in place which allow you to send in a master of your short for low cost encoding, which they then replicate, print and post for you each time they get an online order for your film. While you will have to pay for this service, it will save you the hassle of having to become your own distributor; the last thing you need to do when you are writing your next film is schlep back and forth to the post office to mail DVDs!

✳ **Best v Best's Penny Nagle** is interviewed on page 187; **Cinema 16's Luke Morris** is interviewed on page 167; and **Brent Hoff** from **Wholphin** chats with Ingrid Kopp on page 189

Cable and Satellite

Many dedicated short film channels are springing up. In the UK, they are available on either the Sky platform or cable television. A lot of these companies are at fledgling stage and as such they do not have the viewing figures yet. But given time, it likely that one or two will come to the fore and be excellent places to view shorts. You need to be aware of whatever contract you are signing with a company like this. Ideally you do not want to give away too many rights. As they are often accessed via satellite, the channel requires the full territory of Europe. If you sign an exclusive deal then you rule out any potential revenue generating sales to other channels across Europe. Where possible sign a non-exclusive deal.

Some of the channels around the world are:

Propeller TV	www.propellertv.co.uk	UK
Movieola	www.movieola.ca	Canada
Zed	www.zed.cbc.ca	Canada
IFC	www.ifctv.com	USA
Current TV	www.current.tv	USA

Mobile phones and hand-held devices

Most people would watch something on their phone when they have 5 minutes on the bus, or 30 seconds standing in a queue. Therefore, this is a natural place for shorts to be available. All the major sales agents are doing deals with mobile phone networks, and many of the companies with the hardware – Sony PSP, mobile phone companies, dual MP3/Video players - are establishing relationships with some of the VOD content providers I mention below.

When thinking about a mobile as a place to screen your short, consider how it will look on a phone screen. If your film relies on a lot of visual detail, then it may not work on a very small screen. Also length is important, generally the shorter the better for phones. It is worth looking out for competitions for mobile phone shorts commissions. One company that is leading the way on these commissions is Yorkshire based Blink Media (www.blinkmedia.org).

✳ Check out our interviews with **Evan Fleischer** from **IFC** on page 211; and **Jason Meil** from **Current TV** on page 209

Online and video on demand

Increasingly it is becoming obvious that more and more shorts will be screened either via the web or on video on demand (VOD).

The web is a perfect home for shorts. A few years ago it was difficult for budding filmmakers to see short films other than at festivals or at 2am on television. Now there are hundreds of shorts on many websites around the world. It is a great opportunity for those making films to see what is out there and to immerse themselves in the world of shorts. It helps to give a filmmaker an understanding of what works in a short, how the narrative, be it traditional or not, is key to the success of the film and what the market is looking for.

VOD allows users to select and watch content which can be delivered through and interactive television system or online. Anyone who receives their televison now via cable or satellite and subscribes to a service such as Sky+ in the UK or Tivo in the US already has access to VOD, this is in the form of replaying previously screened telelvison programmes and buying films straight from your television. You can select the title you wish to view, you enter a pin code then can then pause, rewind and fast forward as you would a standard DVD. Most providers also offer movie on demand services (pay per view) and most networks are developing plans to make their back catalogue of films and and new titles to viewers via video on demand for viewing on television sets. Whilst this is not yet fully in use for shorts, it is only a matter of time before the channels will be crying out for quality content. The service is very new in the UK, but expect it to really take off over the next 12 months.

Online networks and sites are also entering the running and with platforms and hardware merging, you might soon regularly watch films you have downloaded online through your television system. Below you'll find a number of important sites and companies which have established themselves in the internet short film market, some of which have them available for download. This is not a definitive list.

www.bbc.co.uk/filmnetwork

This site screens films from UK filmmakers. Generally the films are screened once they have had some festival exposure. The site is a community for filmmakers and has space for you to include details of yourself and your work. There is also space for people to comment on films. The site also has filmmaker video diaries, festival diaries and hi resolution downloads.

www.revver.com

User upload media site which pays filmmakers or content producers everytime someone watches the advertisement embedded into the end of their film file. Site also encourage users to share the video file (and again, creator is paid each time the ad is viewed).

www.britfilms.tv

The main purpose of the site is to entertain and to inspire budding filmmakers. Anyone can submit, and they ask you to sign a licence agreement if they select your film for one of their channels (they have the Short Film Channel; Bang Festival (non-competitive) and Bang International).

www.minimovies.com

This is a video download site whereby you submit a film. Users pay to downloaded films to view on their computer or iPod and the filmmaker gets USD$1 per download.

www.atomfilms.com

Atom Films is one of the largest internet short film websites. You submit your film for selection and if it is picked up, they will pay an advance and then a share of the advertising revenue pool – the more your film is viewed, the more revenue you receive. It is advisable to have a good look at their site before submitting a film. They have a certain style of film that works well for their audiences and although the selection is diverse, the slant is more towards funny, youth oriented films.

www.lovefilm.co.uk
This is the UK's online DVD rental company and short films can be viewed for free on their site, though they are also testing the market by making some award-winning shorts available for a small fee.

www.myspace.com
The famous site is now doing for film what they have long done for music: encouraging people to use the network to share art and ideas. Filmmakers upload short films; viewers find quality work via other user recommendations and networks. Shooters also curates short films for the site and provides weekly indie film news.

www.pawky.com
US-based site where users can upload their films and join the pawky community of film fans. Films are vetted before they go live and hence they tend to be of a better standard than most user-upload site.

www.nano-tv.com
America's first short film channel, offering continuously updated content featuring talent both fresh and familiar.

www.itunes.com
The renowned music download site has moved into the world of film. You can buy feature films to download, but they also offer shorts as free downloads. The deals have been done via sales agents rather than directly with filmmakers.

www.shootingpeple.org
Shooting People are launching a new online film channel that allows members to upload films they have made and worked on, and also watch the work of other members (a great resource for filmmakers looking for collaborators, crew or cast).

When uploading or submitting a film to an online site, be it for streaming or download, it is essential to carefully read the terms and conditions to which you are agreeing. Make sure you understand what the site is asking of you. (Are all the clearances in place because you may be legally responsible if not? What you are giving to the site – do they have the right to sell the film on to a third party? Can you decide later to take your film off their site?) Even though you are probably only ticking a box with some of these sites, this is in effect a contract, so read it carefully.

✳ Revver's Steven Starr is interviewed on page 207

The point is to get it seen
Although all of this may seem quite daunting, it is worth considering the amount of time you put into writing, raising finance, directing, producing and editing your film. If it does not get shown you will feel cheated. Take some time to get to know what your opportunities and avenues are for sales. The market for shorts is rapidly changing, but with internet access it's easier to keep abreast of advances and opportunities. Your film has the potential to be screened all over the world particularly at festivals or on the internet. If you can get a sales agent on board but understand their role and what they expect of you. Finally you have a worldwide audience available to you so put as much energy into marketing your film that you undoubtedly will have put into getting it made.

Distribution Profile:
The Mobile Cinema

www.shootingpeople.org/mobilecinema

Every year Shooting People puts together a tour of the best short films made by our members in our very own Mobile Cinema.

For two weeks each year, we send 'Shooter' filmmakers, the Blaine Brothers, out into the wilds of the UK armed with only:

> a projector;

> a map;

> a mobile phone and a laptop;

> a portable DVD player;

> a DVD collection of fantastic shorts from Shooting People members; and

> a friend called Adam who owns BETTY THE VAN.

The guys drive across the UK publishing BETTY THE VAN's latest location and a number to call on a daily Mobile Cinema blog. Any member of the public wanting to host a screening then rings and the team head off to screen the films wherever they are called: town halls, bars, football training grounds, people's living rooms, and on one memorable occasion, they successfully gate-crashed a cinema multiplex.

Their wry observations describing the hard sweat and joyous tears of Mobile Cinema are published daily on the blog (including a 12hr trip to the Shetland Islands one year and a 14hr wait after they missed the first boat…). Mobile Cinema is now preparing for its next juggernaut, an on-road adventure all the way from NY to LA.

Have Cinema. Will Travel

Producer Luke Morris,
on Getting your short film seen and Cinema 16

www.cinema16.co.uk

Can you give us the distribution highlights for each of your short films thus far?

Our first film, *Je t'aime John Wayne,* premiered at TCM Classic Shorts competition, it won there and then played in Berlin, Cannes, was BAFTA nominated and finally won the European Film Award. We also sold it to French Connection who turned it into a one-minute cinema advert. That was just lucky – it happened to fit into the campaign they were doing at the time.

Luke Morris has been both a short film buyer *and* a seller. As a producer and latterly a co-director, he worked with director Toby MacDonald on three multi-award winning short comedies: *Je t'aime John Wayne* (2000); *Mexicano* (2002) and *Heavy Metal Drummer* (2005). He is also the producer of the hugely successful DVD series **Cinema 16**, which includes short films from established names in cinema – Alexander Payne, Mike Leigh, Todd Solondz, Lukas Moodysson – alongside strong new emerging directors. Here, we ask him to share some of his distribution and exhibition experiences.

Mexicano was our second short – it also starred Kris Marshall - and it premiered in Directors' Fortnight in Cannes. In 2005 we made *Heavy Metal Drummer,* which premiered in Berlin then played at Clermont Ferrand. The print is very well travelled – London, Bristol, Sweden, Rio, Sydney, Austin and LA, to name a few recent destinations. There were also different opportunities for this one because it's a music film. It played at Coachella, which is California's Glastonbury, on a huge outdoor screen between bands. I liked the idea of it screening to a music crowd.

With *Je t'aime John Wayne* also approached Metrodome [UK distributor] to release our film with Lukas Moodysson's feature *Together.* I'd seen it at a market, loved it, and just thought it was a good match. We said to them we'd do some promotion and try to get another few hundred people into the film: friends, family and friends of friends. An organisation called Short Circuit paid for about 20 prints. Metrodome knew of our short, liked it, and were really supportive.

Is it harder now for filmmakers to do this theatrically?

I think you have to approach the right distributor with the right film at the right time because, ultimately, it costs them money, and so there has to be a real advantage to them doing it. It's going to be near impossible with a studio film playing any multiplexes because the advertising time is so tied up, and frankly speaking, they're just not going to care. But there are movie chains like City Screen in the UK, for instance, which are more interested in film culture and can see a value in that kind of thing. For it to be viable I think the film would need to have some profile, some awards behind it, or some kind of hook, for the distributor to even be interested and it would almost certainly have to be an independent distributor, working with an exhibitor like City Screen.

What about TV sales? Is it difficult to sell a short film to TV in the UK now?

The only company who has every really bought shorts in the UK is Channel 4 and they don't seem to be doing it much any more, as far as I can tell. They used to have Shooting Gallery, a late night slot for shorts, where they would regularly buy films, albeit for a tiny fee. It's a shame; it's very different to France where they really recognise the importance of short films, not just in terms of production but also distribution. The French TV channels are obliged by the government to pay healthy sums for local short films now. We sold *Heavy Metal Drummer* to Canal + and got a couple of thousand euro. If it had been a French short they would have been obliged to pay around €10,000. They recognise the value of short films in France, and really support them.

Based on your experience, what does TV pay?

They tend to pay by minute so the longer your film, the more you might get. Then it varies form territory to territory - you might get a few hundred euro in Finland or a couple of thousand in Europe for a 5 or 10 minute film. Of course, there are exceptions. Generally they acquire the rights for two or three years.

Did getting nominated for the BAFTA for *Je t'aime John Wayne* make a major difference to your distribution prospects?

Festivals and awards ceremonies are the great for getting industry attention. When there are thousands of short films made each year, people just don't have time to watch them all and festivals and awards can act as a filtering process; the best stuff is meant to rise to the top. Awards make life easier for TV buyers and development people. But that's not to say awards always get it right.

Do you think it's important to have an exhibition strategy for your film, or should you just screen your film anywhere you can?

When you are talking about a short film, I think you need to be aware of what possibilities are out there. If you are trying to convince funders to back you, it's good to be seen to know how it works and where your film will find an audience. But in terms of 'strategy'... well, the exhibition possibilities for any short are limited to the few platforms that show them.

In reality, you are much better off spending your energy in having a good idea and executing it well because ultimately there is no point having a strategy for a film that doesn't work. More often than not you're just trying to get your film shown wherever you can – though of course you want to know which the best festivals and what distribution opportunities exist. It's only when you have a film that's doing really well that you are in the lucky position of being able to choose where you're film plays.

> **"If you are trying to convince funders to back you, it's good to be seen to know how it works and where your film will find an audience"**

Do you sell the films yourself, or do you have a sales agent?

I've never had a sales agent. We were approached but didn't want to do it. Because *Je t'aime John Wayne* was doing so well, the buyers came to us, and I think that's generally true of films where you have awards success early on.

Having said that, trying to market your film to short film buyers yourself, as a filmmaker or producer, is usually a waste of time unless your film is winning major awards. They attend the festivals, they watch the films, and talk to each other; it tends to be the same few films which get picked up. They don't pay too much attention to lobbying from filmmakers themselves. Sales agents do have the attention of the buyers and do screen films for them.

If you sell your own short, you have to have the time to deal with delivery and have a basic understanding of contracts and licences. When I was making these shorts, I was also working in the film industry – as a Producers Assistant and then at the UK Film Council as a Production and Acquisitions Assistant in the

Premiere Fund - so I understood how these things worked. But if you're a first time filmmaker with no experience, you do need to get someone on board, be that a lawyer to give you advice or a sales agent. Servicing sales can be a time consuming business too.

Another benefit of having a sales agent is that they often sell films in packages by theme as well, so you may be better off than you would be as a stand-alone film.

If you are selling your own film yourself, ultimately you have to be aware that it is a buyers' market and there is not much room for negotiation.

> "If you are selling your own film yourself, ultimately you have to be aware that it is a buyers' market"

Are there other commercial possibilities for short films like online sales?

The big problem for people making shorts in terms of recouping revenue for them is the fact that people are now used to getting short films for free. The problem with online is that there are going to be *even* more films available for nothing. Look at BBC Film Network or Channel 4 website, which are all free. Many companies also use short films as a way to pull people in to get them used to the technology and ready to purchase feature films. Free sites devalue the short film commercially, but I am not sure it's going to change radically because filmmakers are hungrier for their film to be seen than these sites are to acquire them.

When you are making a short, you need to be realistic about whether there is any commercial value you on it... are people willing to pay for short films? Of course, people don't make short films to make money, but I do think it's important to be aware of just how limited the opportunities are to recoup the money you've spent making your film. If you are asking people for cash – especially friends and family – you will probably want to be honest with them about what the potential commercial opportunities are.

Do you have any contract tips for filmmakers?

The big problem is that you aren't in a position to negotiate unless there is competition for your film. You want to look at the commission rates obviously, and also consider whether exclusivity is absolutely necessary. Sometimes, it is necessary for a distributor or a sales agent because they can't do their job without it. Also, check that the TV stations aren't asking for digital and online rights. Often they'll try and add these into the contract for no extra money when they have no plan about how to exploit them.

Essentially you just need to make sure that both parties have a contract that they are happy with.

Can you give us a little background on the Cinema 16 series?

I started it for two reasons. On the one hand, it was about giving people access to shorts. I had just made *Je t'aime John Wayne* with Toby [MacDonald] and neither of us went to film school. We learned by watching other people's films but discovered that accessing them was really hard to do. At the time they were just hard to find. The only places you could see them were at festivals and occasionally on late night TV.

I thought there were other people like me who wanted to see these films and that the films deserved to be seen.

The other imperative was releasing *Je t'aime John Wayne* and giving it a life. The festival circuit lasts about a year and once that was done people were still asking about seeing the film, but we couldn't direct them anywhere. Releasing the film in the context of Cinema16 was a way to keep it alive.

The basic idea was to have a high quality threshold and have a good combination of early films from big directors, which can be a great source of inspiration, alongside award winning film from new filmmakers. When I put the first Cinema16 together I think there was a perception that there wasn't an appetite for short films and people wouldn't be willing to pay for them but I felt that wasn't the case, and that they just hadn't been put together in the right way yet.

Do you have a sense of who the audience is for the DVD?

I think you have to be honest and say that the main audience for shorts are filmmakers, aspiring filmmakers, people who are interested in the moving image and movie buffs. Although some shorts have broken out into the mainstream – like *George Lucas in Love* and *Terry Tate*, they tend to be exceptions. The short film world, in the traditional sense, is quite an internal thing. That's probably because you have to look for them, and they don't come looking for you.

Are you doing any VoD sales for the Cinema 16 series yet? Or do you have plans to?

Because Cinema16 is working well on DVD the question on when and if to go online needs some thought.

But one thing I think we are still seeing is that filmmakers and rights holders are still suspicious of, or nervous about digital - how it is controlled and accounted. It's true that if you have a library of short films then you are going to feel differently to someone who has just made one valuable film who might be more protective of that film.

Obviously attitudes to VoD will have to change in the same way that they did for the music industry. These are certainly interesting times in terms of digital conversion with the film business. On a bigger level, you only have to look at iTunes and what's going on with the studios to see there is still a resistance there.

Do yourself a favour: what not to do when submitting your film to a festival

We've spoken with lots of programmers in the course of researching this book, and have come up with a list of big 'no-no's, which they seem to mention again and again when asked to give filmmakers submission advice.

DON'T:

> Submit too much flashy supporting material. Keep it clean, simple and professional. Overly expensive press kits or EPKs seem to set off warning bells with most programmers who feel the film should do the talking.

> Miss the deadline. This is important. These are set because festivals have tight publication deadlines to meet and most won't accept submissions which are even a day late.

> Badger the Festival to find out if you are in. Yes, you want to know, but so do the other 578 filmmakers who sent in a short film. Many festivals now offer submission deadlines that give information about when you might expect to have heard. If they don't, it might be worth just sitting tight, unless you have a conflicting offer from another festival, that is.

> Argue with the programmers if you are not invited. Of course, you are within your rights to ask why your film was not accepted, but be aware that many bigger fests get thousands of short film submissions. Since they can't possibly offer this info to all filmmakers, they might make it a policy not to give feedback at all. However, if they do give you feedback, stay respectful and professional at all times. You aren't going to change their mind by arguing what a stupid mistake they've made in depriving audiences of the chance to see your film. They remember filmmakers who are rude and it can make a difference next time you submit a film.

Digital Screen Network

Will the Digital Screen Network help get short films on the big screen?

The UK Film Council is in the process of rolling out a programme which optimists hope will have a positive impact on the long-term future of short film screenings in UK cinemas. Outside of London and the bigger UK cities, seeing a wide variety of work on the big screen is difficult (if not impossible in smaller towns). The Digital Screen Network (DSN) is the cornerstone of the UKFC's strategy for addressing this problem and getting specialised (or non-mainstream) film into cinemas.

The theory is that the lack of variety and non-mainstream fare is in part due to the high costs of making and transporting 35mm prints, so if delivery costs can be lowered, distributors and exhibitors will be willing to take more risks.

Being able to deliver your short film to a wide range of cinemas on a digital format will certainly make it cheaper and easier for filmmakers. But will more freedom to take risks mean *exhibitors* are more committed to short films?

How the DSN works

The Network is a 'virtual network' of 240 screens, which are located in approximately 200 cinemas.

In return for the UKFC's financial contribution which will allow cinemas to install expensive digital projection equipment, network cinemas will devote a set percentage of playing time to specialised programming.

The UKFC will also contract each cinema for a certain number of programming slots which will be booked centrally by UKFC sources. These additional slots are likely to consist of educationally orientated content, archive material, and potentially, short films.

One of the key advantages of digital projection equipment is that prints can be delivered on much cheaper formats, and in the future, perhaps delivered digitally to cinemas for one-off screenings. Short films, which can be downloaded quickly, may be the first to benefit from digital delivery if and when it becomes a reality.

What the critics say

Critics argue that the UKFC's definition of 'specialised' film is too vague and that films which are already commercially viable under the old system – *Fahrenheit 911*, *Sideways*, *Eternal Sunshine of the Spotless Mind* – are what the more commercial cinemas in the Network (the big multiplex chains which make up a significant part of the Network) will choose to play to satisfy their commitment to the programme.

There is also no specific mention of short films in their definition of 'specialised', which seems a missed opportunity. This means that it's likely that only the cinemas which already have a commitment to cinema culture and to making short film exhibition part of that culture, will continue to screen them – but the good news is that this programme might just make it easier for them to pursue this strategy.

How you can help short films realise big screen potential?

It's important then that when short films screen in cinemas that we go and see them! They'll never become viable public exhibition formats unless there is a market for them, and filmmakers are generally a guilty bunch when it comes to this. We moan about our films not getting into cinemas, but truth be told, we rarely go and see others when they are screening. We have to make it clear that there is a small but dedicated audience who wants to see short films play in their favourite cinemas. If we do that, then who knows – we may be looking at getting back to the 'good old' days, when shorts regularly screened at the movies.

The Interviews

Short film distributors and exhibitors tend to see hundreds of short films a year, and they are also best placed to understand how the short film industry is developing and changing.

With this in mind, on the following pages you'll find interviews with people who buy, sell and programme short films for some of the top web and TV outlets, sales agents, DVD producers and festivals in Europe and the US - from Sundance Film Festival and Current TV, to Shorts International, Aspen Shortsfest and Cinema 16. Through these interviews, we hope to give you insight into how short film exhibition currently works, and a glimpse of where it's heading in the next few years.

Short films in UK cinemas
Catharine Des Forges

www.independentcinemaoffice.org.uk

What is the ICO?

The ICO is the national support organisation for independent cinema in the UK. We aim to support and develop audiences for a diverse range of world cinema. Our main activities are film programming and advice, film bookings, touring programmes, artists' moving image development, training and consultancy.

How often do you programme short films into your cinemas?

We do a number of touring programmes to cinemas around the UK which include short films - for example, a package of Encounters Short Film Festival highlights and the aMovies artists' commissions.

Can you still get a short film screened in the cinemas? Outside of festival contexts, it's a difficult proposition. Yet there are ways, and the UK's Independent Cinema Office (ICO) is facilitating some of these screenings. Here, we talk to **Catharine Des Forges** who is the Director of the **ICO**, and who produced short film *Seafood* with Writer/Director Robin Baker.

What kind of deal might a short filmmaker expect for a cinema screening? Is there a standard fee? Who pays for print or tape transport?

It really depends on whether you have a sales agent or not. If you do, then you would expect a fee for a screening as they would negotiate this on your behalf and not allow anyone to screen the film if they don't pay for it. However many cinemas won't expect to pay a fee to show a short and if they are asked for one, they won't pay it and the film won't get shown. Rare exceptions might be if your film is an Oscar© or Bafta winner which might really be in demand; people have been known to charge £40 a screening. Normally if an agent/distributor is involved the fee would be much more likely to be around £15. Print/tape transport is up for negotiation but obviously having your short screened with a feature for two weeks, for example, is a fantastic opportunity and the cinema may expect you to cover costs.

Why do cinemas not show more short films?

Many cinemas have quite restrictive deals with their advertising contracts, which means that they have to show a set reel of ads, which will take up time. In addition, they have to show trailers and the more shows of a film they put on in a day the more revenue they will make. If a short is longer than 5 minutes it can impact heavily on this by adding to screening time, affecting show times, number of performances, staff shift patterns and therefore revenue. Playing shorts does not bring in additional income even though it's nice to do. Showing shorts programmes does happen but again, co-ordinating them is time-consuming and as most of them do not have regular distributors, arranging transport and screenings uses valuable resources. Many cinemas would like to show more shorts but simply don't have the resources or time to do so. In commercial cinemas, it would require either different projection equipment or else for a short to be attached to a print and then broken down afterwards – again, time-consuming and something which has no income stream attached. Another reason why cinemas might not show shorts is that they are not often certificated [by the British Board of Film Classification]. There are costs involved in certification and many commercial cinemas won't show uncertificated films.

> **"Many cinemas would like to show more shorts but simply don't have the resources or time to do so"**

Are there practical things a filmmaker can do to help maximise their chances of having a film exhibited?

Think about the audience, make sure you have at least one decent still, a line of sellable copy and either DVD/VHS copies of it. Also really consider the length of your film; if it's too long it will really restrict your exhibition opportunities.

As a filmmaker yourself, what is the biggest lesson you learned on your first short film?

Trust your instincts and the more films you watch, the better filmmaker you will be.

Short films at a major film festival, SXSW
Matt Dentler

www.sxsw.com

Can you tell us a little bit about short film programming at SXSW?

We typically programme around 80 short films every year. For the most part, we select our short films through filmmaker submissions. This probably accounts for over 3/4 of the shorts we end up having at the festival.

Ideally, we want a short film to be *short*. That may be an obvious idea, but increasingly filmmakers feel they can make a short as long as they want. We don't gravitate towards shorts that are features-in-the-making. We want to give priority to films that exist just as they are, and with shorts, that means a short-length story that doesn't drag too long or doesn't end too abruptly.

South by Southwest (SXSW) is a nine-day film conference and festival that takes place every March in Austin, Texas. In its 14 years, SXSW has become one of the US fest circuit's best places to meet other filmmakers and for some friendly networking with the global film industry. Ingrid Kopp talks to **Matt Dentler**, SXSW's Festival Producer.

How is technology changing the short film market, and what you do at SXSW?

I think it's fantastic that technology is opening up avenues for short screening. It makes the landscape much more exciting and much more accessible. In terms of how these new advances effect festival programming, I'd say that exclusivity is still something we wish for. In other words, we're more inclined to programme a short at the festival if we feel it hasn't already played the rounds too much, whether that be at other festivals or online. We want to get an early crack at short films at the festival, so we're discouraged if a film has already found a strong web life. My suggestion to filmmakers on this would be, play festivals first and then go for the web.

What advice would you give to a filmmaker making their first short? What are your 'Do's and Don'ts'?

First and foremost, keep it short. And, just when you think it's as short as it can be... make it shorter. Often, filmmakers forget that a short film will' likely screen in a programme, which means you don't want to stand out as the one film that is too long. You want to get in and get out, that's the beauty of short films. Plus, I would start small, use digital video and a basic story. It doesn't make sense to make your first short be a 30-minute period piece epic. Do something small, and build from there. Good things should follow.

What exhibition advice do you have for short filmmakers?

I think filmmakers should just submit to festivals and accept any and all invitations. Play the hell out of it.

> "I would start small, use digital video and a basic story. It doesn't make sense to make your first short be a 30-minute period piece epic".

Short films at a major film festival, Sundance
Trevor Groth

www.sundance.org

Can you tell us a little bit about short film programming at Sundance? How many shorts do you show?

Sundance shows around 80 short films at the festival. We have both an American and an International competition. The films are programmed in shorts programmes as well as in front of features. They are selected from our submissions, of which we receive around 4,400 each year. There are four short film programmers that watch everything and narrow the field down to about 300, which I watch and then we collectively decide which ones to programme.

Shooting People's Ingrid Kopp talks to **Trevor Groth** about short film programming at **Sundance Film Festival**.

Which Festivals are best for short film viewing?

Hands down the best short film festival in the world is Clermont Ferrand. They do an incredible job in every way of generating interest in and support for short films. They have terrific venues that are filled with enthusiastic audiences. As part of their market, they have an unbelievable database of not only every film in the festival, but every film submitted to them. It is truly a world-class festival.

Another great shorts festival is the Aspen Shorts Fest in the Colorado. They do a terrific job with the programming and they have a great reputation for treating their filmmakers well. Everyone that attends has a fantastic time.

What are you looking for when you select a short for Sundance?

Sundance is primarily a discovery festival, so we are primarily looking for new voices and talents. We place an emphasis on originality rather than polish. A film that displays a unique vision with rough edges is much more interesting to us than a slick film that is reminiscent of something that we have seen before.

Do you think new distribution technologies like VOD and video sharing websites are changing short film markets?

Yes, I do believe there is an ever-changing landscape for short film distribution. A few years ago it seemed like the internet was going to revolutionise the short film world, but people couldn't quite figure out what the revenue model would be. The same thing seems to be happening with cell phones and iPods right now. Everyone is clamouring over short form content but nobody knows how to profit from it yet. I am all for any technology that spreads awareness for short films.

Why do cinemas not program more short films?

Cinemas haven't figured out how they benefit from doing it financially. The cost to benefit ratio doesn't make sense to them but hopefully the new wave of digital projectors will allow cinemas to cost effectively start to take more chances on what they program. Whether it's independent features not coming from a distributor or short films in front of features, I do think it can happen.

"Don't be afraid to edit your film down to what is truly essential".

What advice would you give to a filmmaker making their first short?

Stay true to your vision and know why you are doing it. Too many people make films for the wrong reasons. It should be coming from a place of passion rather than it seems like a fun/cool thing to do. Also, don't be afraid to edit your film down to what is truly essential. Short films don't have the structure that features do and don't need excess to pack a punch. In fact, their impact can be lessened with too much fat. With short films, less is more.

Why are short films important?

Shorts films are as important as feature films. They have been around longer and play an important role in not only developing talent but also in providing filmmakers with alternatives to express their visions.

Short film festivals, Aspen Shortsfest
Laura Thielen

www.aspenfilm.org

Aspen Shortsfest is widely regarded as one of the best short film exhibition platforms in the world, and also one of the most filmmaker friendly places to screen your work. Ingrid Kopp chats with **Laura Thielen**, Executive Director of Aspen Film, who run the Festival.

How is Aspen Shortfest unique in comparison to other fests?

It is distinguished by being truly international and embracing all film genres. It's for both filmmakers *and* audiences – it's a forum where the two can interact and encouraging this interaction is very important to us. Aspen appeals to audiences of all ages. We offer lots of school programmes and take filmmakers into the school – the filmmakers say they get a lot out of this.

We're currently in our 16th year of the Shortfest but shorts have been part of the organisation's history for 30 years. Audiences are 60% local. We show 50-60 shorts each year. We mix genres in every programme – taking people on a cinematic journey, try-ing to introduce audiences to the wonderful experience of short filmmaking.

How do you find your shorts? Other festivals? Films online?

We do an open call for entries. We also rely heavily on recom-mendations and our own research. There is some talent online but if you're looking for pure cinema and great storytelling then it can be hard to find good films on the internet. It's also hard to watch films on a small screen but it's in its initial phase right now and it has potential.

What do you look for in a short? What are your do's and don'ts?

Don't make a film for a festival, make it for yourself. Don't rush a film to make a festival deadline. If a film is worthy, it will find its place in the sun. Some shorts are too long. Get feedback from someone you trust (who isn't too close to you or the film). Get feedback at the script stage and the edit stage but don't do it by committee as this causes confusion.

Aspen has achieved a reputation as a short fest with real industry presence. How have you achieved this?

We provide travel stipends to our filmmakers and honour them as artists so we are respected by filmmakers. The festival also *only* shows shorts – filmmakers don't feel like they're competing with the big guns of features. Creative partnerships start to evolve as a result. It's also an Oscar® qualifying festival. Most of the shorts are in competition but we also have sidebar programmes that are not in competition (retrospectives and family programmes). And finally, established filmmakers sit on our panels and juries and are really inspired by the work they are seeing (e.g. Alexander Payne). Many of them come back year after year because they love the experience and find it so inspiring.

"Don't rush a film to make a festival deadline. If a film is worthy, it will find its place in the sun".

Short film festivals, London Short Film Festival presented by Halloween

Philip Ilson

www.shortfilms.org.uk

Halloween has been working with and promoting short films for many years. For the newcomer, can you give us a little potted history of your work leading up to HSFF?

I started Halloween Society (as it was then) with a school friend Tim Harding in 1994 after we'd attended and screened one of our low budget short films at Exploding Cinema. This bar-cum-live event screening was inspirational as a concept, particularly as there was nothing else happening like this at the time. By late 1994 we'd moved to the 300 capacity 1940's ballroom Notre Dame Hall off Leicester Square and introduced cabaret acts, live music, and visuals to create a spectacular monthly multi-media night which caught the public mood throughout the late 90's.

Since then Halloween has gone through many incarnations, from bringing in a more late 90's club culture vibe and adding name DJs and VJs, which got us picked up by the British Council to become our 'Sensurround' world touring club event. Halloween also held regular feature film and music nights called Full Length at the ICA as well as one-off short film screenings.

London Short Film Festival (aka. **Halloween Short Film Festival**) Director **Philip Ilson** has been curating and screening short films in the UK under the Halloween brand at high profile and well loved events since the early 90s. Who better to ask for a little history on the UK's short film exhibition scene and for his take on short film event and festival screenings?

To sum up, the thing that has held it all together these last 12 years has been the continual influx of short films. With or without the media frenzy for short film at various times through the years, it's a genre that will never go away, which is why we decided to concentrate on an annual Short Film Festival. It's about bringing together our celebration of short film into one time and place alongside the Halloween multi-media brand and ethos, rather than spreading things out through the year.

How has short film exhibition in the UK changed since you started programming short films at Halloween events?

Vastly. Exploding Cinema was pretty much the only outlet in the mid 90's for the growing number of UK filmmakers. Film festivals like London were more 'exclusive' for certain kinds of international short film, so many filmmakers wouldn't even consider entering such a festival. Other film groups came through at this time, such as *Omsk* and *My Eyes My Eyes*, culminating in the *Volcano Underground Film Festival* in 1996. Also, about this time, the web was being used more to showcase shorts, although this outlet didn't yet have the technical specifications to make it a viable option, and many short film sites collapsed.

But as the underground and more alternative short film clubs faded at the turn of the millennium, a new breed of more industry-led organisations sprung up. Futureshorts have aligned themselves with the Soho film industry, getting sponsorship from facilities houses and holding monthly screenings in arthouse cinemas across the UK, and Leapfrog Entertainment moved from Soho industry showcases to their Bitesize Cinema initiative to get short films into multiplexes. Also, DVD has become a viable outlet for shorts in the way VHS wasn't; Warp Films had record-breaking success with their single cheap releases of Chris Cunningham and Chris Morris shorts. onedotzero digital film festival DVDs, the Cinema 16 compilations of shorts by famous directors, the Directors Series of music video filmmakers, and the Shooting People Best v Best compilations of award winning shorts have all brought short films to a wider public in the UK.

"A lot of programming literally comes down to personal taste"

OK, so more about Halloween and programming. What qualities do you look for when you select a short film for the festival?

This is an unanswerable question! A lot of programming literally comes down to personal taste. We do theme our programmes in Halloween (from comedies to horror to experimental to romance etc.), and within these themes we may have drama, animation, documentary, or experimental, so there are no hard and fast rules. We also look for more low budget work that may not get a chance to be seen, specifically for a low budget programme, and last year we introduced a music documentary strand.

You are also one of the programmers for the London Film Festival. Are your selection priorities any different when you select films for that Festival, than they are for HSFF?

Very much so. Firstly, there's far more work to watch and with only a limited number of shorts programmes within the LFF, far less space to programme. With Halloween, if we like a film, we accept it, where as with London, once I'd formulated my programming ideas, even if I saw a fantastic film, if it didn't fit the theme, it might get rejected or I'd pass it on to the other shorts programmer to view for his programmes. Having said this, I tried to make my LFF themes as abstract as possible, so it wasn't restricted to just looking for horror films or romances etc, but within my chosen themes I could have a varied subject matter of shorts.

Are there benefits to screening in a dedicated short film festival, rather than in a sidebar of a general film festival?

This isn't an easy question to answer. A festival as high profile as London or Edinburgh is great for a filmmaker to have on their CV. And to be honest, the screenings of shorts at these festivals do bring in good audiences. Also, other filmmakers will get a chance to see what else is out there in the world. Plus these Festivals have lots of high profile press and thousands of free brochures to give out, so they're hitting a lot of people in their respected cities. The downside is that the vast size of such a Festival means it may have lost the personal friendly face [for the short filmmaker]. Short films are also often seen by some as a less important sidebar, so networking opportunities may not be as forthcoming as at a smaller short film festival. Certainly in the UK, Encounters Festival in Bristol is the most important *short* film festival, with much industry support, and being located in both the smaller city and in one dedicated venue, the chances for networking is far greater. There's also Kino Short Film Festival in Manchester, and in London we try to create the friendly festival vibe with Halloween.

Are there common pitfalls that you see in short films? Things for a filmmaker to avoid?

I'm not a big fan of 'showcase shorts'; having said this, there is some successful work out there that I would put into this category. Film schools are good examples of where it can be more about technical ability than creating meaningful and lasting

work, but I wouldn't say that I avoid graduation screenings as there are always gems and great films within these programmes. I don't know what a filmmaker should avoid, but I would say that whatever you try to make, be truthful. Like any great work of art, it has to come from the heart and for you to believe in it. If you feel your 10-minute short needs an 8-minute tracking shot of someone walking, then put it in. But don't succumb to making things that you feel people want to see.

Do you think the ready availability of short films on the internet is making audiences more reluctant to go to the cinema and to festivals to see them?

This argument is being used for cinema in general. There are always scare stories about audiences dwindling and the death of cinema, particularly with the rise in home cinema entertainments and the web and other alternative forms of viewing film. But nothing beats the collective experience of cinema viewing and hopefully this is the same with Festivals and shorts screenings.

For the filmmaker, what are some of the benefits of having your film screening in a cinema, that new platforms don't offer?

It's giving that collective and immediate experience as you gauge an audience's reaction to your film. You can of course do this on the web with comments and postings, but that loses the immediacy of a live situation; it's a bit like seeing a live band compared to listening to a CD.

Shooting People Films
Penny Nagle

www.shootingpeoplefilms.com
www.bestvbest.com

Shooting People Films is a distribution label set up by filmmakers and for filmmakers, and to explore different models of distribution. Head of Shooting People Films **Penny Nagle** talks about some of the label's short film exhibition and production initiatives.

Shooting People Films started out by releasing Best v Best, a collection of short films on DVD. Can you talk a little bit about this project? Why shorts?

When we first started Shooting People Films as a film distribution label we had little idea that it would develop in the way that it has. Our first release was Best v Best - a lovely collection of award-winning short films from around the globe. It was aimed specifically at people like us - filmmakers who wanted to know who and what was winning at different festivals (for example, a Cannes winner has a very different feel to say, a Sundance winner). There wasn't, and still isn't, anywhere else where filmmakers could see these films together (or even see them at all in many cases!). Most of them play festivals and then disappear. We also thought it would make a great sampler for talent spotters in the industry – producers, funders, other filmmakers who want to check out what the next generation of filmmakers are getting up to.

Little Terrorist
by Ashvin Kumar
(Best v Best Vol One)

It's funny because we were told by numerous physical film distributors (literally the guys who drive the vans to HMV and Virgin) that nobody would buy a collection of short films. Rubbish! We would, if they were good and produced well. It's always been important to us as a distribution label to come up with a fair deal for the filmmakers who have their films on the collection. We're proud of the fact that filmmakers from the first have already seen excellent returns thus far. We're now on our second volume, which has more films and an overall analysis of the short film market from Tricia Tuttle, our DVD producer. She commented that many of films on the collection are exploring serious themes of life, death and conflict, which is interesting given the current political climate and clash of civilisations epitomised in Iraq. *Volume Three* promises to be even bigger and better.

Shooting People Films will continue to release shorts and

The Day I Died
by Maryam Keshavarz
(Best v Best Vol Two)

feature films in cinemas, on DVD and online – but we are also expanding our repertoire to recognise that people's viewing habits are changing with the advent of Youtube, MySpace and Current TV. Shooting People is working on our own Channel too, which should be up and running soon. We have several very interesting partnerships developing which will have an impact on short film distribution and, we hope, on production too. Watch this space.

You have *already* been getting involved at the front end of the production process. Can you talk about your short film competitions?

As a distribution outfit Shooting People Films has had to stay one step ahead of the current film distribution game. For example, with the advent of Peer to Peer networks, podcasting, and video on demand, it has become increasingly important to make film available online. User generated content is a buzz phrase thrown around like digital confetti, yet it has not been fully cracked - until now, we hope. We ran two short film competitions for the Shooting People community, and the wider public - appealing to very different sensibilities. The first, *Destricted*, was a promotional idea to mark the release of the DVD *Destricted* which brings together sex and art in a series of short films created by some of the world's most visual and provocative artists and filmmakers including Larry Clark, Gaspar Noé, Sam Taylor-Wood and Matthew Barney.

The collection of shorts highlighted controversial issues around the representation of sexuality in art, and shooter filmmakers (and others) were invited to upload their own shorts to extend the debate around whether art can be disguised as pornography, or whether pornography can be represented as art, or something else altogether.

We were blown away by the quality of the entries, which were then screened at the ICA. It's fascinating how more spontaneous film challenges like this tend to bring out so much creativity.

The second competition was very different; it was a short film/video competition for Robbie Williams. In this, there were two awards, one from the audience, and one from the Jury (which included Lord Puttnam, Jonathan Ross, Robbie Williams, and commissioners from Channel 4 and EMI). The cash prizes meant that our Technical Director Stu had a constant battle with hackers trying to skew the votes - he developed his own 'weapons of mass detection' and we feel that the results were as fair as possible for filmmakers. Again the standard was fantastic, and the winning entries were particularly superb.

Thanks to the success of this venture, we are now setting up monthly short film competitions for music artists, partnered with Channel 4, The Telegraph, and Edinburgh Film Festival.

Short films on DVD
Brent Hoff

www.wholphindvd.com

Wholphin is a quarterly DVD magazine containing short films, and created by Dave Eggers and Brent Hoff of McSweeney's publishing house. The first issue, published in December 2005 contained otherwise hard to view short films by Miguel Arteta (*The Good Girl*), Miranda July (*Me and You and Everyone We Know*) and Spike Jonze documentary on Al Gore. Shooting People's Ingrid Kopp talks to **Brent Hoff** about short films and his fabulous crazy idea for a DVD magazine.

Tell us about the idea, and why the name?

Wholphin is difficult to spell, impossible to pronounce, and utterly obscure. But does that make it a bad name for a publication? Yes. It is a bad name. But it is descriptively accurate for the types of films Wholphin strives to both make and release. A Wholphin is a recently discovered hybrid cross between a false killer whale and a bottlenose dolphin. It is real, amazing, and slightly disturbing when you try to visualize the moment of conception, and almost completely unknown. The same could be said for most, if not all of the films on Wholphin. When I first heard that dolphins sometimes mate with whales, I wanted to share that news with others. Likewise, when I see a Spike Jonze documentary about Al Gore that has never been released, I want to share it. Dave Eggers, the founder of McSweeney's and an old friend, and this idea just sort of evolved out of our discussions. We had each seen all these short films that were cinematic Wholphins and just we just sort of decided to go for it, hoping people would like them as much as we did.

What do you look for when you select a short film?

When we select, I look for intent. It's hard to explain beyond that, but I succumb to films that are the unabashed result of irrefutable intent. And squid. I like squid.

Do you think the short film market is changing with new distribution technologies like VoD and video sharing websites etc?

I watch films online all the time but prefer the better size and resolution DVDs offer currently. As that quickly changes with technology I'll easily move to VoD, and so will Wholphin.

As for the short film market, remember that end scene in *The Wiz* when everyone takes off their ugly chains and monster

"I seriously think we are about to enter a new golden age of cinema".

costumes and dances around in the rain? That's what's about to happen to the both the short and feature film industry. Once true VoD hits, filmmakers will be able to throw off the repressive time constraints imposed on them by the wicked, bloated traditional media outlet witches, and begin to let stories determine their own running times.

I seriously think we are about to enter a new golden age of cinema as this happens. The influence of marketing and advertising-based priorities on narrative structures long accepted by TV networks and studios are about to be obliterated by the obvious truth that each story has its own inherent perfect length. It will liberate storytelling and produce better films.

Do you think digital projectors will encourage cinemas to have more short film screenings?

I sort of doubt traditional theatres will be swayed, but I can see the proliferation of digital projectors leading to more micro-cinema-type screenings around the country, at book shops, bars, coffee shops, parks, homes and museums, etc. Like the rotating iPod-DJ clubs, except everyone can take turns showing their latest underground short finds.

What advice would you give to a filmmaker making their first short?

Same as for any artistic endeavour; You will make what you intend to make, so if you intend to make a calling card, you will likely end up with a functional calling card, but not necessarily a great film. Intend clearly.

'Don't' think for a minute that your film can't be ruined by a single misstep in writing. It can all crash down in a single awkward line or moment. 'Do' try and add a squid in here and there. Not as a main character necessarily, but just somewhere.

Why are short films important?

Short films are not important. But good films, of any length, that help us better see and understand the world and ourselves, are vital to humanity. As any anthropologist knows, cultures without art do not survive.

Short films on DVD, Short Film Central, Custom DVD
Andrew Goode

www.shortfilmcentral.com

What is Short Film Central?

The Short Film Central site features profiles for the most awarded short films of recent years, showing the events they screened at, the awards they won, and many other details about the films. The website is designed to allow filmmakers and event organisers to log in and update their own profiles at any time, so the rest of the filmmaking community always has the latest information. We also track the festivals and continually add new award-winning films to the database.

www.shortfilmcentral.com

Short Film Central's Andrew Goode talks to us about his system which allows short filmmakers and distributors to sell DVDs directly to their audience, and which allows audiences to custom-make a short film compilation.

For filmmakers, whether they have their own website or not, their film profile on Short Film Central is a mini-site displaying all the information which is of interest to their audience and others in the industry, including images, synopsis and film details, awards and screenings, credits, categories etc.

What is your "Make-Your-Own-Compilation-DVD" system?

We developed this system for the site and it allows film fans to purchase one or more short films on a custom-made DVD. They can simply add available films to a compilation list, add a custom title for the DVD, change the playback order, preview the cost, add it to their shopping cart and pay with PayPal. At our end, we build the DVD with custom menus containing the film information, print the custom label and insert, and send it off to the customer.

Why did you start the site?

In 2003, I finished making an animated short film called *Love Tricycle*, which went on to compete or screen at over 60 international film festivals. I spent a lot of my own money on the production, so I needed to make some back. I knew little about how the festival side of the film industry worked, and when I started seeking information on festivals, I found many lists on the internet were poorly updated. I eventually identified a list of highly-regarded festivals and focused on submitting to them, as well as a selection of smaller events. After the film started getting noticed, I hoped that it would bring some opportunities to recoup some money. We made a DVD of the film with extra 'making-of' materials, and made it available on the film's website. All we had to do then was attract people to the site. The web address was shown after the film's end credits, but disappointingly, it was seldom published on festival websites or printed catalogues.

The experience taught me to not expect much help from festivals in promoting a short film, other than exposing it to live audiences across the world. Such exposure is an important part of marketing a short film, but only by making direct contact with their audience can a filmmaker hope to cover their costs. So in 2005, we started developing Short Film Central with the goals of making the festival selection process quicker and easier for filmmakers, and to provide established and lesser-resourced filmmakers and distributors with a way to recoup money through DVD sales.

How international is your traffic?

The site has been visited by users in over 100 countries. Our registered users (filmmakers and festivals) are fairly evenly distributed across the world.

When you license short films for this service, how do you structure the deals? What might a filmmaker expect to receive each time their film is selected/sold?

Our agreement is non-exclusive, for DVD only at this stage, and can be terminated at any time by either party. A major benefit of our system is that film owners can set their own prices for their films at any time using forms on the website, so they can experiment with charging more for a popular film, or less for a lesser-known film. We do encourage keeping the price at a level where a full DVD of short films would cost about the same as a new feature film DVD, but we don't restrict the price. With films at the recommended price, about ¾ of the cost of a full DVD goes to the film owners, which we think is the best deal around. The film owner can also restrict sales by country if they only hold DVD rights in certain territories, and we have developed a unique copy-protection system to prevent the DVDs from being copied.

What are you looking for and how do filmmakers submit their work to you?

At this time, any short film is eligible to be listed on the website if it has won at least 1 award at a film festival. Film owners with a short film listed or eligible to be listed on the site can contact us through the website, and we'll send some information on our DVD system.

What qualities to do think make a short film creatively successful?

It could be argued that any short film that is actually finished on film or tape is creatively successful, but whether or not it's highly regarded by audiences is another thing entirely. For me personally, the most interesting short films to watch are those with a strong visual/design style - many of those are animated, or display great composition and cinematography. Many great short films make us think about things in a different way, surprise us, or make us laugh. But overall, I think a short film is successful if it holds the audience's interest for its duration and doesn't make them want to reach for the fast-forward button.

What are your future plans for Short Film Central?

We hope to attract more film owners to make their films available on our DVD system - sales benefit them and enable us to continue maintaining the site. We'd also like to make more short film audiences aware of the site as it's their demand for short films which encourages and allows filmmakers to make them. We would like to encourage film fans to support a system which sends their money directly to film owners rather than to exhibitors. Mostly we'd like to see a much wider global audience enjoying the great ideas and images which can only be presented in a short film format.

"Only by making direct contact with their audience can a filmmaker hope to cover their costs".

Short film world sales, Shorts International
Simon Young

www.shortsinternational.com

Can you tell us a little bit about the work that Shorts International do?

Shorts International is the world's biggest short film brand with a catalogue of over 3000 titles. It is the largest distributor of titles to broadcasters such as HBO, Canal+ and Sundance. We have focused in recent years on fast-changing technologies and their impact on the delivery of short form content. The model that the Shorts International team has created has facilitated a commercial life for many short films and given great exposure to many up and coming filmmakers not only through traditional media, but also through cutting edge new media platforms which we have succeeded in establishing ourselves, including SHORTS™ an official provider of short films to iTunes®, as well as SHORTSTV™ and SHORTSTV CORTO™, which are English and Spanish language short film channels made for 3G mobile delivery.

Simon Young, Short FIlm Programmer at **London Film Festival** and Head of Acquisitions at **Shorts International** talks about short film distribution and the changing nature of short film sales in the age of new technologies.

Tell us about the history of the company?

We originally traded as Britshorts Ltd, and the company was established by Carter Pilcher in 2000 as a UK-based internet platform for short films. As the business evolved, we started to focus more on traditional methods of short film distribution, with a keen eye on the technological developments that were changing traditional sales channels for shorts. We started to develop new ways of packaging short films to make them more accessible to these new channels and new audiences.

Our sales model involved businesses such as iTunes and mobile operators, and has allowed us to get short film talent out to a previously untapped market. We changed our name from Britshorts to Shorts International in 2004 as our business developed, our catalogue broadened and we opened 2 new bases in the US.

Where do you try to sell films?

Traditionally our main clients have been TV channels worldwide but particularly outside the UK (which offers virtually no support or (paying) airtime whatsoever to short films). In the last year though, we have launched a groundbreaking VoD deal - with Apple/iTunes in the USA.

Are all of your shorts available through iTunes, or just a small selection?

Only a relatively small selection at the moment - but we are adding to the titles available through our page by releasing new films every month. At present only iTunes in the USA is selling short films but this is expected to expand to other territories as soon as it is possible to do so. The potential for both income and unprecedented exposure to a new audience via a cutting-edge medium [handheld devices] is fantastic news for short filmmakers.

What about the Oscar iTunes downloads in 2006? How was Shorts International involved?

This was an unprecedented success both commercially and in terms of creating massive exposure for short films to a new audience. We set up the deal - between ourselves, the filmmakers, Apple, Magnolia (the US theatrical distributor & indie/ arthouse chain) and the Academy and the results have been fantastic for all involved and have even surpassed expectations.

How many short films are in your catalogue now, and where do you pick up new work?

Approximately 3000. We usually receive several DVD or VHS submissions at the office every day

"There are still far more short films made than there are outlets, so the standard of a commercially successful film is necessarily very high" and we attend the principal short film festivals and film markets throughout the UK, Europe and the USA to look for the best new content. We also work closely with international film schools such as the University of California, The American Film Institute and similar establishments in the UK.

So filmmakers can submit films to you directly?

Yes! Please go to our website www.shortsinternational.com, where you will find a submission form and all the info you need.

Is it easier than it used to be for short films to see distribution/exhibition revenue?

There are still far more short films made than there are outlets, so the standard of a commercially successful film is necessarily very high indeed. We are striving to create high-profile commercial platforms for short films that can provide a financially sustainable business model for all involved. Theatrical exhibition, even for most features, is not a great source of income and so this is not an area in which we specialise - although we do 2 or 3 screenings per year. But having said that, there are plenty of organisations out there who want to screen short films theatrically - they just won't pay filmmakers for doing so (usually).

What are the major growth areas in this sector?

Digital TV through the internet (TV on demand) is the future of home entertainment, or so I am led to believe!

In purely commercial terms, what types of films sell well? Which types don't?

Comedies with well known faces (in the US) are very popular, though Sean Ellis' *Cashback* (UK) has also done very well indeed. More artistic foreign language films have generally had less success - I guess we have to accept that we are catering to a mass market here. And the UK filmmakers' favourite - the downbeat short film about how tough it is to be an underprivileged child on a grim inner city council estate has been done to death. Positive stories and 'universal' comedies are definitely well received.

You also create podcasts for the short film industry and enthusiasts – such as a mini-doc on the Aspen Shortsfest, for example. Can you talk a little bit about why you do this and what your plans are in this area in the future?

We aim to produce a regular podcast to either highlight new releases on iTunes, or address areas of interest within the short film market place - such as film festivals and emerging talent. They gives us a more informal way of communicating with our audience and establishing SHORTS™ as a dedicated short film brand. Short films have traditionally been treated without the deference that features receive so we are producing the podcasts to give our growing audience a taste of the world of short films and a deeper insight into the creative process behind each film.

Do you have any advice for short filmmakers?

Keep it short - literally. I think that far too many short films outstay their welcome. Ensure that you have a really, really great, 100% original script to start with. If you don't feel like it is an important story, which absolutely has to be told, then the film probably doesn't have to be made either! Too many poor quality or mediocre short films get made every year. Many are never seen outside of the filmmaker's immediate circle. You have to make something special, which will rise to the top.

> **"Don't give your film away for free, especially on the internet (at least until you really have exhausted all other options open to you)".**

Using actors who can act will also help!

Don't use commercially available music, which will need to be cleared with the publisher - the cost of this is usually prohibitive, and will prevent the film being seen on TV etc.

And finally, don't give your film away for free, especially on the internet (at least until you really have exhausted all other options open to you). We have been striving for years to create a commercial value for short film, and that is completely undermined when our competitors/peers use shorts as cheap (or rather free) content.

Short Film World Sales
Sydney Neter

www.sndfilms.com

Can you give us a little history of SND Films?

SND Films has been in short film (and documentary) sales since 1994, mostly starting with shorts that screened at the then relatively unknown Sundance Film Festival. This festival turned out to be a great source for quality short films from the USA. Later on in 1996, when the Sundance Channel started, SND had rights to a lot of shorts that they wanted to buy to focus on Sundance as a brand. Now SND has more than 200 titles and some shorts series.

SND Films is one of the world's leading short film and documentary sales agents, which has been going since 1994. Founder and Director, **Sydney Neter** talks about the benefits of having someone sell your short, and about how the sales landscape has changed.

What are the biggest markets/platforms for short film sales now? And what about territories?

The most reliable market is still TV - terrestrial or pay TV. Once these buyers know you and know the quality you're selling, it is a pretty reliable outlet (as long as the buyer's programming slot doesn't disappear!). You always get paid, the license fees are okay and the license periods are usually not too long, or they are negotiable. However, if an internet operator buys your film, your potential audience is suddenly multiplied by a million. So if you're going for audience, and not for money, this is better. The best territories are the 'western' territories or at least those that have a feel for art-house movies; the USA, Canada, Japan, Australia and Europe are the best. Rarely can you sell to South America.

Can festivals be a source of revenue for filmmakers? Should filmmakers expect screening fees from a festival?

It depends. If it's 'just another short', there is no money for it. If you've won a big prize (like an Oscar!) you could actually start asking for screening fees. Gay festivals tend to have a higher screening budget than the regular ones, so they are more willing to pay for screenings (but you should never expect to get rich this way). The truth is that the biggest festivals never pay, as it is considered an honour to have your film play there.

What are the benefits of having a sales agent, and what is the range of commission that a filmmaker can expect to pay their sales agent?

The benefit is always that you're part of the short film catalogue and get publicity no matter what. An agent can sell films in packages, which means only one contract needs to be made. A buyer will always prefer to have one contract for 20 films, rather than 20 contracts that all need to be explained and negotiated. It's too much work for most buyers. Furthermore, the sales agent takes care of the delivery, the paperwork (tax paperwork can be boring and a lot of work for first-timers). Also, sales agents go to visit the buyers, go to markets and festivals to meet them, and are up-to-date when it comes to knowing who's buying what kind of film...and who has ceased buying. The commission is usually around 35%. SND stopped declaring expenses (it's too much administration), so it's 35% net. Though, if a producer has more than one film, we are willing to negotiate on the commission; it's all about relationships.

What qualities are you looking for when you pick up a short film?

I look for well-made films – story-wise and technically. I would go for the 'film look' if fiction, and usually ones which are not totally dialogue driven (though there are always exceptions). Obviously, they need to be fun to look at and entertaining. It could be a thriller or a drama, but comedy is something that's easier to sell. Edgy films are great, but experimental films are out of the question for us. Black and white is difficult to sell too, so I generally stay away from those. Animation is good because it's timeless, and English language films usually sell better. Furthermore, we tend to only pick up films, which are under 17 minutes. Shorts which are longer than this are hard to sell, unless they are around 40 minutes (some stations have 40 minute slots). Of course, known actors are also always good.

Are there certain festivals you go to every year to look for new work? And can filmmakers submit unsolicited films directly to you?

Yes, I go every year to Sundance, Clermont-Ferrand (they also have the biggest short film market in the world), Berlin and the

Toronto Short Film Festival. As for sending a film to SND: Film-makers should first send an e-mail with information about the film, using the address on the website. I will get back to them to let them know if it sounds like something for SND.

There is much talk about how new digital platforms are changing short film distribution. Is this true? Are any of these platforms revenue generating yet?

Yes, they are generating a bit of money, but not for one little short. With regards to VoD rights specifically, it's tricky but not impossible to negotiate separate deals because lots of online platforms go across territories. TV stations want these extra rights too, to make sure that another company isn't going to buy those during their license period. Since the extra money is never *huge*, it's sometimes better to include those rights in the TV sale, or at least let the other competing company have VoD rights after a year instead. There are many ways to make the buyers happy and still earn a bit of money with it!

How do you envision short film distribution/exhibition in 10 years? Will it look similar to the landscape now?

In general terms, I suspect the video stores in the streets will be totally gone once the feature film business has found a way to make download streams smaller (or once the broadband is broader) and thus faster. However, I don't expect TV or internet programmers will disappear. People want to be entertained and I don't think the majority of viewers is interactive. They just want to hit a button and see a program. AtomFilms is one of the short film companies that understands this.

In terms of sales, it's still a people's business and you need to have the so-called 'human filters', so that buyers don't get flooded with amateurish films. The same is true for the consumers/viewers who go to reputable sites for quality. You always need filters to get and maintain quality. Sites like youtube.com do serve a purpose, but as a sales agent I would strongly advise you not to upload your film to these sites because of what I said before about giving films away for free. But yes, if someone else did it, so be it. There is not much you can do about this kind of piracy these days. Let's just hope it's not going to happen to you and me!

Short film event screenings... London, Europe, Future Shorts

Fabien Riggall

www.futureshorts.com

Future Shorts are a London-based organisation that champions short films through a core activity of hugely popular and creative regular short film screenings in clubs and cinemas. But they're not just a national events producer. Around the world – Belguim, Moscow, Paris – an almost a viral network of linked Future Shorts satellite organisations host similar regular short film events in their own cities. Founder **Fabien Riggall** explains some of what they do and how they are working to raise the profile and prestige of the humble short film.

Can you give us some background on Future Shorts?

I started Future Shorts in 2003, originally as a monthly casual get together in Shepherd's Bush [West London] with other film-makers where we would have a drink and watch short films and talk about the films, but it quickly became apparent that there was a big demand for a regular film night, almost like a monthly film festival. We quickly met up with a group from Belgium who liked what we were doing, took the idea back home and then we started exchanging the very best films from the UK for the best new work from Belgium and France each month. The network sort of grew from there. We now have 40 different events per month across Europe. Each city and each country has it's own vibe. Sometimes it's a theatrical venue, sometimes it's a concert hall. It's really just about creating a community of people around the world who share this passion for watching films together as part of a social interactive experience.

Why do you go to such great lengths to find different venues and not just do a shorts programme in a cinema?

I'm really interested in making cinema less stuffy, getting it out of the box of the cinema. We are interested in how people respond to films in a nightclub or a concert hall or a bar where there isn't that pressure to respond in a particular way. I think this may appeal to people who don't necessarily think of themselves as being into 'independent cinema'. I want to see more varied audiences. For instance, we are creating programmes of music-based shorts with filmmakers like Adam Smith (who made The Streets videos) for a kid's charity we are working for called Kids Company.

The received wisdom is that it's usually filmmakers who go to shorts programmes. Do you find that this is the case?

Well, I think it is a little different for us... sometimes it feels more like we are running a music venue or a club. We don't sell our events with the image of a film camera on the flyer; we are highly visual but not presented in a typical way. We show films from around the world – Poland, Iraq - but we do seem to be getting a slightly different audience, not just the people who work in the film industry. I'd like to reach a wider audience in the same way that music does. People are more adventurous with music.

What types of films do you look for?

We have an open submission policy because we have rolling events. I often try to find a lead film and then build a programme around that. With themes, I try to programme as broadly as possible and probe questions from different sides, so a programme about love would examine the subject from many different angles and hopefully make people think and flip the theme. I look for films that work as a programme; it's like making a mixed tape for a friend. Yet, in this case, that friend is an audience of a 100 people. It's not all about my *personal* taste. I try to respond to the audience. I sit in the venue to watch the films with the audience to see what people like, and what doesn't work.

You've recently started acting as a sales agent for shorts, can you talk a little bit about how this fits into what you are already doing?

Well, we only pick up films that we want to show theatrically through our network. We also often screen films with our audiences first to see how they work before we pick them up to sell. A difference for the filmmaker is that we try to be really clear about what we expect. I signed a contract three years ago for my short and I was really bewildered by the process. It was confusing; there were lots of hidden renewals in the contract. When we started distributing, we wanted the process to be as transparent as possible and totally bespoke for the filmmaker. If the filmmaker is very, very busy and wants us to take it over completely, sell it and get it out there, then we'll take it on exclusively. Yet if that filmmaker is someone who has a few things in his pocket, so maybe wants to send it to someone he knows at HBO or whatever, we would consider a non-exclusive model. Obviously, we want to work exclusively so that we can really strategise with that film. What we are also concentrating on with our theatrical screenings is building a trusted brand with audiences around the world which we hope will help with sales, particularly when pay short film downloads like the iTunes model start to be more widely used. We want the Future Shorts brand to act as a quality filter. We want to filter out some of the noise.

What are some of your other plans for the future?

We are talking to the UK Film Council and the Film Distributors Association about the possibility of a monthly feature-length programme of short films which would be treated like a feature film and reviewed by journalists and booked into cinemas. This is now more feasible technically – at least in Britain – because of the Digital Screen Network. It wouldn't have previously been possible to do this because of the cost of 35mm prints, but now many cinemas can project digitally here. This is what we are already doing on a smaller scale with the screenings we do at City Screen [independent chain of Picturehouse arts cinemas in the UK]. Shorts have always been sort of the ugly duckling in a way, but we have a sense that if we can change people's perceptions and get them to perceive these collections as equal to a feature in stature, then the press may review them more, and a wider audience will see them. So we treat it as a feature release. We want to get support for that. Unfortunately, we have a long way to go to change perceptions...

Short film event screenings, NYC, USA, Rooftop Films
Dan Nuxoll

www.rooftopfilms.com

Is Rooftop Films a 'film festival'?

Rooftop Films is more than a film festival, we are a community. We are a collective collaboration between filmmakers, festivals, audience members, venues and neighborhoods. Our goal is to create a vibrant independent filmmaking community that bridges cultural boundaries, and we hope that we can bring artists and audiences together.

Rooftop Films is a non-profit film festival and production collective that supports, creates, promotes, and shows daring short films worldwide and in a weekly summer-long outdoor film festival in New York. Their Summer Series screenings feature new, undistributed, independent films and all of the shows take place outdoors – in parks, along the waterways, in various scenic locations…on rooftops. They don't screen in theatres, but in communities. Shooting People's Ingrid Kopp talks to Rooftop Films **Dan Nuxoll.**

Can you tell us a little bit about short film programming?

Rooftop has always been dedicated to showcasing short films since we started screenings in 1997. More than half of the 47 outdoor screenings that made up our recent Summer Series were devoted to short films. There are a number of reasons that we have always focused on short films. First of all, we love them. We watch thousands of movies each year and it is very easy to get a little tired of conventional plots and story structures. With most feature films – even the better ones – there are often contrivances and filler shoved into the film in order to stretch the work out to feature length. With short films, filmmakers can write and edit their films to the proper length for their subject and be true to their material.

We also like the vibe of an outdoor shorts screening. We have music beforehand and have an intermission as well and it is great to have the audience and the filmmakers milling about and becoming acquainted with the work of multiple artists.

How do you select short films?

The bulk of our selections draw from our filmmaker submissions. We keep our submission fee low to encourage filmmakers to submit ($8.00 if you submit on time). We received over 1800 short film submissions this year alone. We could never put together 20-25 great programs of shorts a year if we didn't get so many films sent to us. But, obviously, we do check out shorts in lots of other ways, too. We go to festivals whenever we get the chance and I peruse all of the programme listings from other festivals to find shorts that sound interesting or unusual or that or that I think might work well with our festival. We get a lot of recommendations from friends and co-workers and I never hesitate to invite a filmmaker to submit to us if their film sounds worthwhile. We do check out shorts online, but we try to avoid showing things that have gotten massive exposure on the internet unless we really, really love the film. Ideally we'll find a film and show it *before* a million people have already streamed it.

What are you looking for when you select a short for Rooftop?

First let me say what we aren't looking for: Rooftop really tries to avoid generic high-concept, high-budget, calling-card films. You see this sort of film at all the mainstream festivals and they bore the audience to death. Instead, we are really looking for films that stand out and speak to us and that were made for their own sake. We don't care about shorts that were made in order to show off fancy equipment or that run through all the tricks that the filmmaker and DoP learned in film school. That's not to say that we don't appreciate craft or the value of a talented production team – we absolutely do. But the first thing we look for is a good story and a carefully considered and appropriate filmmaking style.

> "With short films, filmmakers can write and edit their films to the proper length for their subject and be true to their material".

Rooftop also really tries to show films that portray people and communities and lives honestly and without all of the conventions that populate mainstream media. We prefer subtlety and honesty to contrivance and demagoguery. A lot of shorts out there try to tackle big issues and ideas even though the filmmaker doesn't really have anything new to say about the subject. What's the point? Instead, we look for films that have something to say, even if the issue the film deals with is modest or local or personal.

Is the short film market changing with new distribution technologies like VoD and video sharing websites?

Not so much. It is still close to impossible to make a profit off of a short film, especially if you count unpaid labour, so distribution methods aren't quite transforming the world the way some expected. The fact that people can go out and find shorts on their own raises the bar a bit from a programmer's perspective. Even with Atom Films and YouTube and Current TV and other short film channels and sites out there, I still find it hard to discover a genuinely fantastic film just by browsing around a little bit. Most of the stuff out there is still pretty generic, and I think it will always be the job of the film programmer to sort through the muck and pick out the films that are genuinely unique.

Why do cinemas not programme more short films?

There is no money to be made on a large scale, for a number of reasons, and that makes it hard to get the funding to start up a major distribution company for shorts. First of all, even if you don't take the length of the films into consideration, you have to understand that the major distributors (including those few genuinely independent studios) – whose films account for 98% of the box office – simply don't know how to market unconventional films that don't have stars in them or that are not the works of someone who is considered an auteur of high standing. The best shorts tend to be unconventional, rarely do they have celebrities in the cast, and rarely do major directors work on them. Right off the bat you have '3 strikes' against you. Also, it's obviously impossible to mass-market a *single* short film because nobody will pay to see a 5 minute film by itself. But it is also very difficult to mass-market a *programme* of films because it is hard to market something that has many component parts. These factors make it unlikely that shorts will be theatrically distributed on any large scale any time soon. However, I do think that repertory theatres with loyal audiences can make such screenings work.

Will the roll out of digital projectors encourage cinemas to have more short film screenings?

Absolutely. It already has changed things. It is much easier to compile, ship (or upload) and screen films digitally than it was on 16mm or 35mm, and that makes it possible for microcinemas to put together screenings and present them on relatively high-quality formats. Though theatres will still likely resist short films for all the reasons listed above, microcinemas (as opposed to traditional theatres) will benefit most from the availability of cheap, high quality projectors.

Short Films and VoD/Online Sales, Revver
Steven Starr

www.revver.com

How is Revver different...?

Revver is different from most video sharing services in two ways: First, we are the only video sharing service that reviews each video uploaded (for copyright infringement, pornography, hate speech, etc.) and does not accept copyright infringing content. We also use Creative Commons licensing to protect the owners' rights as 'Revverized' videos are shared. Second, we are also the only service that embeds an ad directly into the video, so that advertising can be served dynamically no matter where the video travels. We also share the advertising revenue with the person who owns the video and the person who distributes the video.

Can online video sites be a viable business?

Most definitely. Revver is already making money, and we have filmmakers who have earned as much as $35K in about one month.

As the gap between producers and consumers shrinks will there be a decline in production values?

After you watch your thousandth cat-on-a-skateboard video online, it might seem that way. But the reality is that as more professional tools become available to average consumers and as production costs continue to decline, people will produce more high-quality content. Much of what we receive is already television-quality, and it won't be long before it hits the feature-film mark.

Revver may have answered one of the riddles of short film exhibition: how can filmmakers can get paid for uploading their quality content onto the internet? They've created a marketplace for viral videos led by ad revenue where they match every uploaded video with an ad, and encourage viewers to share the video on other sites. They then split the revenue that is generated when a viewer watches the video and the ad – anywhere online - with the video's creator. Revver's Founder and CEO **Steven Starr** talks to Shooting People's Ingrid Kopp.

> ## "Films will be everywhere. You'll be able to stream them on your cell phone, then share that data with the 142-inch plasma screen across the room so that everyone with you can watch too"

How does one find the good stuff on Revver?

We have a search tool, and we do have a section called 'Editor's Picks,' which our internal staff curates. You'll see more organization on our homepage shortly, such as 'Featured Collections' and a spotlight section for our most prolific and successful artists. But everyone on Revver has the same chance to get into one of these categories – there are no 'gate-keepers' if the content is successful.

How is the market for short films changing?

It's exploding! So many more screens are available for programming now than just a year ago. Of course we're looking at all those categories, but we're not in a position to talk about what we're doing... Yet.

How do you envision short film distribution/exhibition in 10 years ?

Films will be everywhere. You'll be able to access them no matter where you are. And you'll be able to stream them on your cell phone, then share that data with the 142-inch plasma screen across the room so that everyone with you can watch too. The internet will be key to this distribution, but it won't look the way it looks today because you won't need any wires to connect to it. It's going to be amazing.

How Revver works:

> Users sign up on Revver's Web site and upload an original video to get started

> Once Revver attaches an ad to the back of the video, users can distribute it anywhere on the Internet

> Users make money (split 50/50 with Revver) according to ad click-through, so the more popular a video is, the more money it makes

> Users don't have to upload a video to make money. They can sign up as an affiliate to host 'Revverized' videos on another web site or MySpace page to earn 20% of the ad revenue (taken off the top).

> It's viral. Users make money no matter where the 'Revverized' video goes online- whether via e-mail, Web site, or P2P network

Short films on TV, Current TV
Jason Meil

www.current.tv

Current TV is a major network devoted to short docs and non-fiction material, and a new model in television networks with a youth orientated non-fiction programme created in part by the people who watch it. Shooters' Ingrid Kopp talks to **Jason Meil**, Senior Vice President, Original Programming & Acquisitions.

Can you tell us what Current TV is in more detail?

Current TV, which launched 1 August 2005, is a network created by, for and with an 18-34 year-old audience. The network shows young adults what's going on in their world, in their voice as programming is supplied in part by the very audience who watches it. Current's 'viewer created content' (VC2) comprises roughly one-third of the on-air broadcast; audiences to submit short-form, nonfiction video 'pods', 'viewer created ads' (V-CAMs), and mobile video. In addition, the network acquires and produces original content. Programming ranges from the hottest trends in technology, fashion, music and videogames, to pressing issues such as the environment, relationships, parenting, finance, politics and spirituality. Current is available in 40 million U.S. homes via Comcast (channel 107 nationwide), Time Warner Cable, and DirecTV (channel 366 nationwide). In 2007, Current also launched in the UK and Ireland on BSkyB.

Can you tell us a little bit about short film programming at Current?

At the moment, Current's schedule consists entirely of short form programmes we call 'pods'. Pods can run really run any length that works best for the content; we've run pods as short as 30 seconds and as long as 20 minutes. Most of Current's pods run between 2 and 10 minutes.

How do you select short films? Festivals? Filmmaker submissions?

Current gets its programming in a number of ways. First, we encourage everyone, even non-professional filmmakers with a story to tell, to contribute to the network by uploading pods to our website at www.current.tv, which gives us what we call our 'viewer created content' or VC^2. Currently VC^2 makes up close to a third of our on-air broadcast. We also acquire material out of festivals, through submissions, and through direct contact with filmmakers and distributors. Once we've formed a relationship with a filmmaker, we are open to commissioning pods as well.

What are you looking for when you buy for the channel?

Current's programming reflects any topic of interest to our audience. There is no "right" production style – we have 'verite' pods and animation pods, pods shot on film and pods shot on mobile phones. We just want the content to be smart, relevant, and absolutely fascinating.

Are you at liberty to reveal how much a short film might sell to the Channel for, and for how many screenings?

Our prices range depending on the content, but our price structure can be found at www.current.tv. How many times a pod airs is dependent on how relevant it is on any given day; a pod about an event that is in the 'zeitgeist' right now will air in heavy rotation, and then will air less frequently or be retired when it becomes less relevant. While it is not a news network, Current is about being just that – current.

What should filmmakers keep in mind if they want to be able to sell their short film to a broadcaster?

> Make something that is compelling.
> Know who your audience is and what the best outlet is to access that audience.
> Make sure you have your legal documentation in order, including appearance releases and music clearances. You can create the most inspired content in the world, but if it can't be cleared for broadcast, it will likely not make it to TV.

Short films on TV, IFC
Evan Fleischer

www.ifc.com

Tell us about IFC's Media Lab?

Media Lab is an online short film destination. Filmmakers from all over the world can upload their films for others to view and vote on, with the top-ranking films being brought to IFC's air on a monthly basis.

What are you looking for when you choose films from the Lab to air on the channel?

We air the films the online audience likes best. The top-ranking films are what we air and if selected, the film will play at least 5 times over the course of a month.

Do you pay a license fee if the film airs on the channel?

We don't pay a license fee, but by submitting a film to Media Lab, a filmmaker grants IFC non-exclusive rights to their film.

What qualities do you think make a short film good? And what are some common mistakes you see in first short film?

They should be short. Concise. Good production values. Strong story. The biggest mistake is when filmmakers try to do too much in their short film. Filmmakers need to remember that it's a *short* film, and it should be treated as its own form. Many filmmakers try to cram a feature length movie into a short film model, and the result is most often miserable.

How is the market for short films changing?

Interest is definitely increasing. The public has become accustomed to viewing short videos on the web, and this appetite is translating to TV as well. There are also more outlets for content available now than ever before. More web sites are hosting video, and there are more opportunities for audiences to consume short form content [**ed:** and filmmakers to exploit their content] in a variety of places: on TV, online, on cell phones, on iPods.

The Independent Film Channel (IFC) is the first and most widely distributed network dedicated to independent film 24 hours a day, uncut and commercial free. Short film content is generally acquired through their website, and while they don't pay license fees for shorts which come via the site, this can be an excellent place for exposure (as always, make sure you understand how it effects your other distribution possibilities before submitting to the site). Ingrid Kopp talks to **Evan Fleischer**, IFC Director of Marketing, Promotions about the Channel's short film strategy.

How do you envision short film distribution/exhibition in 10 years?

That's a good question, and one that *everybody* is trying to figure out right now. People are trying everything in an attempt to figure out the best model. If I told you I knew what it was going to look like in 10 years I'd be full of shit, because *nobody* knows.

"Many filmmakers try to cram a feature length movie into a short film model, and the result is most often miserable"

Contacts

Short film sales agents

Big Film Shorts
 100 S. Sunrise Way #289,
Palm Springs,
CA 92262, USA

(☎) +1 760 219 6269

💻 info@bigfilmshorts.com
www.bigfilmshorts.com

British Film Institute
✉ Film Sales,
21 Stephen Street,
London W1T 1LN

(☎) 020-7436 4014

💻 john.flahive@bfi.org.uk
www.bfi.org.uk

Dazzle Films
✉ 388 Old Street,
London EC1V 9LT

(☎) 020-7739 7716

💻 sales@dazzlefilms.co.uk
www.dazzlefilms.co.uk

Future Shorts
✉ 34-35 Berwick Street,
London W1F 8RP

(☎) 020-7734 3883

💻 info@futureshorts.com
www.futureshorts.com

KurzFilmAgentur Hamburg
✉ Friedensallee 7,
D-22765 Hamburg, Germany

(☎) +49-40-39 10 63 19

📠 +49-40-39 10 63 20

💻 sales@shortfilm.com
www.kurzfilmagentur.de

Microcinema International
✉ 1636 Bush Street,
Suite 2, San Francisco,
CA 94109, USA

(☎) +1 415 447 9750

📠 +1 509 351 1530

to submit a film:
✉ 1528 Sul Ross,
Houston,
TX 77006, USA

(☎) +1 713 412 5120

💻 info@microcinema.com
www.microcinema.com

onedotzero

Unit 212c Curtain House,
134-146 Curtain Road,
London EC2A 3AR

info@onedotzero.com
www.onedotzero.com

Shorts International

25 Beak Street,
London, W1F 9RT

(✆) 020-7734 2277

📠 020-7734 2242

simon@shortsinternational.com
www.shortsinternational.com

SND Films

P.O. Box 15703,
1001 NE Amsterdam,
The Netherlands

(✆) +31 20 404 07 07

📠 +31 20 404 07 08

nfo@sndfilms.com
www.sndfilms.com

Short film screening initiatives & networks

Bitesize Cinema

info@bitesizecinema.com
www.bitesizecinema.com

TAKE NOTE: Put together regular touring packages of high quality, often award-winning short films to screen at venues in the UK. They also have plans to release a DVD of short films and invite submissions of films.

British Federation of Film Societies

info@bffs.org.uk
www.bffs.org.uk

TAKE NOTE: act as organising body and central information service for film societies all over the UK.

Future Shorts

info@futureshorts.com
www.futureshorts.com

TAKE NOTE: UK-based organisation which hosts regular high profile short film screening events all over the world, releases DVD compilations, and acts as a short film sales agent.

Mobile Cinema

www.shootingpeople.org

TAKE NOTE: Mobile short film screenings on demand from 3 guys in a van. You say where!

Rooftop Films

info@rooftopfilms.com
www.rooftopfilms.com

TAKE NOTE: NYC-based non-profit 'film festival' and production collective that creates, promotes, and screens daring short films worldwide and in a weekly summer rooftop film festival in NYC.

Websites and digital channels for short film

Movieola

www.movieola.ca

TAKE NOTE: Canadian digital channel devoted entirely to shorts

Atom Films

www.atomfilms.com

TAKE NOTE: Long-running online site for viewing shorts – hit and miss quality but has 1000s of films. Also buys some of its content so worth supporting!

IFC Media Lab

www.ifc.com

TAKE NOTE: Independent Film Channel's online site for viewing shorts. Highest rated shorts are considered for broadcast on channel.

Fourdocs

www.channel4.com/fourdocs

TAKE NOTE: Classic archive and contemporary doc shorts

Channel Four

www.channel4.com/film

TAKE NOTE: Great selection of short films from the C4 and Film4 collections.

Cinema Bank

www.cinemabank.co.uk

TAKE NOTE: 'Portal' with short dramas, docs and music videos

IFILM

www.ifilm.com

TAKE NOTE: User upload site, lots of content but variable quality.

It's Electric

www.itsallelectric.com

TAKE NOTE: Showcase short films from their 50 Quid Film Festival

Last Independent

www.lastindependent.tv

TAKE NOTE: A site set up by Birmingham-based production company

MySpace

www.myspace.com

TAKE NOTE: User upload site with short film networking

Pawky

www.pawky.com

TAKE NOTE: User upload short film site with some element of curation (and hence, better quality work)

SP Channel

www.shootingpeople.org

TAKE NOTE: New online film channel of members' films

Tank TV

www.tank.tv

TAKE NOTE: User upload short film site. Other users review your films and you can read short scripts online

Trigger Street

 www.triggerstreet.com

Current TV

 www.current.tv

TAKE NOTE: Doc shorts digital channel established in US and newly launched in UK in Spring 2007. Viewers submit doc short 'pods' on news and current events and some work is commissioned.

Key short film festivals

Aspen Shortsfest

 110 E Hallam St,
Suite 102 Aspen,
CO 81612, USA

 +1 970 925 6882

 +1 970 925 1967

 trigney@aspenfilm.org
www.aspenfilm.org

WHEN? April

TAKE NOTE: Films in competition are eligible for over $20,000 in prizes.

SUBMISSION COST? $35-$55 depending on when submitted

WHEN'S THE DEADLINE? November

Bilbao International Festival of Documentary & Short Films

 Colón de Larreátegui,
37 - 4°,
Apdo. 579,
48009 Bilbao, Spain

 +34 94 424 86 98

 +34 94 424 56 24

 info@zinebi.com
www.zinebi.com

WHEN? November

TAKE NOTE: Several major awards with cash prizes.

SUBMISSION COST? free

WHEN'S THE DEADLINE? September

Clermont-Ferrand Short Film Festival

 La Jetee,
6 place Michel-de-l'Hospital,
63058 Clermont-Ferrand Cedex 1,
France

 +33 473 91 65 73

 +33 473 92 11 93

 info@clermont-filmfest.com
www.clermont-filmfest.com

WHEN? February

TAKE NOTE: This is arguably THE biggie on the short film with a market with many buyers and exhibitors. Also has several prestigious cash prizes.

SUBMISSION COST? free

WHEN'S THE DEADLINE? October

Encounters Short Film Festival

 1 Canons Road,
Harbourside,
Bristol BS1 5TX

 0117-929 9188

 0117-929 9988

 info@encounters-festival.org.uk
www.encounters-festival.org.uk

WHEN? November

TAKE NOTE: Biggest UK short and animation festival. Includes a buyers market

SUBMISSION COST? free

WHEN'S THE DEADLINE? May

FlickerFest International Short Film Festival

 Bondi Pavillion,
PO BOX 7416,
Sydney,
NSW 2026, Australia

 +61 2 9365 6888

 info@flickerfest.com.au
www.flickerfest.com.au

WHEN? January

TAKE NOTE: cash prizes

SUBMISSION COST? $35AUD

WHEN'S THE DEADLINE? September

Going Underground International Short Film Festival

 Tempelhofer Ufer 1a,
109 61 Berlin, Germany

 +49 (0)30 2529 1322

+49 (0)30 2529 1322

festival@interfilm.de
www.interfilm.de

WHEN? November

SUBMISSION COST? free

WHEN'S THE DEADLINE? August

Halloween Short Film Festival

Halloween Short Film Festival,
c/o Curzon Soho Cinema,
99 Shaftesbury Avenue,
London W1D 5DY

info@shortfilms.org.uk
www.shortfilms.org.uk

WHEN? January

TAKE NOTE: Lots of prizes, fest has filmmaker friendly event vibe

SUBMISSION COST? free

WHEN'S THE DEADLINE? October

Hamburg International Short Film Festival

 KurzFilmAgentur,
Hamburg e.V.,
Filmhaus,
Friedensallee 7,
D-22765 Hamburg, Germany

 +49 40 39106323

+49 40 39106220

festival@shortfilm.com
www.shortfilm.com

WHEN? June

TAKE NOTE: Prizes also include one for best 'no budget' short, and fest has a big international market.

SUBMISSION COST? free

WHEN'S THE DEADLINE? February

Huesca Film Festival

Avda. Parque, 1-2, 22002 Huesca, Spain

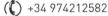 +34 974212582

+34 974210065

info@huesca-filmfestival.com
www.huesca-filmfestival.com

WHEN? June

TAKE NOTE: Lots of prizes with main winner getting an automatic short-listing for the US Academy Awards best Short Film.

SUBMISSION COST? free

WHEN'S THE DEADLINE? March

KinoFilm: Manchester International Short Film Festival

 42 Edge Street,
Manchester M4 1HN

 0161-288 2494

0161-281 1374

 john.kino@good.co.uk
www.kinofilm.org.uk

SUBMISSION COST? free

Los Angeles Short Film Festival

 1610 Argyle Ave #113,
Los Angeles, CA 90028

+1 323 461-4400

info@lashortsfest.com
www.lashortsfest.com

WHEN? September

TAKE NOTE: Home of Hollywood so has the industry glitz, if that's what you are after...

Oberhausen International Short Film Festival

Grillostrasse 34,
460 45 Oberhausen, Germany

+49 208 825 2652

 +49 208 825 5413

 info@kurzfilmtage.de
www.kurzfilmtage.de

WHEN? May

TAKE NOTE: This is a biggie on the short film circuit. 16 prizes and a video library for buyers

SUBMISSION COST? free

WHEN'S THE DEADLINE? January

Palm Springs International Festival of Short Films

1700 E Tahquitz Canyon Way,
#3 Palm Springs,
CA 92262, USA

+1 760 322 2930

+1 760 322 4087

info@psfilmfest.org
www.psfilmfest.org

WHEN? August/September

TAKE NOTE: Prizes worth $70,000 in cash and lots of Hollywood attention

SUBMISSION COST? $30-60 depending on date submitted. Discount for students

WHEN'S THE DEADLINE? April, June

---

* TOP 6 Short Fest Heavyweights

Aspen Shortsfest, USA

Clermont-Ferrand Short Film Festival, France

Encounters, UK

Palm Springs International Festival of Short Films, USA

Tampere Film Festival, Finland

Toronto Worldwide Short Film Festival, Canada

Tampere Film Festival

 Box 305,
FIN-33101 Tampere, Finland

📞 +358 3 223 56 81

📠 +358 3 223 0121

💻 office@tamperefilmfestival.fi
www.tamperefilmfestival.fi

WHEN? March

TAKE NOTE: Biggie with lots of prizes including Prix UIP short which is automatically short-listed for European Film Awards

SUBMISSION COST? free

WHEN'S THE DEADLINE? December

Uppsala International Short Film Festival

 PO Box 1746,
751 47 Uppsala, Sweden

📞 +46 18 12 0025

📠 +46 18 12 1350

💻 info@shortfilmfestival.com
www.shortfilmfestival.com

WHEN? October

TAKE NOTE: Many awards including one for Best Children's Film

SUBMISSION COST? none

WHEN'S THE DEADLINE? June

Worldwide Short Film Festival

 2489 Bayview Ave.
Toronto, ON M2L 1A8 Canada

📞 +1 416 445 1446

📠 +1 416 445 9481

💻 shortfilm@cdnfilmcentre.com
www.worldwideshortfilmfest.com

WHEN? June

TAKE NOTE: Quickly becoming major fest. Numerous awards include one for best screenplay.

SUBMISSION COST? $15 per film

WHEN'S THE DEADLINE? February

Key specialist festivals

Amsterdam International Documentary Film Festival

 Kleine-Gartmanplantsoen 10,
1017 RR Amsterdam, The Netherlands

📞 +31 20 6273329

📠 +31 20 6385388

💻 info@idfa.nl
www.idfa.nl

WHEN? November

Anima – Brussels Animation Film Festival

📧 Folioscope asbl,
Avenue de Stalingrad 52,
B – 1000 Bruxelles, Belgique

📞 +32 2 534 41 25

📠 +32 2 534 22 79

💻 info@folioscope.be
folioscope.awn.com

WHEN? March.

TAKE NOTE: Awards for best short films in international, student and children's film categories

Animafest – World Festival of Animated Films

📧 Koncertna Direkcija Zagreb,
Kneza Mislava 18,
100 00 Zagreb, Croatia

+3851 450 1191

 +3851 450 1193

animafest@animafest.hr
www.animafest.hr

WHEN? June

TAKE NOTE: In even-numbered years, fest is solely devoted to short animation (under 30 mins); odd years are for features.

Annecy International Animated Film Festival

c/o Conservatoire d'Art et d'Histoire, 18 ave. du Tresum, BP 399 74013 Annecy, France

 + 33 4 5010 0900

+ 33 4 5010 0970

info@annecy.org
www.annecy.org

WHEN? June

TAKE NOTE: special awards for work by student filmmakers.

Britdoc

Britdoc Events Ltd, PO Box 51376, London N1 6WX

020-7366 5650

020-7366 5652

 jackie@britdoc.org
www.britdoc.org

WHEN? July

TAKE NOTE: Brilliant new festival and doc conference. Great place to meet makers, buyers and comissioners.

Cinema du Reel – International Documentary Film Festival

Bibliotheque Publique, d'Information Centre, 25 rue du Renard, 75197 Paris Cedex 04, France

+ 33 1 44 78 44 21

+ 33 1 44 78 12 24

cinereel@bpi.fr
www.bpi.fr

WHEN? March Short Film

TAKE NOTE: Prize worth 2500 euros.

Cinemagic – World Screen Festival for Young People

3rd Floor, Fountain House, 17-21 Donegall Place, Belfast BT1 5AB

028-9031 1900

028-9031 9709

 info@cinemagic.org.uk
www.cinemagic.org.uk

WHEN? November/December

TAKE NOTE: short film prizes receive £500

Créteil – Festival International de Films de Femmes

Maison des Arts, Place Salvador Allende, 940 00 Créteil, France

+ 33 1 49 803 858

+ 33 1 49 804 10

 iris@filmsdefemmes.com
www.filmsdefemmes.com

WHEN? March

Dublin Lesbian and Gay Film Festival

 c/o Nexus,
Tower One,
Fumbally Court,
Fumbally Lane,
Dublin, Ireland

(📞) + 353 1 4158414

📠 + 353 1 4730597

🖥 dlgff@ireland.com
www.gcn.ie/dlgff

Fantasporto – Oporto International Film Festival

 Rua Anibal Cunha,
84 – sala 1.6,
4050-048 Porto, Portugal

(📞) + 351 2 2207 6050

📠 + 351 2 2207 6059

🖥 info@fantasporto.online.pt
www.fantasporto.com

WHEN? February

Feminale – International Womens' Film Festival

 Maybachstr, 111,
D-50670 Cologne, Germany

(📞) + 49 2211 300 225

📠 + 49 2211 300 281

🖥 info@feminale.de
www.feminale.de

Hot Docs Canadian International Documentary Festival

✉ 110 Spadina Ave,
Suite 333,
Toronto ON M5V 2K4, Canada

(📞) + 1 416-203-2155

📠 + 1 416-203-0446

🖥 www.hotdocs.ca

WHEN? April/May each year

Leipzig International Festival for Documentary and Animated Film

✉ DOK Filmwochen GmbH, Grosse
Fleischergasse 11, 041 09 Leipzig,
Germany

(📞) + 49 341 308640

📠 + 49 341 308 6415

🖥 info@dok-leizig.de
www.dok-leipzig.de

WHEN? October

✻ www.shootingpeople.org/shortsbook

Download a free calendar of Shooting People's Top 40 short film animation festivals!

We created the shortlist based on filmmakers' experiences. Which are the best festivals for getting you to the next level? Which ones hand out cash prizes? And which ones show filmmakers the best time?

London Lesbian and Gay Film Festival

✉ National Film Theatre,
South Bank,
London SE1 8XT

☎ 020-7815 1323

📠 020-7633 0786

🖥 www.llgff.org.uk

WHEN? March/April

Mix: New York Lesbian and Gay Experimental Film Festival

✉ 79 Pine Street,
PMB 132,
New York,
NY 10005, USA

☎ + 1 212 742 8880

🖥 info@mixnyc.org
www.mixnyc.org

WHEN? November

onedotzero

✉ Unit 212c,
Curtain House,
134-146 Curtain Road,
London EC2A 3AR

☎ 020-7729 0057

🖥 info@onedotzero.com
www.onedotzero.com

WHEN? September

TAKE NOTE: focus on digital cinema including pop promos and commercials

San Francisco International Lesbian and Gay Film Festival

✉ Frameline,
145 Ninth Street # 300,
San Francisco,

CA 94103, USA

☎ + 1 415 703 8650

📠 + 1 415 861 1404

🖥 info@frameline.org
www.frameline.org/festival

WHEN? June

TAKE NOTE: the 'Cannes' of gay film fests - get in here and you'll get loads of other fest invites

Sheffield International Documentary Festival

✉ The Workstation,
15 Paternoster Row,
Sheffield S1 2BX

☎ 0114-276 5141

📠 0114-272 1849

🖥 info@sidf.co.uk
www.sidf.co.uk

WHEN? October/November

All-around film festivals

There are a number of sites online with thorough info about the big film festivals already (see www.britfilms.co.uk, or Shooting People's downloadable poster of the top 40 festivals). So, instead of duplicating that info here, we decided to list the film fests that we think best showcase short films (either with awards and prizes or with a large screening focus on shorts).

AFI Fest: American Film Institute Los Angeles International Film Festival

 www.AFI.com/AFIFEST

WHEN? November

TAKE NOTE: Fest has competitive short film section

DEADLINE? July

Bradford Film Festival

www.bradfordfilmfestival.ac.uk

WHEN? March

TAKE NOTE: 'Shine' award for Best New Short Film (selection by jury)

SUBMISSION COST? none

DEADLINE? January

Berlin International Film Festival

www.berlinale.de

WHEN? February

TAKE NOTE: Berlinale includes approximately. 60 short films across competitive sections with many prestigious short film awards. Berlinale also hosts the Talent Campus for 500 emerging filmmakers from all over the world. Talent Campus gets filmmakers together for screenings, workshops and seminars – great way to meet the international industry (see www.berlinale-talentcampus.de).

SUBMISSION COST? none

Cannes Film Festival

www.festival-cannes.fr

WHEN? May

TAKE NOTE: awards Short Film Palme d'Or (the Competition's highest honour) and Cinefondation short film screenings highlight the work of new emerging talent and student filmmakers.

SUBMISSION COST? none

Cambridge Film Festival

www.cambridgefilmfestival.org.uk

WHEN? July

TAKE NOTE: no short prize but good audience fest with increasingly good industry presence in UK

Cardiff Screen Festival

 www.cardiffscreenfestival.co.uk

WHEN? November

TAKE NOTE: DM Davies Short Film Award has cash and in-kind prizes

of up to £20,000 and film must be from a Welsh filmmaker, a resident of Wales, or someone who attended a Welsh college or university and must be made in Wales.

SCREENING FEES? none

Cork International Film Festival

www.corkfilmfest.org

WHEN? October

TAKE NOTE: competition for short films of under 30 minutes, with awards for Best Irish, international and gay and lesbian short films.

SCREENING FEES? none

DEADLINE? June

Edinburgh International Film Festival

www.edfilmfest.org.uk

WHEN? August

TAKE NOTE: short film award for best British short

SCREENING FEES? none

DEADLINE? May/June

Leeds International Film Festival

🖳 www.leedsfilm.com

WHEN? November

TAKE NOTE: Louis Le Prince Award (Best International Fiction Short); World Animation Award (Best Animated Short); Yorkshire Film Award (Best Short made in the Yorkshire)

SCREENING FEES? none

DEADLINE? Aug/Sept

Locarno International Film Festival

🖳 www.jahia.pardo.ch

WHEN? July

TAKE NOTE: Leopards of Tomorrow prize to the best short film (films of up to 20 minutes)

SCREENING FEES? none

DEADLINE? May

The Times BFI London Film Festival

🖳 www.lff.org.uk

WHEN? October

TAKE NOTE: Turner Classic Shorts Award judged by industry big-wigs and with a tasty cash prize and broadcast on TCM.

SCREENING FEES? none

DEADLINE? July

Melbourne International Film Festival

🖳 www.melbournefilmfestival.com.au

WHEN? July/August

TAKE NOTE: Major Ozzie short film competition, with prizes of more than $35,000 in various categories.

Rotterdam International Film Festival

🖳 www.filmfestivalrotterdam.com

WHEN? January

TAKE NOTE: Tiger Cub Award goes to the Best Short Film

SCREENING FEES? none

DEADLINE? November

Pusan International Film Festival

🖳 www.piff.org

WHEN? October

TAKE NOTE: Awards go to best new Asian short and an international short

SCREENING FEES? none

DEADLINE? July

Raindance Film Festival

🖳 www.raindance.co.uk/festival

WHEN? October

TAKE NOTE: has big focus on shorts with 20 short film programmes and hosts the British Independent Film Awards with a major shorts prize

SCREENING FEES? £15 for a short

DEADLINE? July

South by Southwest (SXSW)

🖳 www.sxsw.com

WHEN? March

TAKE NOTE: gives winners and runners-up awards in several short categories – narrative, experimental and animated as well as a music video award.

SCREENING FEES? $25 for shorts

DEADLINE? December

Sundance Film Festival

 www.sundance.org

WHEN? January

TAKE NOTE: Special Jury Award for Best Short Film and a number of other significant short film prizes

SCREENING FEES? $25 -70 depending on sub-mission date

DEADLINE? August-September

Tribeca Film Festival

 www.tribecafilmfestival.org

WHEN? April

TAKE NOTE: Short Film Competition which gets good industry attention in the US

DEADLINE? January

---

* **www.withoutabox.com**

Planning on submitting your film to lots of fests? If so, this is an excellent time-saver for filmmakers. Complete a master application form online and upload stills and press materials, and these can be sent to the participating festivals you want to enter as their deadlines arise. Submission fees can also be paid online. You can also sign up for email updates to be notified about upcoming festival deadlines. All standard services are free for filmmakers.

Section Six:

Resources

Tasty Shorts: Contributors' Recommendations

As we interviewed key film professionals during the research for this book, we asked them what shorts they love. Here are some of the highlights; some are obscure; some are easily available online. This is your own personal short film treasure hunt, have fun tracking them down. It will be well worth the effort!

Brent Hoff, Wholphin (US DVD Magazine)
Fork by Mike Mitchell; *A Stranger In Her Own City* by Khadija Al-Salami is art as Berthold Brecht intended it: "Not a mirror to reflect society, but a hammer to shape it."; *Day 37* by Dillon Hagerty is about space and waste and it is truly funny

Trevor Groth, Sundance Film Festival
In no particular order, I love: *Golden Gate* (Fernando Mereilles), *Rejected* (Don Hertzfeldt), *Wasp* (Andrea Arnold), *Two Cars One Night* (Taika Waititi), *Bugcrush* (Carter Smith), *Five Feet High and Rising* (Peter Sollett), *Architecture of Reassurance* (Mike Mills)

Luke Morris, Cinema 16
Many of my favourite shorts are on the Cinema16 DVDs – *Gasman* (Lynne Ramsay); *The Man Without a Head* (Juan Solanas); *Vincent* (Tim Burton). But of those that aren't, because they can't be released for legal reasons or I couldn't get them, I would mention *Heavy Metal Parking Lot*, *Les Mistons* and *Zero de Conduit*.

Simon Young, Shorts International and London Film Festival
These are my favourite short films (well, 16 of them anyway) off the top of my head and in no particular order: *Sweet* by James Pilkington; *Je T'aime John Wayne* by Toby MacDonald; *Bailongas* (Disco Biscuits) by *Chiqui Carbante*; *Bawke* by *Hisham Zaman*; *What About The Bodies* by Simon Ellis; *Palindrome* by Philip Barcinski; *Home Road Movies* by Robert Bradbrooke; *Bugcrush* by Carter Smith; *Lighten Up* by John Viener; *DEF* by Ian Clark; *Mother* by Sian Heder; *Mule* by John Hardwick; *The Librarian's Dream* by Jon Wright; *Call Register* by Ed Roe; *Handicap* by Lewis-Martin Soucy; *Delusions In Modern Primitivism* by Daniel Loflin. Apologies to anyone I've forgotten who I shouldn't have....

Ingrid Kopp, Producer and Head of Shooting People office in the US. Ingrid hosted the US based interviews in this book
Crumbs... I hate doing this because suddenly my mind goes utterly blank. Here are few that spring to mind: *Terminal Bar* (Dir. Stefan Nadelman); *Snack and Drink* (Dir. Bob Sabiston); *Wet Dreams and False Images* (Dir. Jesse Epstein); *Two Cars One Night* (d. Taika Waititi); *Five Feet High and Rising* (d. Peter Sollett); *Tyger* (Dir. Guilherme Marcondes); *Heavy Metal Parking Lot* (Dirs. John Heyn, Jeff Krulik); *C'etait un rendez-vous* (dir Claude Lelouch); *Every Boy I've Fucked* (Dir. Jennifer Matotek); *Undressing My Mother* (Dir. Ken Wardrop); *Je T'aime John Wayne* (Dir. Toby MacDonald)

Robin Baker, short filmmaker, *Seafood, Christmas Merry*, and Curator of British Film Institute's Mediatheque at the National Film Theatre (see www.bfi.org.uk for more about the Mediatheque).
For inspiration and pure pleasure: *The Vampire* (Jean Painlevé, 1945); *Duck Amuck* (Chuck Jones, 1953); *O Dreamland* (Lindsay Anderson, 1953); *Holiday* (John Taylor, 1957); *Scorpio Rising* (Kenneth Anger, 1963); *Powers of Ten* (Ray and Charles Eames, 1977); *Foutaises* (Jean-Pierre Jeunet, 1989); *A Summer Dress* (François Ozon, 1996); *Early Frost* (Pierre Pinaud, 1999); and *Wasp* (Andrea Arnold, 2003)

Cath Le Couteur, filmmaker and Shooting People founder

My Wrongs 8245-8249 AND 117 (Dir. Christopher Morris); *Bugcrush* (Dir. Carter Smith); *Le Cheval 2.1* (Dirs. Kirk Kirkland, Stephen Scott Hayward); Jan Svankmajer's food trilogy; *Stalk* (Dir. Leigh Hodgkinson); *Sissy Boy Slap Party* (Dir. Guy Maddin)

Chris Blaine, filmmaker

The Wrong Trousers by Nick Park; *Creature Comforts* by Nick Park; *Knitting A Love Song* by Annie Watson; *The Monk And The Fish* by Michael Dudok De Wit; *The Orange Tree* by Simon Kent; *Monsters* by Rob Morgan; *Journey Man* by Dictynna Hood; *Telling Lies* by Simon Ellis; *Foley St* by Tim Clayton and Rob Crowther; *Je T'Aime John Wayne* by Toby MacDonald; *Earthquake!* by James Brett; *My Back Garden* by Lee Kern; *Konsekwens* by Charlotte Baxendale; *City Spirit* by Alex Turner; *Push* by Steven Hore; *Baboon On The Moon* by Christopher Duriez; *Tea* by Barney Cokeliss; *Gone* by Matthew Thompson; *Rabbit* by Run Wrake; *Green Monkey* by Rob Sprackling; and *Hammerman* by Andy Shelley

Two Cars One Night, Taika Waititi

Matt Dentler, programmer, SXSW

Some of my favorite shorts of the last years are: *Nevel is the Devil* by Peter Craig; *K-7* by Christopher Leone; *Redemptitude* by the Zellner Brothers; *First Date* by Gary Huggins; *Shortstop* by Risa Machuca & Fanny Veliz; and *Hiro* by Matthew Swanson.

Daniel Mulloy, Award-winning filmmaker

Don't Be Afraid (Dir: Vera Neubauer) Powerful and influenced a generation of filmmakers such as Mathieu Kassovitz (*Le Hain*); *This Morning* (Dir: Lucy Mulloy) The most compelling short I've seen. A tender look at two incredible kids; *Before Dawn* (Dir: Balint Kenyeres) A beautifully shot and incredibly constructed film that knocks you flat; *La Jetee*, (Dir: Chris Marker) Shaped a hole genre of film and generations of filmmakers; *First Date* (Dir: Gary Huggins) A raw, funny, and touching film made on video for a couple of hundred dollars. Santiago Vasquez gives the best performance I've seen in a short; *The Christies* (Dir: Phil Mulloy) A powerful cutting and disturbing animated depiction of a family devastated by the mundanity of existence; *Undressing My Mother* (Dir: Ken Wardrop) A beautiful and touching film, made with such humility and power that it's unnerving; *Matrix Ping-Pong* (Dir: unknown) A web phenomenon that could be the most viewed short with a fantastically simple premise and execution; and *Small Boxes* (Dir: Rene Hernandez) A faithful and powerful depiction of how hard it can be to get a job when you leave school and have nothing.

Matthieu de Braconier, The Bureau and Cinema Extreme

There are so many brilliant shorts out there. Some get lots of attention and are then never mentioned again. Some are quite discreet at first, but become real classics. Others impress from day one. Lots of short film directors have gone on to make features. Not all their shorts are exceptional, but when one is thinking of the good ones it's hard not to think of *Gasman* by Lynne Ramsey; *Le Signaleur* by Benoit Mariage; *The Sheep*

Thief by Asif Kapadia; *Passionless Moments* and *Peel, An Exercise in Discipline* by Jane Campion; *Fierrot le pou* by Mathieu Kassovitz; *Last Round* by Thomas Vinterberg; *Le Batteur du Bolero* by Patrice Leconte; *The Burning* by Stephen Frears; *The Grandmother* by David Lynch and my all time favourite; *E pericoloso sporgersi* by Jaco Van Dormael.

Neil Hunter, filmmaker, features *The Lawless Heart*, *Sparkle* and new short *The Sickie*

The two that come to mind are Jeunet's *Foutaises'* and Leconte's *Bolero Drummer* (*Le Batteur de Bolero*). Simple ideas perfectly executed

Andy Gordon and Christos Michaels, producers *Hibernation*, co-writers of *"The Sound of Money"*

We have gone for some British ones and when they are good they do really stand out: *The Cat With Hands* (Dir. Rob Morgan) Brilliantly executed and cinematic masterpiece; *Broken Heart* (Dir. Matt Mconaghy) A thrilling short film with tension throughout, and a great script; *The Sheep Thief* (Dir. Asif Kapadia) A brave and unusual story for a young director with some very accomplished moments; *How To Tell When A Relationship Is Over* (Dir. Tony Roache) Very funny and poignant film and all in under 90 seconds; *City Paradise* (Dir. Gaelle Dennis) Stylish work of art to be savoured on the big screen; and *The Banker'* (Dir. Hattie Dalton) for its confidence in style and fine acting performance.

Kelly Broad, filmmaker (producer, *The Banker*)

Family Portrait (Dir. Patricia Riggen) is an amazingly evocative portrait of a family facing the darkest days of poverty in New York, and I love *Heavy Metal Drummer* (Dir. Toby McDonald) for the way it captures the pent up interior life of an outsider just looking for a way to escape.

Jess Search, Shooting People and Channel 4 British Documentary Film Foundation

Two of my all-time favourite innovative short docs are animations. *Snack and Drink* (1990) was one the first - and still uplifting - mixes of documentary and animation. Bob Sabiston's 4-minute film follows a boy with autism into a 7/11 to buy a snack and drink (watch it online: http://www.sputnik7.com/servlet/asxplayl-ist/1/56/snac/file.asx). And of course, *Creature Comforts*, are some of the first films from the Aardman Animation team. They are always worth a re-run for their inspired characterisation of quite everyday interviews (there's one up on Atom: www.atomfilms.com/film/creature_comforts.jsp).

Laura Thielen, Director Aspen Shortsfest

I love films that express something about being human in a way that is personally visceral. I also have huge respect for people who understand the form, whether it be documentary, animation etc, and can use this craft to show you the world in a way that you never thought to look at it before. Some favourites: *A Day in the Country* by Jean Renoir; Adam Elliot's animation; *Wasp* by Andrea Arnold (I love the way it cinematically renders its emotional content); *City Paradise* by Gaelle Denis; and *In God We Trust* by Jason Reichman.

James Mullighan, Creative Director, Shooting People

Tricia asked me to pick my favourite shorts. Ever. Really? May as well have asked me to pick my nose with my foot, such is the difficulty of the task. So: I've narrowed my selection to a strictly 'after 2am' list for those darker, lonelier hours (perhaps best served with a bellyfull of something brewed from the hearts of blue agave plants): *We Have Decided Not To Die* (Dir. Daniel Askill at www.wehavedecidednottodie.com); *Smack My Bitch Up: Prodigy* (Dir. Jonas Ackerlund); *The Eel* (Dir. Domenic Hailstone on MySpace); *Come to Daddy: Aphex Twin* (Dir. Chris Cunningham); *Electronic Performers: Air* (Dir. Laurent Bourdoiseau on www.independ.net); *Surfer: Guinness* (Dir. Jonathan Glazer); *Terminal Bar* (Dir. Stefan Nadelman on RESFEST Shorts Vol 3).

25 short films to watch for free on the internet

For live links to these shorts, go to www.shortfilmsbook.com

Wasp (Dir. Andrea Arnold, UK 2003, 15 mins)

A young mother struggles with her responsibilities as a parent, and her desire to be young.

Short film Oscar winner in 2005.

http://www.channel4.com/film/reviews/film.jsp?id=130231

Me (Dir. Ahree Lee, USA 2004, 2.30mins)

Beautiful experimental doc in which the artist photographs her own face every day over 4 years.

http://www.atomfilms.com/film/me.jsp

Fishy (Dir. Deva Palmier, UK 2003, 10 mins)

An unemployed misfit falls in love with her goldfish.

BBC Talent, joint Runner-Up

http://www.bbc.co.uk/dna/filmnetwork/A5087306

Tyger (Guilherme Marcondes, Brazil 2006, 4 mins)

Beautiful experimental animation based on William Blake's poem "The Tyger".

http://guilherme.tv/tyger/

The Sheep Thief (Asif Kapdia, UK 1997, 24 mins

Multi-award winning short about a young boy caught stealing a sheep who is branded and cast out of his village.

http://www.channel4.com/film/reviews/film.jsp?id=137725

Nits (Dir. Harry Wootliff, UK, 10 mins)

Seven-year old James has nits and wants his mum to check his head. His mum has other things on her mind.

http://www.bbc.co.uk/dna/filmnetwork/A13205990

Binta and the Great Idea (Dir. Javier Fesser, Spain/Senegal 2004, 30 mins)

A small girl sets out to change the life of her cousin in a Senegalese village.

http://www.ifilm.com/ifilmdetail/2771644?ns=1

What's Wrong With this Picture (Dir Jeffrey Travis, USA 2003, 2mins)

Three year-old Aidan gets more than he bargained for when he draws a new picture in this animation

http://www.pawky.com/featured/what_s_wrong_with_this_picture

Last Train Ride (Gokhan Okur, Turkey 2006, 4mins)

Dreamy animation about the soullessness of modern commuter life – fabulous score.

http://www.atomfilms.com/film/last_train_ride.jsp?channelKeyword=channel_artsy

Monster (Dir. Jennifer Kent, Australia, 9mins)

A hassled single mum and her young son are haunted by the child's visions of a monster.

http://www.atomfilms.com/sw/content/monster

Spin (Dir. Cath Le Couteur, UK , 10 mins)

Polysexual tension emerges at a teenagers' party during a game of spin the bottle.

http://www.bbc.co.uk/dna/filmnetwork/A6360220

One to Watch (Dir. Isobel Anderton, UK, 5 mins)

Two best friends like the same guy.

http://www.bbc.co.uk/dna/filmnetwork/A4165445

Terminus (Dir. John Schlesinger, UK 1961, 33 mins)

BAFTA winning observational doc about the comings and goings at Waterloo station.

http://www.channel4.com/fourdocs/archive/terminus.html

Free Speech (Dirs. Ben and Chris Blaine, UK, 5mins)

Dirty talk gets serious as a couple discuss their fantasies in the bath.

Stars a pre-football factory Danny Dyer and Jacqui Oceane..

http://www.atomfilms.com/af/content/free_speech

D.E.B.S. (Dir. Angela Robinson, USA, 11 mins)

Super-agent spoof meets high school love story between two girls in this camped-up award-winner.

http://www.planetout.com/popcornq/db/getfilm.html?64136

Love Me or Leave Me Alone (Dir. Duane Hopkins, UK, 15 mins)

Two teenagers try to express their feelings for each other in the subtle and cinematic short.

http://www.bbc.co.uk/dna/filmnetwork/A9968124

Where Have All the Insects Gone (Dir. Lee Kern, UK, 3 mins)

Evocative personal documentary about childhood and torturing insects.

http://www.channel4.com/fourdocs/film/film-detail.jsp?id=20145#

Snack and Drink (Dir. Bob Sabiston, USA 1990, 4 mins)

A boy with autism into a 7/11 to buy a snack and drink in this short doc.

http://www.sputnik7.com/servlet/asxplaylist/1/56/snac/file.asx

David the Great (Dir. David Hughes & Jacqueline Wright, UK, 3 mins)

Melancholy comedy on B&W Super 8 film.

http://www.bbc.co.uk/dna/filmnetwork/A12476540

The Cat with Hands (Dir. Robert Morgan, UK, 3 mins)

Stop-frame animated legend about a cat who wants to be human.

http://www.lovefilm.com/product/detail.html?product_id=68590

O Dreamland (Dir. Lindsay Anderson, UK, 12 mins)

Anderson's brilliant 1956 documentary looks at a funfair in Margate.

http://www.channel4.com/fourdocs/archive/o_dreamland_player.html

Rubber Johnny (Dir. Chris Cunningham, UK, 6 mins)

Johnny is a shape-shifting mutant child kept looked in a basement for scientific observation. Part music video for Aphex Twin, part experimental short from Warp Films.

http://www.lovefilm.com/product/detail.html?product_id=57242

Mercy (Dir. Candida Scott-Knight, UK 2004, 14 mins)

Excellent drama with Natalie Press about a bullied boy at school who exacts revenge.

http://www.channel4.com/film/reviews/film.jsp?id=145026

Everything Hits at Once (Dir. Divya Srinivasan, USA 2001, 4 mins)

Short from on of the **Waking Life** animators using same technique set to the music of Spoon.

http://www.sputnik7.com/vod/film/filmvideos/

Gone (Dir. Matthew Thompson, UK, 10mins)

A boy witnesses a horrific event at a teenage party and is incapable of acting to stop it. An extremely well-scripted and directed drama.

http://www.bbc.co.uk/dna/filmnetwork/A3437787

Nik Powell, On film school
Director of the National Film and Television School

" 'Everything you need to know about filmmaking can be learnt by any reasonably intelligent person in an afternoon' said Orson Welles'. True if you are a great actor, a successful Broadway producer and a radio star with RKO studios at your disposal. Otherwise I recommend film school"

Nik's 3 Good Reasons To Go To Film School

One of the UK's top film producers, **Nik Powell** embarked on an entrepreneurial career in the 1960s, when he set up Virgin Records with Richard Branson. His long partnership with Stephen Woolley, with whom he founded Palace Pictures and Scala Productions, brought an unrivalled slate of award-winning features to the screen, including *Mona Lisa* and *The Crying Game*. More recent films include *Ladies in Lavender*. In addition to being the Director of the NFTS, he is Vicechairman of the European Film Academy, an elected member of the British Screen Advisory Council, the Council of BAFTA and the PACT Council, an he sits on the board of GEECT, the European Grouping of Film and Television Schools.

1. You have access to equipment, facilities, expertise and skills that you wouldn't always be able reach as an entry level filmmaker

2. At one of the better film schools, you'll receive teaching from experienced staff and get Masterclasses with leading practitioners in the field

3. You will meet, and most importantly, work with peers who may become lifelong collaborators.

Film Schools Contacts

Yes, there are many good film school programmes around the world, but lists of them can be incredibly overwhelming. To help you get started on your search, we have chosen eleven schools, which offer programmes with an international reputation.

On the basis that two of the major reasons for going to film school are access to teachers of international repute with professional experience, and the opportunity to meet potential collaborators, we've gone with the principle of "bigger is better" in making this list (though it may not be what *you* are after...).

UK

Bournemouth University (The Media School)

 Bournemouth University,
Weymouth House,
Talbot Campus,
Poole,
Dorset BH12 5BB

(☏) (01202) 965360

📠 (01202) 965530

💻 media@bournemouth.ac.uk
www.media.bournemouth.ac.uk

London College of Communications

 University of the Arts London,
School of Media,
Elephant and Castle,
London SE1 6SB

(☏) 020-7514 6800

📠 020-7514 6848

💻 a.heath@lcc.arts.ac.uk
www.lcc.arts.ac.uk

London Film School

✉ 24 Shelton Street,
London WC2H 9UB

(☏) 020-7836 9642

📠 020-7497 3718

💻 info@lfs.org.uk
www.lfs.org.uk

National Film and Television School

✉ Beaconsfield Studios,
Station Road,
Beaconsfield,
Buckinghamshire HP9 1LG

Outside London

(☏) 01494 671234

📠 01494 678708

💻 info@nfts.co.uk
www.nfts.co.uk

USA

American Film Institute

✉ 2021 North Western Avenue
Los Angeles,
California 90027, USA

☎ + 1 323 856 7600

📠 +1 323 467 4578

🖥 shardman@AFIonline.org
www.afi.com

California Institute of the Arts

✉ School of Film/Video,
24700 McBean Parkway,
Valencia,
California 91355-2397, USA

☎ +1 661-255-1050

🖥 admiss@calarts.edu
film.calarts.edu

New York University, Tisch School of the Arts

✉ 721 Broadway,
12th Floor,
New York,
NY 10003, USA

☎ + 1 212 998 1517

🖥 special.info@nyu.edu
www.nyu.edu/tisch

University of California at Los Angeles (UCLA)

✉ School of Theater, Film and
Television,
405 Hilgard Avenue,
Box 951361,
Los Angeles,

California 90095-1361, USA

☎ +1 310 825 5761

📠 +1 310 825 3383

🖥 webmaster@emelnitz.ucla.edu
www.tft.ucla.edu

University of Southern California (USC)

internship opportunities

✉ School of Cinema-Television,
University Park Campus,
Los Angeles,
California 90089, USA

☎ +1 213 740 8358

🖥 admissions@cinema.usc.edu
www-cntv.usc.edu/

Australia

Australian Film, Television & Radio School

✉ PO Box 126,
North Ryde,
NSW, 2113, Australia

☎ + 61 02 9805 6444

📠 + 61 02 9887 1030

🖥 www.aftrs.edu.au

Art Centre

Canada

Vancouver Film School

 198 West Hastings Street,
Suite 200,
Vancouver,
British Columbia V6B 1H2, Canada

📞 +1 604-685-5808

📠 +1 604- 685-5830

🖥 admissions@vfs.com
www.vfs.com

Others

There are many other good international schools these are also worth a mention:

North Carolina School of the Arts, School of Film-making (www.ncarts.edu); The National Film School of Denmark (www.filmskolen.dk)

Polish Film School Lodz (www.filmschool.lodz.pl)

University of Texas at Austin (www.rtf.utexas.edu)

For a full list of Skillset accredited Screen Academies in the UK go to www. skillset.org

London also has a growing number of good film courses – Metropolitan Film School (www.met-filmschool.co.uk) and London Film Academy (www.londonfilmacademy.com) offer a variety of diploma and short courses, and The Script Factory (www.scriptfactory.co.uk) offer well regarded short courses in screenwriting and script development.

For additional information, and to download extra materials and clearance forms which are in this book, go to www.shootingpeople.org/shortsbook

Other Film Organisations and Contacts

Training

New Producers Alliance (NPA)

 www.npa.org.uk

TAKE NOTE: Membership organisation for independent, new producers which stages regular events and training.

Raindance

 www.raindancefilmfestival.org

TAKE NOTE: Indie filmmakers org, which also holds annual festival. They also have film training courses and publish a series of useful books.

The Script Factory

 info@scriptfactory.co.uk
www.scriptfactory.co.uk

TAKE NOTE: Major screenwriters' organisation offering training, events and development services including a reading service for short film scripts.

Guilds, Orgs & Unions

BECTU (Broadcasting Entertainment Cinematograph and Theatre Union)

 info@bectu.org.uk
www.bectu.org.uk

TAKE NOTE: Trade union for workers in the film industry who work 'behind the camera'.

British Academy of Composers and Songwriters

 info@britishacademy.com
www.britishacademy.com

TAKE NOTE: Represents composers and songwriters of all genres

British Film Designers Guild

 enquiries@filmdesigners.co.uk
www.filmdesigners.co.uk

TAKE NOTE: Site has a database of members' credits

Directors Guild of Great Britain (DGGB)

 info@dggb.co.uk
www.dggb.co.uk

TAKE NOTE: Trade union for directors across in all media

Producers Alliance for Cinema and Television (PACT)

 www.pact.co.uk

TAKE NOTE: Trade association which represents interest of independent television, feature film, animation and new media industries.

The Writers' Guild of Great Britain

 www.writersguild.org.uk

TAKE NOTE: Guild of professional writers in all media.

Contributors' Biographies

Ben and Chris Blaine

Having just completed *Hallo Panda*, for The Film Council and Film4 through their Cinema Extreme scheme, the Blaine Brothers are making the transition towards feature filmmaking. They will be part of the Guiding Lights mentoring programme, through which they working with Gillies McKinnon. Featured in Screen International's "Stars of Tomorrow 2006", Chris and Ben are self-taught filmmakers who have learnt their craft over the course of making eleven short films and numerous music videos (and according to them, "by mistakes, flukes and a lot of hard work"). Previous work includes a video for Art Brut's debut single, voted the second-best cartoon video of all time by MTV2, the cult documentary *Rocklands* and the BAFTA short-listed films *Russell Square*, *Burnt Bernard*, and *Free Speech*, which was also nominated for best film at Rushes in 2004. They are passionate supporters of British film culture, having mentored and produced films from other directors including Alex Turners' RTS Student Award nominated animation, *City Spirit*. Ben is on the panel for the BBC Film Network and since 2004 the Blaines have been working with Shooting People, the UK's leading community of independent filmmakers, running their Mobile Cinema, a traveling showcase of shorts by talented new filmmakers in the UK, which has connected them with filmmakers and audiences up and down the country.

The Blaine Brothers are represented by Jean Kitson at MBA

www.charlieproductions.co.uk

Andy Gordon and Christos Michaels

Andy and Christos produced John Williams' multi-award-winning short film *Hibernation*.

Andy is an experienced producer of short films. His first commissioned short drama *Guardian Angel* won several international production awards including the coveted Silver Plaque for best short at The Chicago International Film Festival. It was screened at selected cinemas and on ITV. Since gaining an ITV production scholarship Andy has worked on a number of high profile programmes with leading international production companies including the BBC, Carlton TV and LWT. Christos has many years' experience of the business side of the film industry. He currently runs the UK and International Business Affairs department for one of the leading independent film sales and distribution companies. Before that he was an entertainment lawyer for Harbottle & Lewis and Chrysalis Visual Entertainment where he acted on behalf of many well-known producers, financiers, actors and agents on films such as *East is East* and *Kevin & Perry*. In each role he has been involved in the development, finance, production, sales or distribution of a large number of films, both from the UK and US, with budgets ranging from micro to blockbuster.

www.soundfilms.co.uk

Lisa Gunning

Lisa Gunning has worked as a Film Editor since 1998. Based at The Whitehouse, an editing company with offices in New York, Los Angeles and Chicago, she is acclaimed as both a feature film and commercials editor, and has also worked on a number of award-winning short films. Her feature work includes *Breaking and Entering* (d. Anthony Minghella); *Killshot*, a feature in post-production which is directed by John Madden and Exec Produced by Quentin Tarantino; and *Pump up the Volume*, a documentary by Carl Hindmarch. Her short film work includes Cath Le Couteur's *Spin* which screened in Berlin and Cannes Film Festivals, and her commercial work campaigns have included Nike, Levis, Guinness, Orange, Nokia, Coke Cola, Renault, Adidas, Johnnie Walker, British Airways and Sony Playstation.

Ingrid Kopp

Ingrid Kopp began her career in television in the Documentaries department at Channel 4 Television in the UK. While there she worked across both original commissions and documentary acquisitions and ran a series of workshops for young filmmakers. She moved to New York in 2004 to work as an Associate Producer for a number of independent production companies and is currently heading the US office of Shooting People. She is strangely obsessed with nineteenth century science and wrote her Masters thesis on electricity even though she doesn't know how it works. She loves short films.

Cath Le Couteur

Cath Le Couteur: an ex NFTS graduate and Cannes Cinefondation resident. Cath has made over 7 shorts that have been screened at Cannes, Edinburgh and Berlin, won multiple awards on the festival circuit and been sold worldwide. Cath is now in development with two feature film projects and is the co-Founder of Shooting People.

Marilyn Milgrom

Marilyn divides her time between work as a freelance script consultant and as Senior Tutor with the Script Factory, for whom she devises and delivers training programmes for writers and developers of both features and short films. Her previous career had several different chapters – actor, casting director, TV producer/director of documentaries and drama, producer of short films – but her obsession with story has been at the heart of all of them.

Marilyn has run screenwriting workshops in Mumbai and Jerusalem and has been a tutor at film labs in Brazil and Singapore. She is also a regular tutor on EKRAN, a MEDIA-funded script development programme at the Andrej Wajda Film School in Warsaw. In the UK she has worked with a range of up and coming screenwriters, including writer/director Amy Neil on her short film *Can't Stop Breathing*, which was nominated for a BAFTA, a BIFA for Best British Short 2005, was the winner of Scottish BAFTA for Best New Work and was the film that won Amy the Katrin Cartlidge Foundation Award in 2005.

Méabh O'Donovan

During 12 years in London Méabh O'Donovan spent some time working as a producer but has concentrated her career in Film & Television in the areas of sales, marketing and promotion, including working for CNN International and Jane Balfour Films. In 1999 Méabh moved to Sheffield and set up Short Circuit, a project which funded the placing of short films in front of features in the cinema. In this time, Méabh was also head of Marketing for Yorkshire Media Production Agency. From the project stage of Short Circuit, the concept has expanded into Short Circuit Films Ltd, a company which covers all aspects of short film promotion and marketing as well as bespoke distribution training seminars.

Jess Search

Jess is the Chief Executive of The Channel Four British Documentary Film Foundation. The Foundation was set up in 2005 and funds filmmakers as well as running the BRITDOC festival. Before that she was Commissioning Editor for Independent Film and Video at Channel 4 from 2000 until January 2005 where she focused on documentary new talent, innovation, polemical and high impact films including *My Foetus, Dying for Drugs, Alt TV, Pornography the Musical, Adam Ant: The Madness of Prince Charmin* and *The Texas Season*. She is also the co-Founder, with Cath Le Couteur, of Shooting People, the UK's independent filmmakers' community with over 30,000 members worldwide (www.shootingpeople.org). She has produced a number of short films for Cath Le Couteur, including the award winning *Spin* and *Starched*.

Pixeco

Whilst still at primary school, Pixeco had already decided that it wanted to be an astronaut. However, having failed the medical on an administrative error, it made it's mind up to become a Design Studio. Now graduated from Company University in 2004 it spends it's time keeping Creative Director, James Franklin (29) and Senior Designer, Giles Marsh (26) off the streets. Pixeco is based by the sea and creates design for broadcast and film organisations.

www.pixeco.com

Index

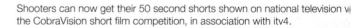